S32

THE DRAMA OF EVERYDAY LIFE

THE DRAMA OF EVERYDAY LIFE

Karl E. Scheibe

HARVARD UNIVERSITY PRESS

Cambridge, Massachusetts

London, England

2000

Library of Congress Cataloging-in-Publication Data

Scheibe, Karl E., 1937–
The drama of everyday life / Karl E. Scheibe.
   p. cm.
Includes bibliographical references and index.
ISBN 0-674-00231-8 (alk. paper)
1. Psychology. I. Title.
BF121 .S328 2000
150 21—dc21   99-043533

For Wendy—
my dancing partner

CONTENTS

When I began to learn Portuguese thirty years ago in preparation for a sabbatical in Brazil, a young Brazilian composer of popular music, Chico Buarque de Hollanda, became my favorite. His lyrical poetry is delicious; his melodies, once heard, are unforgettable and seem natural and perfect. Here is a line from one of his songs: "*Eu hoje fiz um samba bem pra frente, dizendo realmente o que é que eu acho.* (Today I have composed a samba right up front, really saying what it is that I think.)"

That is how I regard this book. It is a statement right up front—in the sense that it takes a radical (that is, fundamental) position on the nature of psychological truth. The position I take—that psychology must view life as drama and must not try to explain away drama—is not new, but I believe its statement here is fresh. Also, in this book I say what I really think on this topic, and I say it in a way that suits me. Psychologists take pains to back up their assertions with experiments and other reliable empirical compilations—what I think of as scorekeeping. I respect this methodology, and in a limited way, I employ it. The reader will find some new scorekeeping on the giving of proper names, on the incidence of schizophrenia in Connecticut over the last generation, and on the behavior of the stock market. Also, where it seems convenient and relevant, I do cite the corpus of conventional psychological research. But I discovered early in my career that much of what I read in the journals just doesn't stick. Rather, I have found psychological instruction in the most unlikely places—in the questions of my students, in the testimony of my clinical clients, in poetry, in literature, in the newspaper, in reflections on my own experience, in visits to shopping malls and casinos, theaters, restaurants, and churches—places familiar and foreign. Relying on these observations of everyday life, I treat in this book a series of topics both abstract (for example, seriousness, indifference, authenticity) and concrete (for example, teaching, gambling, schizophrenia). The general objective is to show that a dramaturgical approach to psychology is both useful and exciting—useful in the sense that it might be applied in the arenas of everyday life, and exciting in that it provides unexpected illumination for some familiar and important problems.

After an opening chapter, I have organized the book in a way that corresponds to William James's analysis of the consciousness of self (James 1890, vol. 1, ch. 10). The subjective "I" is what James referred to as Pure Ego—not an empirical self, but a source of dynamic interests. Seriousness, indifference, and boredom, the topics of Chapters 2–4, are not traditional motivational categories in psychology, but a dramaturgical approach gives them just this significance. The first of James's empirical selves is material. Chapters 5–8 discuss costumes and cosmetics, the marketplace, excess, and eating and sex as features of the material world that figure prominently in the drama of everyday life. James's conception of multiple social selves is represented by Chapters 9–12, which deal with a variety of arenas wherein social life is acted out—casinos, dance floors, mental hospitals, and classrooms. James referred to the third empirical self as spiritual. Chapters 13–15 discuss the meaning of piety, of gifts, and of being chosen, and the question of authenticity—what is real, what is a copy, and does it sing?

But this is, after all, a book, not a samba. This is a pity, for had I the talent of a poetic *sambista* like Chico, I might then reach a much larger audience and teach them more effectively. Sometimes poets can come right to the center of a major psychological truth simply by reflecting carefully on the experiences of everyday life. Then, if they have the heart and the art, they may express that truth in a way that convinces utterly, because the poem strikes an immediate resonance with the known but inchoate and unarticulated experience of people, convincing them without footnotes or the citing of sources. At the very least, the psychologist ought not to shun such truths because of their naked form.

A clear example of this sort of thing is a poem by Kenneth Koch (1994), "One Train May Hide Another." Koch took the title of this poem from a sign at a railroad crossing in Kenya, a warning to people who might be walking, unaware that a moving train might be concealed behind another. From this observation he developed the general insight that one idea may hide another, that one memory may mask another, that our current troubles may hide many other possible concerns, that today's headlines obscure most of the important news, that the fixation of our attention on one possible danger makes us vulnerable to something else that could kill us. The recent film *Wag the Dog*, based on the conceit that the President of the United States might be saved the embarrassment of a sexual indiscretion if a war with Albania were quickly produced, was yet another expression of this psychological and dramatic truth: we tend to believe what we see, and we only have time and attention to see so much.

If I could whistle or sing such truths as may be found in these pages, I surely would do so, for that would be a good deal less effort for me and much more likely to be appreciated by my audience. Our dramatic forms change as technology permits. Nowadays, if you truly have a statement to make, you should make a movie—not write a book, a play, or a poem. Surely if Shakespeare were alive in our times he would be a screenwriter, and a most successful one. But I could not think to translate this book into either a song or a movie. Just to put it into words was trouble enough.

I agree with George Orwell, who said: "Writing a book is a horrible, exhausting struggle, like a long bout of a painful illness. One would never undertake such a thing if one were not driven on by some demon whom one can neither resist nor understand" (1946/1968, 7). Even so, after one has been sick for a while, recovery can also be a sad prospect. There it is—the major source of our dramatic interest is now no longer a process but rather an object. Soon I will no longer live the production of this book, but will have to live with it as finished product. I noticed one day a volume by John Updike in a remainder sale. My heart sank—for if this is the fate of Updike, then what is to become of my poor efforts? Few of all the produced artifacts of human culture, precious few, are for the ages.

I confess this melancholy thought here neither to diminish myself nor to disparage my work, but rather to illustrate an important psychological and dramatic point. Like sharks who must swim in order to breathe, human beings must be in play, or in *the* play, if you like, in order to retain their psychological vitality. The play requires the Other, with whom some cyclic exchange must be achieved and maintained. The Other may be an audience, may be God, or Nature, or the Company. We keep going—remembering, unlike the shark, to rest and to dream.

This leads me to predict that some fair project will bid for my attentions and comprise material for my dreams after this one is cleared to the end. One book may hide another.

Goethe defined genius as "the faculty of seizing and turning to account every thing that strikes us" (in Richardson 1995, 172). Without making any claims about genius, I do say that two features of this assertion are worth the attention of psychologists. First, that one should have the courage to imitate, to seize anything that seems worth seizing and to turn it to account. Second, that one should have the courage to overturn, to be subversive of what we are given. In these pages I demonstrate a certain ruthlessness in seeking and seizing such materials as are within my reach. I also exhibit a confidence in my own everyday experiences as fortification for the assertion of a truth or a principle, something I was explicitly told *not* to do as a beginning student of psychology. But experience ripens understanding, and it is time for me to set aside the constraints of youth. I may be mistaken, of course. At least I have the satisfaction of stating my convictions; the reader can be the judge of their use and interest.

THE DRAMA OF EVERYDAY LIFE

A QUOTIDIAN PSYCHOLOGY

Everyday is all there is.

—Joan Didion

We arrange our days in cycles and seasons. We punctuate our lives with holidays and anniversaries, conventions and ceremonial gatherings. We collaborate with others to give shape to our days—inventing projects, saving our resources, then spending them, inquiring always to find out what is new, then passing on quickly to what is newer still. We count our days from certain especially remarkable events, such as the birth of Christ or the Covenant with Abraham or the Declaration of Independence. The years are alike in length and natural seasons; and yet the years of war command special and prolonged attention and even study, as if something depended upon our getting all of the details right. We seek occupations that will offer us variety and stimulation, and we seek to fill our leisure time with hobbies and exercise programs and feasts. We seek vacations from the monotony of our towns and homes, often to suffer considerable expense and pain. The idle rich, not content to be idle, buy expensive toys and endure synthetic privations. Ordinary people contrive to create regal pageants. Some young people (and some not so young), in order to avoid the bleakness of conformity to reason, choose instead the vertigo of easy highs. For the old, there is shuffleboard and talk of pains and operations. We dramatize. All of us. Every day.

These commonplace observations pose a challenge for psychology. Without an understanding of dramatic context, it is difficult to account for why someone would become a suicide bomber, or why a professional athlete might consider himself underpaid at a million dollars a month, or why there are now so many cases of dissociative identity disorder, attention deficit disorder, and eating disorder, and so few new cases of schizophrenia.

These are among the questions that puzzle me—the sorts of questions that demand an intelligent and intelligible response from psychologists. Yet it seems to me that psychology—despite its diversity, despite its evident prosperity as a science and as a profession, and despite some remarkable successes in certain delimited areas—is not generally successful in offering convincing and satisfactory accounts of a wide range of events in our everyday lives. The historical reason for this limitation of psychology is the universalistic pretension of our science. The drama of everyday life is in constant flux. Psychology has had a hard time learning to swim comfortably in the river of history, for the old pretension was for the swimmer to explain away the river.

We need a quotidian psychology—a psychology that will help us to understand why so many children are bored to death at school, why politicians can behave in an overtly stupid fashion and pretend that no one notices, why academicians—intelligent and honorable people—often allow their public and private discourse to degenerate into childishness and indifference. I wonder that my students, while evidently much more sophisticated and involved in expressing their sexuality than were college students of my generation, profess considerable confusion about the scripts they might follow in cultivating genuine romantic relationships.

A quotidian psychology, or a psychology of everyday life, should enable us to understand—if not predict and control—the unfolding dramas around us. Such a psychology, I propose, must be enriched by the incorporation of the principles and the language of the theater. What are the precedents for such an enterprise?

PRECEDENTS AND PRECONDITIONS

Two famous books of the past century have "everyday life" in their titles. I refer, of course, to Freud's *Psychopathology of Everyday Life* (1901/1965) and Erving Goffman's *Presentation of Self in Everyday Life* (1959). At first glance, these landmark works may seem to have little in common. Freud's work is one of the founding documents of psychoanalysis—a painstaking and eloquent argument for an inner psychic determinism. Freud defended the radical proposition that there are no psychological accidents—that slips of the tongue, forgotten words and names, common minor twitches, tics, and bungled actions (grouped under the opaque term "parapraxes") are strictly determined expressions of unconscious urges—urges that cannot be expressed directly because of the repressive force of the outer layers of the personality. Freud's book is quintessentially psychological in that he conceives the mechanisms and processes at work as intrapsychic, with the external social world serving only as an oppositional force to inner dynamics. Goffman's book, by contrast, eschews the inner psychological world in favor of the interaction order—the horizontal nexus of social exchanges. A quote from Santayana serves as an epigraph of this founding document for the study of impression management—in part: "It is not urged against cuticles that they are not hearts." Goffman preferred to study cuticles he could see rather than hearts he could only imagine—or could not quite imagine.

The language in Goffman's book is explicitly drawn from drama—used, he suggests, as metaphorical scaffolding for the structured study of managed impressions. Freud's use of drama is rather different. For him, dramas, such as Sophocles' play about Oedipus, are expressions of an inner psychological necessity. For Goffman, the necessity is presented by the drama, and actors are tossed about and controlled by its terms. Freud reduces drama to psychology; Goffman reduces life to drama, leaving out the psychology.

But both have "everyday life" as their range, and both focus strongly on errors, mistakes, misunderstandings. Freud's catalog of slips and bunglings is not drawn from remarkably deranged or unusual people but from ordinary folk, including his family and colleagues as well as his patients. Goffman's observations of the arts of impression management are simply drawn from that part of the ordinary world falling into his range of vision. But no one is exempt or excluded from his cold-eyed analysis of the differences between impressions "given" and impressions "given off"—of individuals posturing and preening and colluding in ways that meet dramatic requirements, engaged in a soulless striving for social approval and self-enhancement. Both books were written early in the publishing careers of their respective authors; but even so, both managed to be magisterial—establishing for each author a reputation for keen observation coupled with interpretive ingenuity. "Freudian slip" has become part of our general vocabulary, causing even nonbelievers to blush. Goffman has pervaded our language less than Freud, but because of his skill in interpreting how we wear our selves, he has reinforced doubts about whether there is a self, after all, beneath the apparel. Armed with these manuals, one might see the common stuff of everyday life with eyes newly opened—if the field is suffused with the light of skepticism.

It will not do to note the contradictions in the approaches of Freud and Goffman and to say that they cancel each other out—so that we can begin with a fresh slate. Of course, Freud's rigid psychic determinism is no longer widely accepted, and doubts are justified about how he tailored his stories to suit his theoretical and his personal interests. Goffman's antipathy toward psychology was perhaps justified by the shape of psychology in his times (mostly stimulus-response behaviorism or psychoanalysis), but the notion of the empty self has outlived its heuristic purpose. Even so, the legacies of Freud and Goffman must continue to receive respectful attention in the construction of a new quotidian psychology.

Since Goffman's death in 1982, psychology has changed in such a way as to become much more hospitable as a companion to drama. Cognitive psychology is firmly established as the main focus of what used to be experimental psychology, and cognitive psychologists have discovered that they must be interested in story, in how stories are constructed and remembered.[1] Narrative psychology has become established as a major way of addressing issues that were formerly the province of static theories within personality and social psychology.[2] Kenneth Gergen's (1973) landmark paper "Social Psychology as History" has been followed by many other works that have strengthened the relationship between transient culture and psychology. American psychologists have started to read European literary theorists and social critics, such as Bakhtin, Benjamin, and Moscovici, as a way of enriching and broadening the conceptual tools they can bring to bear on quotidian psychology.

The orthodoxies of the past lie shattered all around us. A remarkable example is Donald Spence's (1982) revision of classical psychoanalysis in *Narrative Truth and Historical Truth*. The advantage of shattering orthodoxies is that one may proceed, as Spence has, to develop a line of inquiry in a way that follows practical interests, without fear of being attacked along the way by offended sacred monsters.

Jacob Moreno worked and wrote in an era when orthodoxies were most powerful, forcing his brilliant and innovative work on psychodrama to the margins of eccentricity and exclusion. Moreno's name is simply not to be found in contemporary psychology texts. More surprising still, he is not cited in the current spate of work on narrative psychology, or even in an admirable compendium of work on the dramaturgical tradition within sociology, *Life as Theater* (Brissett and Edgley, eds., 1990). Yet Moreno not only had powerful insights about the theatrical character of human life but developed from his ideas a set of revolutionary therapeutic practices. Group psychotherapy owes more to Moreno's genius than to any other single source. Because he was a psychiatrist, yet anathema to the dominant orthodoxies of psychoanalysis, Moreno built his theoretical house in a region set apart. Born in Rumania and reared in Austria, he lived and worked for the most productive part of his life in the United States. However, the psychodramatic tradition seems more alive and prosperous in Europe and Latin America than it does in his adopted country. Those who knew him suggest that Moreno certainly wanted recognition for his accomplishments; it seems an ironic twist that while his influence has been mighty, his name has receded into the shadows.[3]

Among Moreno's visitors at his institute in Beacon, New York, in the 1940s was Theodore R. Sarbin, a young psychologist who had just received his doctorate. Sarbin was strongly attracted to Moreno's ideas about social roles. He also had the advantage of spending the greater part of a postdoctoral year at the University of Chicago, where the spirit of George Herbert Mead was still strong, reinforcing further Sarbin's belief in the power of a social and dramaturgical perspective in the interpretation of human life. Sarbin developed a role-theoretical interpretation of hypnosis and later wrote a critique of so-called mental illnesses based on role theory.

A critical event in Sarbin's professional history is illustrative of the principle that identities are shaped by events in the drama of everyday life. After Sarbin left his clinical practice for an academic position at the University of California at Berkeley, he happened to read an article by Theodore Newcomb entitled "Taking the Role of the Other." He wrote a long letter to Newcomb, detailing his reactions to the article, including some critical comments. Newcomb responded with appreciation. Later, Newcomb suggested to Gardner Lindzey that Sarbin be invited to prepare the chapter on role theory for the *Handbook of Social Psychology.* That chapter effectively established Sarbin as "Mr. Role Theory" within psychology. Another series of dramatic accidents resulted in my coming to study with Sarbin as a graduate student at Berkeley, all unknowing that this confluence of lives would give lasting shape to my own identity and career.[4]

Sarbin has provided a philosophical foundation for a dramaturgical psychology. Following the suggestion of Pepper (1942; see Sarbin 1977), he proposed that the appropriate world hypothesis for psychology is not mechanism, but contextualism.[5] The second foundational concept is that of constructionism—the idea that social objects and categories do not have a natural existence apart from people who create and sustain them (see Sarbin and Kitsuse, eds., 1994). Third, Sarbin has shown that many of psychology's central terms can be seen as fossilized metaphors.[6] Among the dead metaphors that have been subjected to his mission of demythification are hypnotic trance, mental illness, schizophrenia, anxiety, and hallucination (see Sarbin 1950, 1967a, 1967b, 1968; Sarbin and Mancuso 1980).

COMPLEMENTARY APPROACHES

Whether or not one accepts the problematic notion of postmodernism, the present era in psychology is different from the era just past. At the risk of offending some sensibilities and ignoring some major fights, I prefer to think of it as a "post-polemical" era—or to put it more positively, an era of theoretical pluralism.[7]

Freud and Goffman wrote their books at times of major polemical embattlement. Both defined themselves by staking out positions that were radically different from the prevailing orthodoxy. Freudian psychoanalysis, in turn, became one of the most stultifying and captivating orthodoxies of the twentieth century. Goffman and Moreno before him were to a degree excluded from their respective professional establishments, and their career stories can be told in part as struggles with those establishments.

The arguments about contextualism, constructionism, and demythification have been heard and have had their impact—if only in encouraging a much greater tolerance of divergent theoretical positions than was prevalent earlier in this century. For my present purpose—that of suggesting a proper and fruitful relationship between psychology and drama—all of this precedent has set the stage. This makes it possible for me to articulate a position that is not likely to be offensive or threatening, as it might have been at an earlier time.

Let us say, after William James, that psychology is the "science of mental life"—a science that is fundamentally contextualist and constructionist, the terms of which must be metaphors, recognized as such. I believe that the essence of drama is transformation: seeing one thing as another (envisaging a potato as a human body and toothpicks as arms and legs, seeing puppets and dolls as being like people); or becoming something else (pretending to be a doctor or to be sick or to be deaf, assuming a character, enacting a role).[8]

I see three possible relationships between psychology and drama:

1. Psychology can be viewed as the science that explains or accounts for drama.
2. Drama can be viewed as accounting for psychology, as well as for everything else.
3. Psychology and drama can be viewed as complementary approaches to truth and understanding—at the same conceptual level, with frequent borrowings back and forth.

The first of these positions has been customary within psychology. Freud used his psychology to account not only for the psychopathology of everyday life but also for the artistic creations of da Vinci, the development of religion, the humor in jokes, and the origins and cultural dissemination of Greek myths. Behaviorists were no less ambitious.

Skinner could present an account for just about everything within his view by referring to principles of reinforcement. The enterprise known as psychohistory was in this sense psychologically reductive—psychology being viewed as somehow more fundamental than history.

One may see the opposite relationship in several forms. Western psychology has been dismissed in classical Marxist dogma as yet another manifestation of the everlasting struggle of bourgeois culture to maintain its class domination. Radical forms of symbolic interactionism within sociology similarly dismiss psychology as having anything at all to bring to the table—for the very idea of a table is thought of as a product of symbolic interaction. Goffman is not quite the same as a symbolic interactionist, but even so he saw no essential need for a psychology to supplement his accounts of activities within the interaction order. A more recent example is provided by a book entitled *Inventing the Psychological* (Pfister and Schnog, eds., 1997). The essays in this book present arguments about the ways psychological ideas and concepts have been shaped by mass media, the arts, economics, and domestic life.

But the times do not require the reheating of polemical debates. Rather, I wish simply to posit a complementary relationship between psychology and drama and to suggest that this union presents the best promise for a useful quotidian psychology.

The complementarity of psychology and drama is not a difficult conception. In fact, it has the virtue and beauty of simplicity. Let me provide some examples.

The drama of everyday life is enveloping—but it is not always dramatic in the sense of being distinctive or gripping. Imagine traveling along in a car, listening to the radio, thinking absently about past or future—unaware of any drama in the moment. But the sudden appearance of lights and sirens on a car rapidly approaching from the rear results in an immediate dramatic transformation. The heart begins to race; palms sweat; excuses, explanations, pleas begin to form in one's head. The police officer strides up as you open your window. "License and registration, please," she says, following the script. A dramatic transformation occurs in the little circle formed by the officer and the driver, with passengers in supporting roles. It will be an item—something worth talking about—a dramatic intensification of an otherwise unremarkable time.

Or imagine that a Spanish-speaking tourist is detained at a Canadian airport security checkpoint, for he looks a bit suspicious to the agent, and the agent doesn't speak Spanish. Somehow, a background of common knowledge pervades the scene. A massively fatal airline crash occurred less than a month ago. It happened a thousand miles away, to be sure. But baggage is examined more thoroughly now than it was a month ago, and no one complains. The Spanish-speaking tourist seems to accept the terms of the drama, for he too is aware of the famous crash under suspicious circumstances. In this way, and in millions of other little episodes enacted in airports around the world, the dramatic force of a remote event is brought to bear on countless lives. In time, this singular event will cease to be a force in the conscious lives of the population, but it will gradually be assimilated into a generalized apprehension about air travel, perhaps making some incremental difference in regulations adopted here and there.

An airline accident is horrible. Yet, macabre as it may seem, the horrible has positive value—as a glance at movie advertisements will show. An airline crash provides news, interest, many strong stories. The *New York Times* ran capsule histories of each of the 230 victims of the TWA crash that occurred on July 17, 1996. These little dramas increased tremendously the impact of the event in the minds of readers. While the world attended to the protracted investigation of this event, which seemed dramatically required, thousands of other deaths occurred outside the margins of the news, and were safely ignored.

Since the beginning of the O. J. Simpson scandal in 1993, network evening news stories involving homicides have increased in the U.S. media by some 721 percent, while actual homicides have diminished by 20 percent. Dan Rather says, "The O. J. story convinced a lot of people that kind of story will put people in front of the set . . . I felt the pressure strongly after that."[9] The media have capitalized on the power of murder stories to draw an audience. If the American public has the impression that celebrity murders are on the increase, this is a matter of dramatic manipulation rather than a realistic perception.

Topics within psychology include fear, attitudes, decisions, reflexes, prejudice, distortions of judgment—and all of these topics are contained in the dramatic vignettes here sketched. And not only contained—I enter the stronger claim that our understanding of the psychology of fear, attitudes, and so on is illuminated better by their operation in the drama of everyday life than by experimental abstraction. Another case will strengthen the connection between the drama of everyday life and psychological topics.

CYRANO'S ADVANTAGE

Cyrano de Bergerac had a problem—but he also had an attitude. Aware of his nose and burdened to think of it as a disability, he presented his interlocutors with a dilemma. Should they look at it—thus confirming their awareness of his disfigurement? Or should they dissimulate—looking away as if he had no such outstanding feature? Either way, Cyrano's wrath would be entirely justified. When there is no way of meeting or avoiding the gaze of a person with a problem and an attitude, that person has Cyrano's advantage.

Despite his eloquence, Cyrano's passion remained a secret to his beloved Roxanne, for he was forever barred by his own sense of disability and fear of rejection from revealing his heart. He died pathetically—willfully denying himself the confession of love that would have made his life complete. Here dramatic pathos is clearly connected, via its Greek origin, to pathology—the suffering brought on solely by circumstance. Cyrano's advantage comes with a terrible cost.

Goffman noted the pervasiveness of this dilemma for those who interact with physically handicapped and stigmatized persons:

> We will feel that the stigmatized individual is either too aggressive or too shamefaced, and in either case too ready to read unintended meanings into our actions. We ourselves may feel that if we show direct sympathetic concern for his condition, we may be overstepping ourselves; and yet if we actually forget that he has a failing we are likely to make impossible demands of him or unthinkingly slight his fellow-sufferers. Each potential source of discomfort for him when we are with him can become something we sense he is aware of, aware that we

are aware of, and even aware of our state of awareness about his awareness; the stage is then set for the infinite regress of mutual consideration that Meadian social psychology tells us how to begin but not how to terminate. (Goffman 1963, 18)

Cyrano's advantage places the person with a stigma at least temporarily in a position of moral superiority. But such a position has its cost. A brilliant student, who had had a leg amputated because of cancer, told me that he constantly wondered how other students viewed his infirmity. He usually chose not to call attention to his artificial leg. But how then was he to explain his limp, or his inability to participate in certain student activities, such as a pick-up football game? In time, he came to realize that his disability imparted to him a certain arrogance and the right to have it. He justified an unwillingness to take the role of the other, for he was convinced that most others were quite unable to see the world from his perspective. The result was a moral distance between him and his fellow students, and some bitterness on both sides.

Cyrano's advantage is at once psychological and dramatic. It can be merely a label for a certain awkward social situation that most of us have faced. But it can and should be the sort of thing that provokes further thought and reflection in the psychologist. As a psychotherapist, I have often encountered situations in which a client has the conditions for such an advantage—and its corresponding cost. The challenge is to find a way to meet such a person—who has AIDS or terminal cancer or who is very old and infirm—at a level that confers respect and dignity and yet is not at all patronizing. It is not easy.

THE REQUIREMENT OF SELF

The self is a psychological construction—a term invented to stand for something that is commonly experienced and yet cannot be described or expressed directly. For a long time, psychologists and sociologists, in their need to be objective, have avoided worrying about the self. For all of Goffman's brilliance, this is a conspicuous problem with the Goffmanian drama—his characters have no depth. Depth is another metaphor, of course, and the obvious question is, "What do you mean by depth?"

In reply, I assert that depth implies selfhood. And by selfhood I refer to what Jung meant by Self, what James meant by Pure Ego, and what Mead meant by the subjective "I" as opposed to the objective "me."[10] Sarbin has argued that our identities are constructed largely by "imaginings stimulated by stories read or stories heard [that] provide the plot structures for one's self-narrative" (1997, 67). And yet individuals are selective about how their identities are constructed, and this selectivity is self-guided. The self is an abstraction, but a necessary and useful abstraction to account for the reflexivity of human thought. Identities are more open to observation; social markers make the task of identification rather easy.

The distinction between self and identity can be illustrated by the differential responses elicited by the twin questions "Who are you?" and "What are you?" Sarbin reports that the former question typically produces responses in terms of conventional social roles—names, occupations, statuses, places of origin, and the like. The latter question, by contrast, produces more cosmic responses—a human being, a soul in a body, a temple for the spirit. The actor, as it turns out, is not just a robot or an automaton who plays roles as if programmed to do so. The actor also has inner agency, or self, and that self has at least a vote in determining the identity or identities to be assumed.

I have found it helpful to think of self and identity in terms of a two-dimensional model. Self implies the vertical dimension and identity the horizontal. Jung, as a boy, thought of all his interactions with his classmates as limiting and in some ways false. Jung consistently used the metaphor of verticality to refer to his self—alone now and somehow more true, with the heavens above and the earth below. One thinks of him seated on a stone, meditating in solitude—wondering if something in the stone is conscious of his being conscious of the stone.[11] If meditation is the connective act of the self, conversation is the connective act of identity. Conversation is conducted horizontally—with our social companions and mates. Goffman studied only the horizontal interaction order. The vertical interaction order is less open to inspection. But without its inclusion, our capacity to understand the drama of everyday life is gravely reduced.

People are different, not just in the superficial respects of the roles they play and the identities they assume, but also at the fundamental level of self. Jung's theory of psychological types may or may not be right in its details, but it is a theory about the conformation of the self according to certain polarities—masculinity-femininity, introversion-extroversion, and so on. We are not all *given to be* alike. And the way we are *given to be* determines, at least in part, how we become placed and located in our social dramas.

The way people tell their own stories illustrates this principle. The author Paul Monette told of his struggles with being homosexual in a heterosexual world. Before he came out, it was as if his self was suffocating. He observed other boys in relation to himself: "And every year they leaped further ahead, leaving me in the dust with all my doors closed, and each with a new and better deadbolt. Until I was twenty-five, I was the only man I knew that had no story at all. I'd long since accepted the fact that nothing had ever happened to me and nothing ever would. That's how the closet feels, once you've made your nest in it and learned to call it home. Self-pity becomes your oxygen" (1992, 1).

The nature of this struggle is not alike for all homosexual men. Roger Brown (1996) declared in his memoir that his homosexuality never made him feel oppressed in this fashion at all. To be sure, for long periods of his life this feature of the conformation of his self was not openly shared with society, and the very title of his memoir, *Against My Better Judgment,* suggests a secret self being revealed. But one might simply say that Roger Brown sailed in more congenial seas than did Paul Monette. Acceptance of his homosexuality never seemed to be an issue for Brown, though the dramas he enacted because of his homosexuality brought him both joy and sorrow.

The old-fashioned idea of a calling, or true vocation, implies a living inner self—responding differentially to such opportunities as are presented.[12] Somehow, one thinks of Mozart as having a natural calling to music, Einstein to science, Emerson to letters, Thoreau to nature, Mark Twain to humor. In each case, it is as if a resonance occurred between a person's inner self and an opportunity for expression and activity presented by the world.

An example of the resonance between the self and dramatic possibilities is presented in a profile of Peter Gomes, campus minister at
Harvard University:

> Gomes was an exceptional student and was consistently elected presi-
> dent of his class, where he was the only black student. A precocious
> child, he had a flair for running things. In the afternoons, he would
> stage elaborate plays in which he acted out *all* the roles while the other
> children were forced to play the "part" of the audience. He also threw
> his energies into the church, where he preached his first sermon at the
> age of twelve. "I loved it for all the theatre and pageantry," he says.
> "Church was for me what the basketball court is to most black kids: A
> place where my imagination was unleashed and I was given free rein on
> a stage." (Boynton 1996, 68)

The distinction between self and identity is also revealed in the
kinds of mix-ups in communication illustrated by Cyrano's advantage.
Our horizontal social dealings do not easily take into account the soulful
nature of the other or of ourselves. One wants to be able to say these
unlikely words to a person without a nose: "Look, I want to talk to you
Self to Self, in a way that is not encumbered by your lack of a nose—a
lack that I notice but that is totally without significance to me." This sort
of thing might be achieved in fact, but it probably matters less what
words are spoken than what is happening with other channels of communication—in particular, the eyes. We generally speak and are spoken
to in a way that respects our presented identities—not necessarily our
inner selves.

Here is a little drama that illustrates the point. A client of mine, call
him Joe, was arrested and sent to jail for heroin possession. When he
boarded the van for transport to the jail, the other prisoners already in
the vehicle denied him a place to sit. Finally, a large black prisoner
moved over and made room for him to sit down. Joe sat down and
murmured, "Hey, man. Thanks for the seat." The reply: "Fuck you.
Don't be thankin' me for anything. Just sit down and shut the fuck up."

On his first meal in jail, Joe carried his tray into the dining hall and
tried to sit at an empty table near a group of Puerto Ricans. One of them
came over to him and said, "You can't sit here. Leave. This is for family."

He found the same treatment from the blacks on the other side of the hall. There were about eight white men in the whole jail. They finally found two tables where it was possible for them to eat.

Later, in a detention center, Joe's roommate—a Latino—asked Joe to move out of their room. He asked Joe three times to move and threatened him with harm if he didn't. So Joe requested another room assignment. The authorities interrogated him about who had ordered him to pack up—but he wouldn't say. He interpreted this episode as part of the power struggle between the gangs and the authorities over who was actually in control of the detention center.

Joe wanted to be recognized not as a white guy but as a fellow sufferer—to make some Self-to-Self contact. "Hey, man," was his invitation. The lack of reciprocation—in the van and in the later episodes—left him feeling pathetically isolated, very much as Paul Monette must have felt isolated by the straight world, and as Cyrano felt because of his self-imposed isolation from Roxanne.

The drama of everyday life must be described in a way that respects both self and identity. The story of self is more difficult to tell than that of identity, resulting in such awkward titles as *Against My Better Judgment*. Indeed, Jung's main autobiographical memoir, *Memories, Dreams, Reflections* (1965) contains plenty of evidence of editing—by him first of all, and then by his family after his death. In particular, he was not entirely forthcoming about his mistress of forty years, Antonia Wolf, or his flirtations with many of his female patients and colleagues.[13] Such revelations, given the climate of the times, would reflect badly—or so he and his family must have thought—on his character.

The self is an essential element in the human drama. How does it come to be so?

THE ARBITRARY BECOMES ESSENTIAL

Nothing in the human genotype can be specifically marked for playing basketball, speaking English, composing baroque music, having extramarital affairs, or becoming a physicist or a psychologist. All of these forms of expression are products of human cultural invention, developed thousands of years after the human genome was established by the survival pressures of the ages. Even so, once the human being comes to possess a name, a race, a religion, a national identity, a family, and even the ability to respond to a calling, much is laid down that no longer is a matter of arbitrary assignment and accident. Indeed, one's self and much of one's identity seem—and in a psychological sense truly are—essential.

First in a biological and then in a psychological sense, much that begins as arbitrary becomes essential. At the level of human reproduction, there are billions of possible combinations of particular spermatozoa with particular ova for any pair of sexual partners, and of course billions more combinations of sexual partners. Out of these multiple billions of possibilities, only a few conceptions occur. But once conception occurs—we have to say arbitrarily or adventitiously, given the huge number of voided possibilities—the genotype for that individual is established in its essence.

Arbitrary things continue to happen after birth as well. A name is selected—perhaps from a name book with thousands of entries. By inspection, the young creature is assigned to a gender category, and by ascription, to a racial, national, ethnic, and religious identity. Viewed from the perspective of the ages, all of this is quite arbitrary—the product of myriad successive accidents.

And yet when we look into the mirror we do not see an accident. We see and we feel an essence. We own our names and our faces, our families, and even our place in the world—be it noble or humble—as essential elements of our being. These are the starting points for the dramas we enact in the world, and we are careful and selective about how we are transformed by circumstances. We have a general reluctance to change our essential features or to suffer mistakes in how we are called, recognized, acknowledged. We either deny or forget that it is all so improbable, so unlikely, so unnecessary, so arbitrary.

The stages we are thrust upon also have something necessary about them. The rural boy feels the country in his soul. The urban sophisticate will not take to the farm. The arbitrary becomes essential.

This formulation seems particularly helpful in thinking of religion. One who reflects from a disinterested perspective on the plethora of world religions will have a difficult job justifying one's own religious tradition as being uniquely correct. As Mark Twain said, "The ease with which I see my neighbor's religion to be false suggests to me that my own may be false also." And yet, we are what we are—arbitrarily of course, but also essentially—Christian, Jew, Hindu, Muslim, Buddhist.

Religion, itself, is not just an arbitrary piece of theater, though theater it certainly is.[14] It is that form of theater specifically developed to help us cope with the most difficult moments of crisis in the human drama—birth, marriage, and death. In between, religion provides us with sacred stories—sacred fictions, if you like—that are instructive about such matters as blessings, moral duties, and how to deal with existential fears. The whole mythological structure conveyed to us through religion is marvelously instructive. To study the history of religion or to search for the historical Jesus is to be forced to recognize that our particular tradition is quite arbitrary—that things could have turned out quite differently. But if we remember that what was once laid down arbitrarily can and does become an essential feature of who we are, then it is possible to accept the mythic truths to which we are heir. *Credo quia absurdum est.* Someone has said that the soul responds to three different modes—mathematics, music, and myth. If we neglect the arbitrary myths that speak essential truths of our condition, we do so at our peril.

THE ESSENCE OF DRAMA

The essence of drama is transformation. This formulation comes from the Russian dramatist and actor Nicolas Evreinoff. Evreinoff emigrated from Russia to Paris in 1925 and remained there until he died in 1953. His writings are more like philosophical treatises than descriptions of the theatrical crafts. *The Theatre in Life* (1927) is a provocative and radical statement of Evreinoff's views, including a development of the central idea that drama is transformation. Transformation is the key to magic, to miracles, to the fascination with watching things grow or be destroyed:

> Man has one instinct about which, in spite of its inexhaustible vitality, neither history nor psychology nor aesthetics have so far said a single word. I have in mind the instinct of transformation, the instinct of opposing to images received from without images arbitrarily created from within, the instinct of transmuting appearances found in nature

into something else, an instinct which clearly reveals its essential character in the conception of what I call theatricality. (1927, 22)

This is why religion can be so dramatic and so interesting. Water is turned into wine, bread into flesh. Christ rises from the dead. God manifests himself in a burning bush. Moses leads his people out of slavery. Joshua, after imitating Moses' Red Sea trick at the river Jordan, accomplishes some major magic with horns and shouting at Jericho. God promises atonement, or redemption, or salvation—transformations all, differing only in detail. The dead are raised, the blind made to see, and the sick made well. Take away the transformative qualities of religion—take away the magic of the myths—and what remains is dramatically impoverished and deadly, a desiccated ethical culture society, stale and reeking of age.

Evreinoff watched children play and noted that the child is always acting, pretending, inventing, imagining. For the child, the doll is not just a doll—it is imbued with spirit, with imaginary qualities. The child spends much of its time in exercises of transformation—dressing up like adults, playing soldier, Indian, doctor, nurse, mother, father, sports hero. One of my own sons loved his Smokey the Bear costume, complete with ranger hat. My other son would join in any enterprise that would give him a uniform. Clark Kent becomes Superman, Billy Batson becomes Captain Marvel, Ninja Turtles are creatures in metamorphosis, as are Power Rangers, and Barney is a dinosaur turned half human.

Modern science is transformative magic both in its origins and in its applications. Chemistry was born out of alchemy, the ancient quest to transform base metal into gold, to find the elixir of life, to work miracles with matter. Modern chemistry is more amazing in its practice than alchemy was in aspiration—for it has discovered ways of transforming petroleum into tires, mold into life-saving drugs, and snake venom into an antitoxin. When I was a child, my chemistry set came with two manuals. One was for a series of experiments, numbered sequentially from the most elementary to the most advanced. The other was a book of magic tricks, including making invisible ink, combining two colorless liquids to make a wine-colored fluid, and softening the shell of an egg so that it could be inserted into the neck of a milk bottle. It was great stuff, all of it involving transformation—the essence of drama. Scientists are enthralled with the magic of dramatic transformation—it is what they are mainly about.

The sequel to the observation that drama is essentially transformation is the obverse principle that the lack of transformation is stasis, is constancy of condition, is boredom. This seems to me of the utmost psychological significance; for boredom, as I will argue in Chapter 4, is the paramount motivational issue of our times. Boredom is the other side of drama. The psychology of boredom is not so simple, for boredom cannot be simply controlled by stimulus complexity. Thoreau was not bored in the woods at Concord—he could find diversion in a shrub oak.[15] But my bet is that he would have been deathly bored by watching an hour of MTV.

DRAMATIC CIRCLES AND CYCLES

Piaget observed that children begin to display circular reactions in the sensory-motor phase of their cognitive development. Before two years of age, a child will engage in a repetitive series of actions if those actions are followed by some regular and reciprocal response. The sucking response is an example. A more advanced case is throwing a rattle out of the crib, to have Daddy pick it up and return it, only to throw it again, for Daddy to return it again, and so on. It is a primitive game of catch. Piaget, Vygotsky, and others who have looked at language learning have identified these circular reactions as critical to language acquisition and to cognitive development in general. Piaget notes that the circles enlarge over the course of development, so that the child becomes capable of engaging in dramatic play with more and more remote objects. Vygotsky (1962) enters the correction that language becomes more tightly centered as development proceeds, so that the person becomes able to carry on internal dialogues rather than relying upon others for reciprocation. The point to note is that development is a dialectical and dialogical process, in a moral as well as in a cognitive sense, as Bakhtin has argued.

My emendation of Evreinoff's principle is that drama is not transformation alone but rather transformation that is engaged by the protagonist in a circular process, analogous to a game of catch. A conversation is a circular process and is dramatically interesting as long as both parties remain engaged. A college course is a circular process—presentation of material followed by a student's recitation followed by the teacher's evaluation of that recitation—an instance of what Goffman referred to as the "rule of threes" in human interaction. The young Little Leaguer pitches a tennis ball against the garage door for hours on end—the other in a game of catch need not be a person—until the parents are driven to distraction. The movie *Field of Dreams* is filled with magical transformations—dead baseball players coming to life and the like—and ends with a touching scene of Kevin Costner's character playing catch with the ghost of his dead father. Hunting and fishing are circular processes—interesting only if the game or prey is really out there somewhere. In all of these cases, the drama depends upon engagement in the circle. Broken circles represent boredom. If you ask students in a typical junior high school what they think of their classroom experiences, you will hear them say that they are bored. It is as if the classroom is full of broken circles.

EPIPHANIES

In our quotidian psychology we need a way to include epiphanies—and I think that the idea of dramatic circles is just such a way. The art critic Robert Hughes has said, "When you boil it all down, that is the social purpose of art: the creation of mutuality, the passage from feelings into shared meaning" (1996, 34). Art and theater can provide epiphanies—momentary visits to a new region of truth—transforming in their power. I remember experiencing such an epiphany when I attended a concert of the Russian pianist Sviataslav Richter more than thirty years ago. Music, like mathematics and myth, speaks to the soul. That evening I came away inspired—not to become a pianist, but to do something with my own talents to approximate the joy I saw emanating from those well-trained hands.

Sometimes quite ordinary experiences are imbued with this epiphanic power—not requiring heady interpretation; merely requiring an open attitude of receptivity in order to receive what is there, to be part of the circle.

I remember sitting in a bin of recently harvested wheat on my uncle's farm when I was eleven years old. The color of the wheat was golden yellow. The grain bin seemed to contain a superabundance of wheat—so much quantity was itself impressive. Grain lies in a bin in a natural and easy way after just coming out of the combine. It is warm to the touch and uneven in its wavy surface, but regular. You can reach your arm down deep into the bin—warm, dry, all wheat, all the way down. Remove your arm and an indentation remains, and you can brush it away if you wish and make a little groove or ditch on the surface. It all seemed so perfect, so clean, so simple, so useful, so completely good. The farm all seemed good—the animals, the tractors, the open fields, the barn, the white frame house. I remember thinking that I loved the farm, and wanted from the depth of my being to be forever in the midst of these simple, lovely, clean, useful, and good objects—to smell and feel and taste the wheat always.

I remember also the first time I heard the words of the famous World War I song "How You Gonna Keep 'em Down on the Farm, after They've Seen Paree?" It was at a small-town harvest festival in Illinois, right after World War II. I remember at once admitting and resisting the implicit and unrelenting response to the question in the song: you can't keep 'em on the farm. And I knew I myself would not stay on the farm, even though I had not yet seen Paree (and would not for another forty years). This was another epiphany—like the contemplation of the wheat—but sadder in its meaning and result.

Sometimes the circles that start as little epiphanies loop forward into the future, forming the dramatic sense of events realized long afterward. Benjamin Lee Whorf was brought up as a Methodist Episcopalian and at some point in his childhood began to question the truth of scripture and its relation to the theory of evolution. This led him to the problem of translation, and from there to a general concern with language and its relation to thought. Becoming an expert on Mayan language has little to do with a boy's questioning the Bible. But for Whorf these were part of the same dramatic circle.[16]

A similar example is provided in the work of Solomon Asch, who became famous as a social psychologist for his experimental work on social conformity. As a boy of seven, he attended his first Passover celebration. An extra glass of wine was poured, and he was told it was for the prophet Elijah. His uncle told him that the wine would recede as the invisible Elijah took a sip—and so it seemed to the impressionable youth. This magical transformation occurred only in the boy's mind—a fact he was later to appreciate. He transformed this insight into one of the most fruitful hypotheses in the history of experimental social psychology.[17]

Circles of meaning, then, large and small—these are the elements of the drama of everyday life. Circles connect the protagonist to transformations—of nature, of others, of the passing scene, of the protagonist's own identity—and these are the essence of drama. Solitary confinement is the most severe punishment ever devised for human beings, because it prohibits any participation in circles of meaning and thus eliminates the possibility of drama.

DRAMATIC BOXES

I find it fascinating that many theorists of the self have used the geometric form of the circle to represent the self—James, Lewin, Jung, and Leary come to mind at once. Perhaps there is a geometry that is the natural mathematics of the soul—incorporative of myth and music. Jung also considered quaternity to be feature of this geometry, and the conjunction of the circle with quaternity forms the essential feature of the mandala image.

Goffman considered the metaphor of the frame to be essential to the understanding of social life, and he devoted an entire book, *Frame Analysis* (1974), to this theme. By frames he meant the set of socially constructed understandings that make up the context for any specific interaction.

To appropriate and extend these geometric ideas in a way that will be useful for the drama of everyday life, I propose the metaphor of boxes—or frames with a third dimension. I suggest that we all live in boxes. Our boxes are not uniform, to be sure. And we do not always live in the same box, but move around from one to another. Even when outdoors, under the full and limitless sky, we are psychologically in a box—for I think it patent and obvious that the notion that we live in a universe without limits is an artificial and scientific idea, and one that is not achieved phenomenologically without great difficulty. Let me now illustrate the potential utility for quotidian psychology of adopting this cubic metaphor.

Imagine a conventional stage—a place where conventional actors present conventional plays before a conventional audience. We, as members of the audience, are privileged to peer into a box, for the fourth wall of the stage is conveniently invisible or transparent. Within this box, all the actions occur—circles in the square. A variant of the classical proscenium stage is "theater in the round"—where perhaps three of the four walls are transparent, but which always retains a solid fourth wall, or at least an invisible basement, from which mysterious region actors can make their entrances and exits.

Actors, onstage, are transformed. If you have ever seen a dramatic production and then later encountered the actors offstage, perhaps at a restaurant or at a party or even backstage—you will have noted the transformation. Accents, postures, costumes, lighting, and makeup have their effects, and the range of those effects is breathtaking.

Evreinoff says, "When I am in the theater I do believe in the immortality of man's soul, while in real life I am only trying to believe in it" (1927, 146). A person's convictions can change with the setting, and Evreinoff suggests that his beliefs while onstage are firmer than they are when offstage. Perhaps this offers a hint of the apparent contradiction many of us in the academy have observed between the conviction and sturdy resolution of our colleagues while teaching in their classrooms and their pusillanimous vacillation and indifference in a general faculty meeting. Change the box and you change the person.

The stage can be a refuge for the actor when life off the stage becomes strained. The director Mark Lamos describes a time after the death of his father when he was an actor in Joe Orton's comedy *Loot,* which involves a good amount of farcical stage business about a coffin and a dead body. Through riven with grief, Lamos managed to rehearse and perform:

> During the day, I grieved; during performance I laughed at death.
> Actors who go on performing through illness or heartbreak speak of

the beneficent effect of "Dr. Greasepaint"—because you lose yourself inside a life whose outcome is known to you, it's a life shared with people in the dark and a community of actors, it's a life that pulsates with more boldness and therefore—miraculously manages to both transcend and acknowledge our existence. The great plays—comic or tragic—work within us this way: sustaining, validating, transforming. (1996a, 1)

Boxes provide transforming perspectives. This is essentially the same point that the drama theorist Kenneth Burke (1969) makes in presenting and defending his position on perspectivism. No fixed view of our reality can do justice to its features, for those features change in their meaning and significance depending on the perspective that is taken. This entire argument about a dramaturgical approach to psychology is nothing but a perspective, a particular point of view brought to bear on our subject matter—ourselves and the world we live in. The special advantage of this perspective is that it enables us to see the intimate connections between the drama of our everyday lives and our psychological processes—our perceiving, thinking, social relations—and our pathologies. Nothing in this argument negates the potential value of a biological perspective, or a sociological perspective, or an economic perspective, or a perspective induced by taking some psychedelic drug. I do not argue for the equal value of all these perspectives, for each has a range of pragmatic utility. An unsatisfactory view of reality is one that cannot shift perspectives—so that one stays all of the time in the same box. No transformations, no drama, and the result is predictable and boring.

I have visited boxes of slam poets, square dancers, skeet shooters, schizophrenics, alcoholics, drug addicts, deconstructionists, missionaries, fishermen and farmers, football players, sports car buffs, bagpipe players, and country clubbers—boxes of Carnaval-jumping Brazilians, fraternity pledges, and church deacons as well as psychologists and professors of various sorts. If you are blessed with a reasonably long life, you will compile your own interesting list of boxes—little theaters wherein the play is earnest and the players all convinced of their grasp on reality. To some of these boxes I come as a visitor only, as a tourist or observer, more or less awkwardly placed, depending on the hospitality. In other boxes I am a full participant, losing myself in the action.

MORAL AMBIGUITIES

All of this shifting about might suggest a certain moral looseness. Viewing life as theater can evoke fears of moral corruption. Emerson evinced such fears. Emerson was certainly a master of the theater of the podium, and was compelled in his life to some astonishing dramatic gestures, such as opening the coffin of his long-dead first wife in order to view her corpse, thus somehow assuaging his grief or assuring his sanity. But he reserved some of his most vitriolic criticism for the life of the theater. As Robert Richardson has noted, "He railed against the 'poison and rottenness' and the 'existing viciousness of the drama,' concluding that 'theatre is the sewer in which the rebellious vices exhaust themselves'" (1995, 42).

Of course, he has a point. Professional theater, like professional religion, tends to draw some rather narrow and vicious types into its ranks. The world of theater seems to have a morally liminal quality about it—the very term "legitimate theater" suggests that the illegitimate kind is not far removed. It is as if those who embrace so openly and easily the possibility of transforming themselves from their respectable identities into something entirely alien are not, in the end, to be trusted as stable characters. Goffman pointed out that we have a moral stake in maintaining the consistency of the selves we present. Those who are willing to be actors are playing with a power to be feared.

The theater is, after all, real. That reality can be terrifying and terribly distorting. A particularly grim case of theatrical distortion is provided in *Actors in the Audience* (1994) by Shadi Bartsch—a remarkable work on the politics and theater of ancient Rome. Bartsch makes the case that some Roman emperors used theatrical performances as a way of testing the fealty of their subjects—or, put otherwise, of using their subjects to gratify their insatiable and unspeakably cruel egos. Nero, for example, would perform some musical numbers, while his soldiers and henchmen would survey the audience to see the degree of enthusiasm manifest in the applause for the performance of their divine leader.

Thus the privilege of safely observing a performance on stage through the invisible fourth wall was violated for these audiences. Instead, they were turned into actors—and if their act was not sufficiently convincing, they would be picked out and punished with sword or club:

> The audience's response to the performance itself, not their protest against political measure or taxation, is now the criterion for their punishment; and although they are spectators it is they who are watched, set as it were on-stage themselves and compelled to play a role they do not feel . . . Nero literally constrained his audience to be actors . . . the interaction of the emperor and audience in the theater provides . . . a dramatic parallel to the insidious relations obtaining between the emperor and his subjects when the stage was far from sight. (Bartsch, 1994, 9–10)

It seems a long distance between children playing peek-a-boo, engaging in the innocent exploration of the world's dramatic possibilities, and wicked Nero dispatching those subjects in his audience whose show of appreciation seemed insufficiently sincere. The drama of everyday life is inclusive of these extremes and of vast reaches between them. All of life is not drama. We are not on all of the time—not even to ourselves. We sleep. And some of the time we are simply not engaged, not connecting with any exterior circle—either by the meditations of our selves or by conversations out of our identities. But insofar as we truly live, we cannot keep from acting.

But now a question arises. This blurring of the line between conventional theater and the drama of everyday life creates a sense of confusion. What is to be taken as serious and what as pretense? How can we tell when to take things seriously? I explore this question in Chapter 2.

SERIOUSNESS

All the world is not, of course, a stage,
but the crucial ways in which it isn't
are not easy to specify.
—Erving Goffman

Considering human life as drama brings both promise and peril. The promise is that we can understand human thought and conduct by first knowing the roles we play and the particular demands of the settings wherein the play takes place. The peril is that this approach can seem absurdly unfixed; for if all conduct is contextual, and if we are all just acting all of the time, then how can the individual finally be described, how is a scientific psychology conceivable, and how do we avoid a footless relativism and a theoretical nihilism? How do we avoid concluding, in the words of the Beatles, that "nothing is real, and nothing to get hung about, Strawberry Fields forever"?

DRAMA AND THE SERIOUS

These considerations have led me to explore the warrant for taking the dramaturgical approach to psychology seriously, and in turn to explore the general problem of seriousness. Why are some forms of human activity regarded as serious and some not? Once sensitized to this word, I found a general resonance of my concern throughout Goffman's writings, in which seriousness appears to be a pervasive, if unacknowledged, motif. I offer some examples from *The Presentation of Self in Everyday Life* (Goffman 1959):

When an individual plays a part he implicitly requests his observers to take seriously the impression that is fostered before them. They are asked to believe that the character they see actually possesses the attributes he appears to possess, that the task he performs will have the consequences that are implicitly claimed for it, and that, in general, matters are what they appear to be. (17)

Practical jokes and social games are played in which embarrassments which are meant to be taken unseriously are purposely engineered. (14)

The implication here is that an honest, sincere, serious performance is less firmly connected with the world than one might at first assume. (71)

I propose that a consideration of the utility of the dramaturgical approach to psychology brings us hard against the question of seriousness. I propose as well that the meaning of "the serious" must be derived from context and is not absolute.

At once we see a divergence between a dramaturgical approach and that of mechanistic science, with its root metaphor of the machine and the accompanying notion of the replicable event (Pepper 1942). The employment of this world view enables science to posture as ultimately serious, for it makes it appear to be grounded in something timeless and universal. Viewed dramaturgically, the mechanistic scientist appears ludicrously self-deceived because he does not recognize the provisional and confining character of the root metaphor. A contextualist world view, in contrast, exposes its scientist-practitioners to the charge of not being serious—of being mere journalists, chroniclers of events, undisciplined by rigorously applied criteria of truth-value. The root metaphor of the historical event does not imply universality or perfect replicability of events, but just the contrary—that events are conditional, provisional, and intelligible only within unique contexts. Viewed contextually, the meaning of seriousness itself is not absolute but relative. But this meaning is no less compelling or important for being relative.

Seriousness implies a duality, as the quotations from Goffman should make clear—and the duality is between appearance and reality. Seriousness refers to an alignment between appearance and reality, and unseriousness (playfulness, falseness, whimsy, caprice, deception, frivolity) to the lack of such an alignment. The problem of identifying seriousness is complicated because of the possible disjunction between the way the actor intends to be taken and the way an audience actually takes him. And further, a third party might consider both actor and audience to be mistaken as to their seriousness, as an atheist might judge a prayer meeting.

Consider a few cases. The class when called to order by the teacher departs to seriousness.[1] Unruly children in a therapy group become attentive and cooperative—they get serious—when a videotape camera is installed to record the sessions. The swain who asks a father for his daughter's hand is examined to see whether or not he is in the serious mode. Melodrama is amusing; tragedy is serious. Comedy is light and diversionary; humor is resonant, instructive, and therefore serious. Work is ordinarily serious and play is ordinarily not. It is said that modern professional athletes take themselves seriously and their sport lightly (Will 1990). Serious psychology is to be distinguished from pop psychology or Sunday-supplement psychology. The world of opera contains *opera seria* and *opera buffa,* and ironically a *buffa* work such as *The Magic Flute* may be taken more seriously by contemporary audiences than a *seria* work such as *La Clemenza de Tito.* Science is serious. In the introduction to the Harvard Group Scale of Hypnotic Susceptibility, subjects are reassured that they will not be asked to do anything silly or embarrassing, for "we are here for serious scientific purposes" (Shor and Orne 1962, 4).

In all of these cases, the claim as to where seriousness resides is problematic and context dependent. A bullfight can be described, in Hemingway fashion, as supremely serious, with its climactic "moment of truth." Or it can be seen as an elaborately staged frivolity, as full of contrivance and exaggerated posturing as professional wrestling matches in the United States—which are taken with astonishing seriousness by many.

The claim to seriousness is thus like a dart that can be thrown back and forth, with no fixed home. Like a dart also, claims about seriousness can bring pain, as when a novelist learns in a solemn review that her work is not to be mistaken for serious literature, or when a scholar discovers that the claim to seriousness emerging from years of lonely work is not ratified by a jury of peers at the time of a tenure review.

These points about seriousness can be illustrated by an episode that I witnessed some years ago. A famous psychiatrist who advocated the application of psychoanalytic theory to historical material lectured to a sizable audience on his brand of psychohistory. The talk was followed by a commentary from a rather pugnacious historian, who delivered a devastating criticism of the psychohistorical enterprise, depicting the entire effort as a complete waste of time with no redeeming social significance; and more, as pernicious to credulous youth. Later, after the session was adjourned, the host escorted the speaker and his critic to the parking lot. During this walk the speaker attempted to achieve some rapport with the critic with a jocular remark to the effect that both were, after all, interested in a common search for truth. The critic's parting comment was this: "I want you to remember that I was serious—I meant everything I said." This might be seen as a breach of academic decorum, for usually when one breaks the frame of a heated debate, the antagonists are quick to resort to soothing pleasantries, avoiding obvious points of disagreement and inventing ingratiating little jokes in order to create the semblance of solidarity at a level above the fray.

Seriousness is related to dramatic context. The major determinant and index of seriousness is the extent to which the dramatic import of an event can be generalized across a variety of settings. Put another way, seriousness depends upon trans-contextual generality. Many Germans in the 1930s did not take Hitler seriously, considering him a lunatic or a buffoon. This judgment was to be undone by the devastating and enduring impact of the Third Reich on Germany and the world. So too for disorders of the body and the mind. A flu is serious if it impedes one from performing one's daily round of roles. Loss of a leg is more serious than an appendectomy and loss of sight more serious still. Deafness is generally a more serious defect than blindness, because fewer roles are available to the deaf than to the blind (see Sacks 1989). "Serious" is a word that appears frequently in DSM-IV, referring in general to the extent to which a disorder is functionally disabling and enduring—limiting the dramatic contexts wherein one can perform creditably. One cannot qualify as having a major depressive episode unless one shows dysfunctional symptoms consistently for a minimum of two weeks. Individuals who cannot function in a normal range of dramatic contexts because of their withdrawal and isolation and their delusional thinking are called schizophrenic. They seem unable to maintain a stable frame for their thoughts and actions—and thus their thoughts and actions cannot be taken seriously, even though the individuals who have such experiences may take them quite seriously indeed. Whether mental illness or moral verdict, as Theodore Sarbin and Joseph Mancuso (1980) argue, some individuals are in this sense quite dramatically limited; their disorder is serious. (On schizophrenia see Chapter 11.)

THE VARIABLE SERIOUSNESS OF DEATH

It might seem that at the end of this progression of disorders a constant appears—an event of uniform and final seriousness. But the seriousness of death is by no means a constant but again depends upon trans-contextual generality of impact. Let us take a serious case first, one described by Henry Adams after the sudden death of his forty-year-old sister, Louise:

> He had passed though thirty years of rather varied experience without having once felt the shell of custom broken. He had never seen Nature—only her surface—the sugar-coating that she shows to youth. Flung suddenly in his face, with the harsh brutality of chance, the terror of the blow stayed by him thenceforth for life, until repetition made it more than the will could struggle with; more than he could call on himself to bear. He found his sister, a woman of forty, as gay and brilliant in the terrors of lockjaw as she had been in the careless fun of 1859, lying in bed in consequence of a miserable cab-accident that had bruised her foot. Hour by hour the muscles grew rigid, while the mind remained bright, until after ten days of fiendish torture she died in convulsions . . . One had heard and read a great deal about death, and even seen a little of it, and knew by heart the thousand commonplaces of religion and poetry which seemed to deaden one's senses and veil the horror. Society being immortal, should put on immortality at will. Adams being mortal, felt only the mortality. The first serious consciousness of Nature's gesture—her attitude towards life—took

form then as a phantasm, a nightmare, an insanity of force. For the first time, the stage-scenery of the senses collapsed; the human mind felt itself stripped naked, vibrating in a void of shapeless energies, with resistless mass, colliding, crushing, wasting, and destroying what these same energies had created and labored from eternity to perfect. Society became fantastic, a vision of pantomime with a mechanical motion; and its so-called thought merged in the mere sense of life, and pleasure in the sense. The usual anodynes of social medicine became evident artifice. Stoicism was perhaps the best; religion was the most human; but the idea that any personal deity could find pleasure or profit in torturing a poor woman, by accident, with a fiendish cruelty known to man only in perverted and insane temperaments, could not be held for a moment. For pure blasphemy, it made pure atheism a comfort. God might be, as the Church said, a Substance, He could not be a Person. (Adams 1918, 287–289)

This death of a vital woman stung her brother to his core. Conventions regarding nature and society collapsed. Everyday reality was transformed. Comfort was elusive. Even God was called into question. Such a death represents the pinnacle of seriousness, because a life is stopped suddenly when it is in full course. A life rich in drama is reduced at a stroke to nothing.

The death of another woman provides a useful contrast. Alice James, the youngest of the James children (William was the eldest), died at the age of forty-two. She was a woman of remarkable intellectual power, but was frail physically and emotionally. She suffered from "nervous disorders" which kept her bedridden during the last several years of her life, a time she spent in London, under the eye and care of her brother Henry. While in London she was diagnosed as having a potentially fatal tumor. William, upon learning of this, wrote her a remarkable letter:

So far from being shocked I am, although made more compassionate, yet (strange to say) rather relieved than shaken by this more tangible and immediately menacing source of woe . . . Vague nervousness has a character of ill about it that is all its own, and in comparison with which any organic disease has a good side. Of course, if the tumor should turn out to be cancerous, that means, as all men know, a finite length of days; and then good-bye to neurasthenia and neuralgia and

headache, and weariness and palpitation and disgust all at one stroke—
I should think you would be reconciled to the prospect with all its
pluses and minuses! I know you've never cared for life, and to me, now
at the age of nearly fifty, life and death seem singularly close together in
all of us—and life a mere farce of frustration in all, so far as the
realization of the innermost ideals go to which we are made respec-
tively capable of feeling an affinity and responding. Your frustrations
are only rather more flagrant than the rule; and you've been saved
many forms of self-dissatisfaction and misery which appertain to such
a multiplication of responsible relations to different people as I, for
instance, have got into. Your fortitude, good spirits and unsentimental-
ity have been simply unexampled in the midst of your physical woes;
and when you're relieved from your post, just that bright note will
remain behind, together with the inscrutable and mysterious character
of the doom of nervous weakness which has chained you down for all
these years. As for that, there's more in it than has ever been told to
so-called science. These inhibitions, these split-up selves, all these new
facts that are gradually coming to light about our organization, these
enlargements of the self in trance, etc., are bringing me to turn for light
in the direction of all sorts of despised spiritualistic and unscientific
ideas. (in Lewis 1991, 461–462)

So William, instead of railing against the unkindness of fate or
expressing the terror of confronting the unknown, speaks to his sister
matter-of-factly of her impending death, as a deliverance, as a matter of
being relieved of her post and her pain. More, he invokes the positive
hope of the future existence of some part of her self, at least, in this
relieved state. That William knew his subject is revealed in Alice's reply:

A thousand thanks for your beautiful and fraternal letter . . . Of course
I could have wanted nothing else and should have felt . . . very much
wounded and *incomprise* had you walked round and not up to my
demise . . . It is the most supremely interesting moment in life, the
only one in fact, when living seems life, and I count it as the greatest
good fortune to have these few months so full of interest and instruction in the knowledge of my approaching death. It is as simple in one's
own person as any fact of nature, the fall of a leaf or the blooming of a
rose, and I have a delicious consciousness, ever present, of wide spaces
close at hand, and whisperings of release in the air . . . Your philosophy

of the transition is entirely mine and at this remoteness I will venture
upon the impertinence of congratulating you upon having arrived "at
nearly fifty" at the point at which I started at fifteen! 'Twas always thus
of old, but in time you usually, as now, caught up. (in Lewis 1991,
463)

These two examples suggest that the seriousness of death depends
upon the extent of its reduction of life's dramatic range. For Henry
Adams, the death of his sister was shockingly cruel and could not have
been more serious. For William James, though he was not exactly light-
hearted, the impending death of his sister produced a warm and life-
affirming response, even suggesting the sunny possibility of a life beyond. R. W. B. Lewis (1991) notes that William's intense interest in the
paranormal and the supernatural can be dated from the death of his
infant son, just three years after the death of his father, Henry James Sr.
Perhaps these deaths prompted him to bore a hole of possibility through
the confining wall of mortality, in order to reduce the seriousness of
finality. Product of the "will to believe" or not, the prospect of another
world does reduce the intensity of death, for it makes death not an
ending but merely a dramatic transition.

SERIOUSNESS AND VENTURING FORTH

The valuation of seriousness by individuals and by society is not constant
but variable, and this valuation is context dependent in a way that
cannot be described by a simple formula. This point can be illustrated by
a consideration of the ways adventure and seriousness are related.

José Ortega y Gasset argues in *Meditations on Quixote* that the
romantic novel was an imaginative invention designed to provide a
release from the unrelieved seriousness of the Middle Ages. Life can be
like a prison: "Soon after we begin living we become aware of the
confines of our prison. It takes us thirty years at the most to recognize
the limits within which our possibilities will move. We take stock of
reality, which is like measuring the length of the chain which binds our
feet. Then we say: 'Is this life? Nothing more than this? A closed cycle
which is repeated, always identical?' This is a dangerous hour for every

man" (1914/1961, 132). Adventure is a means of shattering the oppressive seriousness of reality. But leaving the castle to go questing involves a cost to those left behind. Someone must mind the castle while the knights are gone. Since it has traditionally been the role of men to go questing while women remain behind in the confinement of domesticity, we can see here an essential element of the feminist protest. Domesticity is serious business, but it is also confining and boring. Adventures introduce the possibility, not only of an escape from this kind of seriousness, but of the achievement of a more exciting kind of serious worth. Today it is the ideal to provide equality of opportunity to the sexes—so that women will have the opportunity to leave the castle to meet the challenge of the wild unknown and men will be allowed to take their turn at mopping.

Adventures are costly and often do not pay off for the large social collectivity. The gambler is likely to play with the rent money, with little thought about who is to pay the losses. Those who seek cheap thrills by experimenting with drugs, profligate sex, or simply bumming around the land are imposing some cost on society, with benefits accruing only to the adventurers. Such people are viewed by society as escapists, and not serious. The explorer, the scientist, the scholar, the author, and the artist also engage in their quests at the expense of the social collectivity. But here the hope is that benefit will eventually return to the collectivity in the form of advanced knowledge, new discoveries, inspirational art—or at least in the form of a great story. Those engaging in socially responsible adventures are considered to be serious—a grant of faith often accompanied by a grant of money.

Sometimes questions are raised by the sponsoring society about the legitimacy of certain forms of adventure, on grounds of seriousness. The ancient Hebrews had no use for pagan sport. Neither did the Puritans. Both societies considered sport to be unproductive and therefore not serious. Recreational drugs are commonly banned, not out of arbitrary meanness, but because of their social costs. Gambling is commonly banned for similar reasons.

Recently, questions have been raised about the legitimacy of the exploratory adventures of scholars and professors in the United States (cf. Bloom 1988), with suspicions being voiced that colleges and universities have ceased to be socially accountable, and that many academic disciplines have become self-serving, unresponsive, and arrogantly defensive. One can imagine scholars who take themselves seriously, but who contribute nothing and communicate nothing to the sponsoring society, and who form enough of a mutual support group to maintain the impenetrability of their capsule from the serious concerns of critics. One can hear both sides ask, with equal stridency, "Are you serious?" Seriousness is a matter of dramatic context: what seems serious from inside the capsule can appear ludicrously self-indulgent and vacuous from without.

Adventure provides a release from the dead and the deadly. It is creative and constructive, even as it is sportive and risky. It is life-creating and life-enhancing, even as it departs from the oppressive seriousness of the closed chamber. Adventure creates drama and story and contributes to the realization of completed identities. Seriousness is at risk in every venturing forth. But without venturing forth there is no valuable seriousness. Without the possibility of adventure, domesticity becomes a painful reduction of life and is statically serious—oppressive. A new and dynamic seriousness is produced when one opens the closed chamber and redraws it—when the prison is exchanged for the arena.

TAKING THEATER SERIOUSLY

One enters the arena from the street, from quotidian life, from not knowing what to say or how to say it, with vague or pointed worries about the job, the family, the project. One leaves the arena, at worst, bored and irritated at having wasted time. But at best a dramatic performance can be exalting—leaving one inspired and energized. One returns to the street, to quotidian life, to the questions of what to say and how to say it, to the job, the family, the project. If all of this is the same as it was before one entered the arena, then the performance wasn't serious theater. But if things are different, better or worse—if events, words, people, even the street itself, seem to have a different aura about them—then it was serious theater, and serious to the degree of general change. Once again, seriousness is a matter of generalizing effects over various contexts.

The world, of course, is not a stage. But drama overflows the ordinary stage. In *Frame Analysis,* Goffman describes a progression from formal theater to unstaged, actual social life. Intermediate points include interactive theater, nightclub acts, performing or telling a story at a party, and spectator events such as sporting contests. And then:

> A little less pure are personal ceremonies such as weddings and funerals. These occasions typically contain watchers, but the latter function as witnesses and as guests and usually come by invitation, not fee. I might add that whereas the wider significance of a contest outcome is often seen as part of recreational life and in one sense unserious, ceremonials tend to provide a ritual ratification of something that is itself defined as part of the serious world. (1974, 126)

Goffman would allow that contests are indeed serious to those for whom they matter. We can see frequently how charged with seriousness are contests producing the most fictitious claims to honor, virtue, and strength (the tears stream shamelessly from the battered senior quarterback and the cheerleader alike, as the clock ticks down to zero and the other side chants, "We're number one!"). The greater seriousness of weddings and funerals is that these rites refer to changes that are widely acknowledged—more enduring in their consequences than an athletic contest.

A public event such as a commencement ceremony provides an interesting case, for as with weddings and funerals, one attends such an event by invitation and as a guest rather than by fee. A commencement is what Sarbin refers to as a "rite of intensification," marking a passage from one phase of life to another in the unfolding of a life narrative. The intensification is provided reciprocally and mutually by the graduates and their witnesses, who are the main parties involved. The presence of professors, officials, speakers, singers, musicians, poets, and attendants increases the dramatic effect of the intensification, as do the flowers, banners, and printed programs. The individuals enacting these supporting roles are typically unaffected by the proceedings—for them the day is routine, only mock-serious.

What is being intensified, being pressed into existence out of thin air and more or less haphazardly accumulated, accredited accomplishments, is an educational degree, now publicly certified and meant to be taken seriously by relatives, potential employers, and still-higher institutions of learning. At the ceremony itself, one is entitled to make light of things or to complain about the length of the talk or its emptiness. One may even skip it, and be awarded a degree *in absentia,* a common practice for less cohesive student bodies, or for degrees already so imbued with seriousness, such as Ph.D.'s and professional degrees, as to make the intensification of the commencement ceremony otiose. But no matter how filled with levity the day, the accomplishment thereof is quite serious—the degree is now official and has a certain cash value. There are limits to the cross-contextual value of a B.A.—it won't do you much good in a flood—but along with passports, drivers' licenses, social security numbers, and of course cash or cash equivalents, advanced degrees are among the most seriously regarded fictions of our time.

Life is in theater and theater is in life; no hard distinction can be drawn between the two, as Nicolas Evreinoff (1927) argued so brilliantly. We find absurdity in life, absurdity in theater, and crystal-clear coherence in both as well. Scholars write about what really was going on in Hamlet's mind, or what could have caused Othello to be so blind in his rage, or Lear so mad. Purely fictional characters are taken most seriously; Anthony Hopkins, who played an anthropophagic and psychopathic psychiatrist in *Silence of the Lambs,* reported that many people were for a time terrified of him. Shakespeare is serious literature—serious because the concepts and conceits, characters, phrases, themes, and ideas he explored and presented have influenced the entire world for hundreds of years.

Evreinoff suggested that the essence of theater is transformation—working transformations, small and large. A gaggle of raw recruits is transformed into an army. The child becomes a student, the student a scholar, the scholar a savant, the savant a guru, the guru a criminal and a fool. I walk down Main Street, greet a friend, buy a newspaper, make a deposit at the bank, and get in my car and drive off. Transformations occur quickly from role to role, or slowly. The seriousness of things is unstable, negotiable, always a matter of potential conflict and challenge. One may not segregate the fictional, illusory, and artificial from the rest of life and regard the residue as serious stuff. On the contrary, we regard as serious any believed-in reality, no matter whether it is a first-order reality or the shadow of a shadow. To refuse to enter into this theatrical play is to take one's own standpoint as fixed and immutable—as deadly serious. It was in this sense that Evreinoff said, "Least of all would I like to be considered a serious man" (Golub 1984, 145).

People are serious about many things. Their seriousness can be tested in many ways, but it always comes down to a matter of generalizing over contexts. If the project of the Crusades in the Middle Ages is not something people could take seriously today, there is no reason to believe that it was not taken at least as seriously in its time as is the modern project of medical research to find a cure for AIDS. James said, "Each world whilst it is attended to is real after its own fashion; only the reality lapses with the attention" (1890, vol. 2, 293). For some realities the attention span is quite long, for others short. Seriousness exists within the confines of that span, great or small.

THE LIMITS OF SERIOUSNESS

In *Homo Ludens,* Johan Huizinga asserts that "God alone is worthy of supreme seriousness, but man is God's plaything, and that is the best part of him. Therefore every man and woman should live life accordingly, and play the noblest games, and be of another mind from what they are at present" (1949, 211–212). The value of a dramaturgical approach to psychology is that it encourages us to be of another mind from what we are at present, to venture out of the encapsulated seriousness of behaviorism, psychoanalysis, Gestalt psychology, object relations theory, social learning theory, or any view of psychology that would be fixed and final. All theories are arbitrary and only provisionally essential. Theoretical encapsulation leads sooner or later to irrelevance; by irrelevance I mean a failure of psychology to extend beyond the boundaries of its own context, and therefore to be serious. The notion of *ars gratia artis* can easily be abused by artists and scientists alike, for self-serving enterprises fail to acknowledge the massive web of mutual dependencies that supports us. The political, social, economic, and cultural supports for our serious work are commonly ignored because they are silent and taken for granted. We can be responsible to the beneficent socius only by refusing to take ourselves too seriously.

The objective of the dramaturgical approach to psychology is to broaden our vision, to avoid the "certain blindness in human beings" with which, said James, we are all "afflicted in regard to the feelings of creatures and people different from ourselves" (1900, 326). James noted the danger of education as a producer of narrow encapsulation rather than as a means of escape from it: "We are trained to seek the choice, the rare, the exquisite exclusively, and to overlook the common. We are stuffed with abstract conceptions, and glib with verbalities and verbosities; and in the culture of these higher functions the peculiar sources of joy connected with our simpler functions often dry up, and we grow stone-blind and insensible to life's more elementary and general goods and joys" (342).

There is a difference between education that protects and reassures and education that liberates and challenges—and there is a place for each. In our reading and listening we look for both—reassurance and challenge. In his essay on the lecture, Goffman (1981) suggests that the lecturer both "protects us from the wind" and conveys to us a picture worth conveying of a reality to which we might otherwise be blind.

The writer Annie Dillard has a similar point to make about reading:

> Why are we reading if not in hope that the writer will magnify and dramatize our days, will illuminate and inspire us with wisdom, courage, and the possibility of meaningfulness, and will press upon our minds the deepest mysteries, so we may feel again their majesty and power? What do we ever know that is higher than that power which, from time to time, seizes our lives, and reveals us startlingly to ourselves as creatures set down here bewildered? Why does death catch us by surprise, and why love? We still and always want waking. We should amass half dressed in long lines like tribesmen and shake gourds at each other, to wake up; instead we watch television and miss the show. (1989, 72–73)

As we read *Don Quixote,* our own days are dramatized, just as Cervantes in reading books of chivalry gained life for his own imagination. Sarbin (1982) has suggested that the Quixotic Principle—the tendency for us to transport into our own lives elements of the dramas and figures of drama we see about us—is a major means for the growth and development of life narratives. The play with believed-in imaginings has serious consequences—projecting across life's contexts and providing enduring enrichments to character.

The serious psychologist must take lightly the ordinary distinction between fiction and reality, for psychological reality is fictive in origin. Our enterprise is played out in revealing and concealing, always with potentially heavy moral consequences. In his autobiographical memoir, *Self-Consciousness,* John Updike has this to say about the moral ambiguity of revelation:

> Fiction, like life is a dirty business; discretion and good taste play small part in it. Hardly a story appears in print without offending or wounding some living model who seems himself or herself reflected all too accurately or not accurately enough—without that deepening, mollifying element of endless pardon we bring to our own self . . . So my art, like my religion, has a shabby side. These memoirs feel shabby . . . a worthy attempt, which is not, in a larger sense, good: the attempt to work an altruistic good through print is generally a mistake, a miscarriage. I am in these paragraphs struggling to expose what should be—in decency, to conserve potency—behind: behind the facade, the human courtesies, my performance, my "act." But there seems, my having gone this unfortunately far, still this to say: one believes not merely to dismiss from one's life a degrading and immobilizing fear of death but to possess that Archimedean point outside the world from which to move the world. The world cannot provide its own measure and standards; these must come strangely, from outside, or a sorry hedonism and brute opportunism result—a greedy panicked heart and substance abuse. The world punishes us for taking it too seriously as well as for not taking it seriously enough. (1989, 231–232)

To assert seriousness is to imply a point of reference that is at least temporarily fixed. And so the preacher preaches—in full voice and full of terrible conviction, so that the congregation trembles. Later, he is seen to quarrel stubbornly with his wife about whether the chicken is overcooked, and so a question arises about seriousness. One is not always serious in the same way, and the way in which one is serious comes from the dramatic context of the moment. Universal seriousness is not possible, for there are too many subworlds, and any one of them can become absorbing, but only at the exclusion of the others. One can dance and sing and be a scholar and a bon vivant, keep in shape by minding one's diet and exercise, be a responsible and informed citizen by reading much, be faithful and true to one's friends and family and congregation, be a fancier of bees and a dedicated housekeeper. Seriousness in any of these callings will commonly compete with seriousness in the others, say what you will about balance; again, a universal seriousness is impossible.

The final word is this: psychology cannot pretend that it has within it some final Archimedean point from which to illuminate, much less move, the world of mental life and human conduct. Instead, we psychologists have the capacity to move about from provisional point to provisional point, making our researches and explorations, clarifying problems and mysteries, but not finally resolving. Our serious commitment is to the movement itself from point to point, awakening ourselves and our audiences to new dramatic perspectives for viewing and experiencing human life; gaining thereby the possibility of extending serious sympathy to conditions not our own and simultaneously losing the limitation of a static seriousness and a resultant self-adulation. The world is not a stage—it is all the stages.

INDIFFERENCE

Neither the whole of truth nor the whole
of good is revealed to any single observer,
although each observer gains a partial
superiority of insight from the peculiar
position in which he stands.

—William James

William James's essay "On a Certain Blindness in Human Beings" is a compilation of cases illustrating the enormous differences from person to person (or from creature to creature) in their interest in and judgment of exactly the same conditions. The dog is amazed that its master can spend hours staring at the pages of a book, and the master does not understand the charming smells of trees and lampposts. The tourist is blind to the North Carolina mountain dweller's pride of place, seeing in his cove clearings unspeakable squalor where the native sees comfort and a sign of victory over nature. One person is frankly bored by natural phenomena, while for Wordsworth (1805/1947, 37):

> To every natural form, rock, fruit, or flower,
> Even the loose stones that cover the highway,
> I gave a moral life: I saw them feel
> Or linked them to some feeling: the great mass
> Lay bedded in some quickening soul, and all
> That I beheld respired with inward meaning.

James's argument about selective blindness can be extended and integrated with a dramatic analysis of emotions and the lack of emotions—indifference or emotional blindness—a psychological opposite of seriousness. My major claim is that indifference to events that might seem to have a *prima facie* claim to emotional significance is related to the dramatic significance of those events or of circumstances in the life of the observer, and is not a result of absolute stimulus value or inner biological events. Also, indifference is selective in the same person. Caring is invested in some objects and utterly withheld from others; this selective investment of caring is intelligible from a dramaturgical point of view. Finally, the range and character of indifferent events and objects vary widely from person to person in a way that is consistent with a person's constructed identity and the relation of that identity to the world. All of this illustrates the principle that dramatic meaning is not absolute but depends upon context or framing.

Since moral judgments about actions are a direct function of selective indifference, it follows that systems of morality are selective and partial as well. The moral quality of objects, and hence their emotional significance, inheres not in the objects but in the way those objects are described by the selective moralist. The same piece of meat can be described as a sizzling sirloin or as the partially burned, excised muscle of a murdered steer. Similarly, right-to-life advocates are fond of storying the unborn fetus, removing it by graphic rhetoric from the realm of the indifferent to the realm of emotional regard. Abortion-rights advocates are careful to describe the fetus as "tissue." Defenders of euthanasia focus on the misery and suffering of the old and infirm, while those who oppose assisted suicide emphasize the sanctity of human life.

Nature is both profoundly indifferent and amoral to life in all its forms. A solitary walk in the woods is comforting, for the trees and creatures of the wild will not reproach us. We are thus free for a while from the judgments and sanctions of our peers, even as we sense that nature neither loves nor hates us. We are moral creatures living in an amoral world. Our capacity to story ourselves and the world about us removes our indifference, if only in part. I claim that our normal condition is to be indifferent to life and death, except our own life and death and then secondarily the lives and deaths of such other creatures, real and imagined, as come to be connected to us in our made worlds. We are not indifferent to objects in our own narrative worlds, even though those objects are made up. The tears in the theater at the death of Ophelia are as real as any others. Art pulls us away from the indifference of nature into our fretful humanity, and there we cry, we laugh, we shudder, we blush. All art is propaganda, as Orwell said, and the intended function of propaganda is to make us care where we were formerly indifferent. Perhaps the passions produced by art are greater in their force and magnitude than those in our quotidian world, where the slump of indifference is a normal posture.

We live in circles of meaning, circles created by our own life histories; our formal and informal connections to other people begin, endure for a while, and are often forgotten—then passing out of the circles of meaning and into the void of indifference. We read of the death of a childhood chum—someone once intimate but now long out of the circles of our active life—and accord it notice, but just a passing sadness. If you want a person to care about something—say the war in Kosovo, the victimization of women, the pestilence in Rwanda, the internecine wars in Russia, the deadly consequences of easy access to guns—you must bring these issues vividly into the person's circle of meaning by words and pictures, dramatically composed and frequently repeated.[1] Consciousness is naturally lazy and retreats easily into indifference; consciousness-raising removes indifference, if only for a while.

Enormous individual differences exist in the capacity to maintain a wide range of conscious and moral interests in the world. Wordsworth roams nature and invests each object with moral life. Thoreau is inspired and alive at Walden Pond, not bored and withdrawn. Whitman exults where other men snore. Listen to Emerson: "Crossing a bare common, in snow puddles, at twilight, under a clouded sky, without having in my thoughts any occurrence of special good fortune, I have enjoyed a perfect exhilaration. I am glad to the brink of fear" (in James 1900, 257). Similarly, Carl Jung (1965) talks to his pots and pans and cannot shake his animistic visions. Annie Dillard, in our time, takes seriously the task of teaching a stone to talk—and says, after prolonged and assiduous observation, "Nature's silence is its one remark" (1982, 69). For those with sufficient imagination, even inanimate objects can enter into dramatic circles.

FUNCTIONS OF INDIFFERENCE

The British Museum is a vast trove of fascinating objects—so rich and so extensive as to beggar human imagination. The objects are silent, as Dillard has noted—but the stories about them are a reprise of all human history. I recall a guided tour through the museum that illustrated the positive function of indifference. After some extensive and fascinating talk about the displays of Sumerian bas-relief sculpture, the Elgin marbles, and the Rosetta stone, our guide strode off without a word to the other end of the museum, taking us wordlessly past huge quantities of labeled and storied artifacts—mountains of antiquities of stone, wood, silver, gold, and ceramic, displays from all over the world of native cultures and their objects—only to stop at last before a display from an archaeological dig in England, where she resumed her discourse. No explanation was offered for her selective interest in a tiny fraction of the museum's artifacts. None was needed, for what else could be done in a mere two hours?

We must be indifferent to much that could command our interest and engagement, for there is simply not enough time and attention to go around. A form of madness can result from an unbridled interest in anything that happens to fall into view. One starts to prepare a meal, only to be distracted by the newspaper, and then a barking dog reminds one, strangely, to put out the trash, leading to a trip through the clutter of the cellar, to rearranging the wrenches on the bench, then remembering to fix a leaky bathroom faucet, noting that the bathroom smells musty, searching for disinfectant, and so on and on, until one may remember at last to go back to the preparation of that meal. A lack of practiced and discerning indifference would make a visit to a bookstore or a supermarket impossible; the selection of a record from a record store or a meal from a large menu would become a nightmarish task. This lack of indifference produces a phenomenon that is known clinically as tangential thinking. Talking with a client who exhibits this kind of thinking is like trying to handle a live eel. We live within our little stories, and react with lively interest only to a small portion of what could command our engagement, allowing the selective anesthetic of indifference to do its work for survival's sake.

GENERALIZED INDIFFERENCE

At an extreme of generalized indifference is a young man deserving the clinical label *alexithymia*—a term applied to patients who have marked difficulty in verbal expression of emotions and a limited capacity for fantasy. Let me call him Alex.

Alex, when I knew him, was the teenage son of a divorced couple. His father was a boat captain and his mother was a practical nurse. He had one older sister. Alex had a tested IQ of about 120, but had been a poor student. At the time of my meetings with him (arranged at the insistence of his mother), he had no friends, no interest in sports, no hobbies, no apparent sexual interests or activities. He did not help with household chores. He was passive, not actively rebellious. When he reached age sixteen he began to stay home from school, often sleeping until mid-afternoon. He lived with his mother, who had brain cancer, and his older sister, who was actively rebellious and had a strong interest in boys. The mother tried to force Alex to go to school, but he refused. She often took him to school and dropped him off at the door, only to have him walk home. She resorted to locking him out of the house, but he simply stayed in the garage all day. She removed the television set from his room, but since this punishment produced no apparent consequences, she eventually gave in and restored it.

At age seventeen Alex was sent off to a military academy. For a while he seemed to be adapting well to the place. However, within six weeks of his arrival he was dismissed for two instances of petty theft and returned home.

In counseling sessions Alex was passive, difficult to engage, but adept at defending his pattern of life. When asked what he would like to do in the future, he said he would like to be a boat captain, like his father. When I pointed out that he would need to complete high school and enter into a training program to obtain this objective, he responded that he was smart enough to pass the tests when he had to. Indeed, he did complete a GED program, to which his uncle ferried him once a week. When I told him that his passivity and lack of cooperation created difficulties for his sick mother (the case at hand was his refusal to shovel snow to clear the driveway, forcing his cancer-ridden mother to do this chore), he simply said that he didn't care. In fact, the response "I don't care" was Alex's most frequent locution, and proved to be as exasperatingly unanswerable as the similar phrase used by Herman Melville's Bartleby, the Scrivener: "I would prefer not to."

Alex did not appear to be terribly unhappy, but his indifference and moral inertia made the people around him miserable. He was not utterly indifferent to everything: he was interested in science fiction, computer games, movies, and boats. But even these objects in his circles of meaning seemed not to be essential, for if any of them was removed, or if an attempt was made to arrange them in a Skinnerian-contingency fashion so as to make him more responsive, he simply ignored the absent object and waited things out. He was capable of spending days on end circulating placidly between bedroom, kitchen, and bathroom. He showed no emotion—neither crying nor laughing. His mother reported that as a baby he had cried very little.

He lived with his mother until she died. Despite her repeated threats to throw him out of the house, and several attempts in this direction, he always wandered back home, and she always took him in again. When his mother died of cancer, he displayed little emotion. He went to live with his father for a time; I do not know what turns his life has taken since then.

While Alex is an extreme case among human beings, perhaps in another sense his attitude toward life is a natural one, amoral as it is. Dillard has this to say about emotions in nature: "It is our emotions that are amiss. We are freaks, the world is fine, and let us all go have lobotomies to restore us to a natural state. We can leave the library then, go back to the creek lobotomized, and live on its bank as untroubled as any muskrat or reed. You first" (1974, 178).

VARIETIES OF INDIFFERENCE

Alex may be indifferent all his life, may never wake up to life's feasts and shows. Indifference typically comes with advancing years, when one may proclaim, like the aging Solomon, "All is vanity and a vexation of spirit." A case in point is the critic Edmund Wilson, who partook most bountifully of life's banquet throughout his long life, but whose memoirs in his later years reflect a continual reduction in his circles of meaning.

Initially his feelings of indifference were transitory. He said when he was sixty-five: "At my age, I find that I alternate between spells of fatigue and indifference, when I am almost ready to give up the struggle, and spells of expanding ambition, when I feel that I can do more than ever before" (in Updike 1994, 159). Eleven years later, the specter of indifference had grown: "When I look back, I feel quite definitely divided from my earlier self, who cared about things in a way I no longer do. All that comedy and conflict of human activity—one gets to feel cut off from all of that . . . One looks down on an empty arena. What were we all doing there?—running about, jostling and shouting, exchanging vital gossip—involved in great world wars now as trivial and futile as we used to think the Balkan wars were" (ibid., 163–164).

So for Wilson, a man of insatiable curiosity and vast appetites, his final emotional state was one of saturnine indifference, and as death approached he could not quite think why he lived or remember the heavy significance of his efforts. That this is not inevitable in the old is proved in Wilson's own observation of Pope John XXIII, whose unceasing efforts as an octogenarian with cancer to modernize the Church he found heartening. Samuel Clemens was bitter and in a rage as he approached death, Igor Stravinsky continued to compose with positive and vital interest until the end, while Wilson was indifferent. One may walk up to death in different ways.

Indifference can be a collective as well as an individual phenomenon. The anthropologist Michael Herzfeld (1992) has written an excellent treatment of collective indifference, *The Social Production of Indifference: Exploring the Symbolic Roots of Western Bureaucracy.* The forms taken by human identity are determined by culturally inherited patterns, stories, narratives, and roles. In the mid-nineteenth century, modern nationalism and racial ideologies, as well as the bureaucratic ethic, emerged as major shapers of identities. The sequel is that the limits of indifference are redrawn to correspond to national and racial groupings. The bureaucrat is entitled to restrict caring and to become indifferent in a wholly new and expansive way. His circle of caring does not extend beyond his own little agency.

CAUSE AND CONSEQUENCE

As our stories are shaped, so are our patterns of caring and indifference. These in turn determine the selectivity of our morality—whom and what we strive to save, and whom and what we are content to let perish. Indifference is opposed to seriousness; it is the reduction or atrophy of caring into the narrowest of circles. Alexithymia is a chronic failure of human caring. The more common case is depression, a protracted episode of reduced caring, in which the suffering person is seen by others as in serious trouble, while the sufferer may welcome sleep more than awakening to the confusing demands of other people.

All of the examples I have cited are consistent with the proposition that emotional reactivity and the lack of it—indifference—are dependent upon the connections between individuals and their circumstances created by their dramatic constructions. The alexithymic person participates in practically no ongoing stories: circles of meaning are tiny, perhaps as a result of an extreme version of what Mary Ainsworth (1989) called a "fearful-avoidant" pattern of childrearing, or perhaps, as Jerome Kagan (1994) suggests, because of a genetic disposition to extreme apathy. The aging person can be deprived of the possibility of continuing to live a storied life, as the infirmities of the body reduce freedom of movement. The collective indifferences of the nationalist, the racist, the bureaucrat are a direct function of historically conditioned identities. A cardinal symptom of depression is an indifference to people, to activities, to objects. One possible cause of depression is the sense of indifference or lack of caring from others—a prospect that can be made more rather than less likely by material success (see Chapter 7).

I have argued that indifference is a natural condition—that none can escape it. But our human capacity to produce and live in a narrative world gives us the capacity to escape from the pervasive indifference of the anthill, the beehive, or the flock. These structures are efficient—much more efficient than our own, in which emotional squeamishness keeps us from eating our own dead. But they are unlike the human socius in the crucial respect of not producing our peculiar forms of passionate caring. It is something of an evolutionary paradox that our material success can bring about a moral turn in the direction of the termite colony. People can act like termites more easily than termites can act like human beings.

Psychology is coming to recognize that human life cannot be understood at all without the premise that we are as much biographical creatures as biological ones. Biography is story, is narrative, is a construction—and it produces feeling in its train, in exchange for natural indifference. We live in seas of dramatic construction and are vigilant to notice the smallest portents of changes in the weather of our own region, and to these signs we are not indifferent. Yet we are thoroughly and naturally indifferent to all outside our ken and to much within it not related by story to our own little areas.

INDIFFERENT REGARD

The story is told of a politician who, after a long and tumultuous life, came at last in fear and trembling to appear before the throne of God for final judgment. The strains of the requiem mass coursed through his head—*Dies irae, dies magna, calamitatis et miseriae.* God loomed above him at a great desk. "What is your name again?" asked God. "Mortimer Smith," whispered the client. "Smith—Mortimer Smith—yeah, here it is. You're okay. Next?" "Okay? Is that *all?*" protested Smith as the attendants hurried him out of the chamber.

For those of us brought up in the Western tradition, it is better perhaps to be condemned to Hell than to suffer the humiliation of such indifference—divine or human. I am told that Buddhist thinking is in this sense opposite to our own—for Nirvana is a not the result of positive striving but rather of the relinquishment of striving, and is itself a state of perfected indifference. The drama of Western life will not admit such a passive premise. For us, being regarded with indifference by those friends and relatives and lovers who are *supposed* to be connected to us by their stories is the cruelest form of punishment.

Members of the Heaven's Gate cult who committed mass suicide in 1997 were manifesting an indifference to human life that was in some cases just the reciprocal of the indifference they experienced from the world. On a videotape made of the group just before their demise, one woman testified as follows: "I don't have any choice but to go for it because I've been on this planet for thirty-one years and there is nothing here for me."[2]

I don't think a tour through the British Museum would have much interested her. Nor would she have been impressed by Wordsworth or Thoreau. She was involved in another story, quite incredible unless you were part of that pathetic community. No circles of meaning connected her to the world outside Heaven's Gate.

The capacity for human caring is a result of being cared for. Those who are not cared for are in danger of falling off the stage.

BOREDOM

Dominant psychological principles are not so much discovered as they are materialized out of the air of the times. Up until the middle of the twentieth century, the central motivational principle within psychology was that of equilibrium—the dominant principle of physics for the action of mechanical systems. Applied to psychology, the idea is that organisms derive their motive force from an energy imbalance of some kind. Tensions within the body or within the mind produce actions that tend to reduce those tensions. Hunger is a model case. As the body burns energy in the form of glucose, a deficit of nutrients is created in blood and tissue. This produces a drive for the ingestion of food and the restoration of the required level of glucose. For Freud, the master motive was sexual in character—but the principle is the same. Libidinal energy arising in the id produces psychic tension. The release of this energy produces pleasure and a restoration of balance. Likewise, the Gestalt tradition in social psychology, represented by such figures as Kurt Lewin and Fritz Heider, made use of the concept of equilibrium to account for social motivation. Individuals are moved to behave by valences and vectors in force fields, and they make evaluations of other people in such a way as to achieve balance. The biological principle of homeostasis is still presented in virtually all psychological texts as an important key to understanding human motivation. It has seemed obvious to many generations of psychologists that the object of life is to rest—poised in equilibrium, in perfect peace, not needing to toil, rather as one imagines a fetus in the womb or a person floating in one of Dr. Lilly's aquatic chambers, sensing no discomfort, neither hot nor cold, experiencing a lightness of being. But if this view of motivation were correct, it would be hard to imagine why such a thing as drama exists in human experience.

My conjecture is that this idea of human motivation is the precipitate of an age of hard work—when the business of living for the mass of people was considerably more arduous in a physical sense than it is in the developed world today. In Clark Hull's famous version of stimulus-response psychology, work is a negative quantity in the behavioral equation—something to be avoided, like punishment. Principles borrowed from physics—conservation of energy and the laws of thermodynamics—provided models for how psychological energy systems must function. Psychological entropy was envisaged as an ultimate goal state—an utter quiescence with no remaining differentials in the distribution of energy. This must have seemed quite a satisfactory motivational principle in the late nineteenth and early twentieth centuries: relief from the demands of physical work was a cardinal objective of life—a reason for joining the ranks of the learned professions, a reason for becoming rich in order to afford idleness.

THE ESCAPE FROM BOREDOM

It is quite difficult to escape intellectual prejudices that were laid down as truth in the classrooms of our youth. It has been difficult for psychology as a whole to escape the prejudice that homeostasis is a master motivational principle.[1] By now, the weight of hundreds of studies and arguments, as well as the persistent reminders of common sense, has removed the principle of homeostasis from its dominant position in the psychology of human motivation. After all, those who have the means for indefinite leisure usually choose not just to rest, as Thorstein Veblen (1934) argued long ago in *The Theory of the Leisure Class*. Rather they engage in conspicuous consumption, build castles, create industrial empires, hunt, fish, race yachts and cars, engage in incautious dalliances, drink too much, and kill themselves in disproportionate numbers. Common people as well, when given the opportunity to pause from their toils, engage in carnivalesque fantasies, go on pilgrimages, put on harvest feasts, spend more than they need to on weddings. An earthenware pot is equally functional with or without ornamentation. But the boredom of quotidian life is broken by the effort to create aesthetic devices for the enrichment of mere function. College students often look bored in the classroom. But they display enormous energy under the less oppressive circumstances of their social lives.[2]

The amount of drama in our lives is not a constant but is highly variable. Boredom is the other side of drama. Drama develops out of boredom—usually, but not all the time. Chronic and unrelieved boredom fits the description of alexithymia, as presented in Chapter 3. But the common sequence is for boredom to serve as a reason for seeking dramatic action as a relief, even though that drama in itself is not always pleasant.

I think of the scores of couples I have seen for marital counseling. Boredom, in one way or another, is always a central issue in their lives—an inability to retain the dramatic interest in their lives together. In many ways in our contemporary society, domesticity is the enemy of drama, for the easy familiarity of the home erodes dramatic interest in favor of boredom. And boredom, in turn, leads one to imagine other dramas in other places with other partners or with no domestic partner at all.

Here is a case. The young marketing executive comes home from work. All day he has been dealing with crises major and minor. He has had to put on a smiling face for clients and co-workers. Coming home to his wife of ten years, now somewhat plumper than she was as a bride, he does not try to make himself interesting or attractive to her. Neither does she try to make herself interesting or attractive to him. They tacitly give themselves permission to coexist with the other without especially trying to please. The home becomes flaccid, without vitality—a neutral staging area where one dresses up only to go out. The place is a mess and no one seems to care. One may flip on the television or try the Internet or read a magazine—masking the inherent boredom of place with diversions without destination. Sex becomes an empty charade. Shorn of the passion that animated earlier unions, the acts of sex become painfully mechanical—imitations of making love.

The divorce, preceded or not by lies and infidelities, is going to be costly and painful—but at least it will not be boring. Even though life after the divorce is likely to be strewn with difficulty and annoyance, it will seem in prospect, at least to one partner, to offer more dramatic interest than the enervating status quo.[3] It is sad that marriage partners often fall into grim silence with each other—for the silence can be more dangerous than argument and battle. George and Martha, in Albee's play *Who's Afraid of Virginia Woolf?* end up rather sheepishly reconciled, after a most inventive and energetic series of games—performed, as it turns out, for the delectation and diversion of each other. It is a revelation to discover that they really do care about each other.

The sociologist Orrin Klapp (1978) has distinguished two types of quiescence—the good (peace, serenity) and the bad (boredom, loneliness). Likewise, there are two kinds of openings to stimulation—the good (excitement, creativity) and the bad (chaos, noise). Klapp notes that we live our lives in cycles of openings and closings—ideally cycling between excitement and peace, but often between boredom and chaos. Klapp makes the point that all stages in this cycle are inherently unstable in that they cannot be sustained indefinitely. Thus the prolongation of peace eventually produces boredom and the extension of excitement inevitably produces exhaustion. Cycles of opening and closing are fundamental to human life—we both wake and sleep. These cycles are also characteristic of drama: there are openings and closings, and both phases can be qualified as good or bad. No play is so engaging that we wish it to go on forever, or even to encroach seriously on our bedtime. Sir Edmund Spenser's epic poem *The Faerie Queen* is truly wondrous, but it has been said that no one ever wished it longer. The rule of life is cycles, not stasis. Too much of a good thing is not good. Too much beauty palls.

Klapp (1986) presents a strong argument that boredom has become ever more conspicuous as a plaint of our times. He shows in detail the increased frequency of themes of ennui, despair, decadence, and apathy in twentieth-century art, drama, literature, and measures of the quality of life. He cites Becket's *Waiting for Godot* and Sartre's *No Exit,* along with surveys of worker dissatisfaction in the United States and epidemic alcoholism in Russia—all suggesting a rise in the level of world boredom, a slow and insidious crisis of lack of interest, banality, and information overload: "A strange cloud hangs over modern life. At first it was not noticed; now it is thicker than ever. It embarrasses claims that the quality of life is getting better. It reduces commitment to work. It is thickest in cities where there are the most varieties, pleasure, and opportunities. Like smog, it spreads to all sorts of places it is not supposed to be . . . The most common name for this cloud is boredom" (Klapp 1986, 11–12).

If boredom is increasing, attempts to escape the tentacles of tedium should also be ever more prominent. Appropriate sequel observations are easy to make: drug use, gambling, the transmutation of news into entertainment, celebrity worship, the hypertrophy of spectator sports, the growth in popularity of fantasy games, and the increased commercialization of sex all strike me as plausibly related to a generalized attempt to escape from boredom. The sad and paradoxical effect of some attempts to escape boredom, such as gambling or alcohol use, is that repeated trials at escape only lead to a deepened depression—a magnified despair born of repeated failures to escape despair.

But this is incomplete and ungenerous, for the escape from boredom will not always result in some kind of individual or social pathology. Indeed, one may move from a bad closing to a good opening—as when an artist is invited to perform on a new stage after a period of inactivity. Artistic, literary, and scientific imaginations can gain a creative charge from a state of boredom. Plenty of evidence can be found for the exercise of these imaginations in our everyday world. We have no lack of new art, new literature, new science. Engaging and authentic drama can be created to answer the need to escape from boredom.

The epigraph to this chapter, from the poet Joseph Brodsky, suggests that boredom is a condition of human life, not just *modern* human life. I think Brodsky is right. I offer the thesis, without extensive argument or evidence here, that boredom appears to be a much more conspicuous problem in our era because of changes in the nature of work, of time, of information, and of redundancy. We live in an urban world, where the pace of events is rapid, where there is a flood of information, much of it quite alien in its significance to our daily lives, and where mass production and mass media produce a bewildering sameness in our lives (see Chapter 15).[4] If boredom is basic to the human condition, it is masked (and masking is equivalent to temporary elimination) by active participation in what seems to be authentic living, supported by a community that has not grown so sophisticated as to have lost faith in itself—to have become alienated. I think of the Shaker communities of the last century as examples of hard-working people who never seemed to be bored. Meaningful work was always to be done, and community support for an arduous way of life was strong. "'Tis a gift to be simple," they sang. Alas, simplicity is a gift that later generations have not wanted. As meaningful involvement in the work of sustaining life has diminished, the potential for realized boredom in life has been revealed. Skinheads and punks and acid rockers are first of all products of abundance in our society. Surplus produces boredom.

In the essay from which the epigraph is taken, Brodsky suggests to the young that they seek not to escape boredom but to embrace it and to learn its lessons—of humility, of limitations to our own significance in the large round of things, of the shape of our passions. "The best way out is always through," says Robert Frost.[5] Brodsky concurs and so do I. As part of the cycle of living, it is well to be out of the drama at times, to permit and go through periods of boredom, or more positively, of solitude. If you view meditation as boring and therefore impermissible, your soul may be starved. The quality of the drama that occurs at the next stage will depend upon the lessons that are learned in the slow darkness.

THE LURE OF DANGER

Many observers of the human condition have noted a tendency toward perversity among members of our species—where perversity means doing things that appear to be against one's interests. Dostoevsky in *Notes from Underground* suggests that if a man's only opportunity for freedom were to go crazy, he would do so out of sheer cussedness. Nietzsche provides an aphorism to similar effect: "To reject the practical, to change the purposeful into the purposeless, the necessary into the arbitrary, and to do it in such a way as to cause no harm, by simply imagining it, out of sheer playfulness, affords joy and pleasure, because it frees us for the moment from the fetters of the necessary, the purposeful, and the practical." Freud asserted that antisocial and self-destructive impulses derive from unconscious processes. I don't think it necessary to posit an unconscious source for such unacceptable ideas. It is more parsimonious to suggest that people have secrets and that the content of these secrets can easily be revealed under suitable conditions. I have often asked students in an introductory psychology class to describe on a notecard something they would like to do if they knew they could do it with no threat of punishment, embarrassment, or reprisal. Here are several responses:

I would stand naked at the top of the Eiffel Tower.

I'd like to smoke a joint in the Oval Office, joined by the President.

I would physically assault my Econ prof.

I want to be a hooker.

Taken together, the responses provide ample evidence that a wild and outlaw temper is easily accessible. We should be grateful that so few undergraduates act out these fantasies.

The urge to engage in unacceptable and dangerous activity is both pervasive and powerful. As a clinician, I commonly encounter people who do things that are not in their interests—who live more dangerously than they should. A wife cheats on her husband—not because she doesn't love her husband, but for the thrill of it. Having an affair with a man at her place of work provides endless intrigue, secret messages, the constant danger of being discovered, the experience of living on the edge. She says, "I can't go on living this way." And yet she chooses to go on living this way. A recovering heroin addict, long since over the physical effects of withdrawal, accepts an invitation from a friend after a Narcotics Anonymous meeting to score some dope—knowing with virtual certainty that this act will mean the end of his job and being thrown out of his father's house. A high school sophomore, already on the edge of expulsion, succumbs to an impulse to moon a busload of girls. A seventeen-year-old girl, a heroin user, brags about being clean and agrees to a urine test, knowing that she intends to use as a sample the bottle of clean urine she is concealing in her coat.

Michael Balint (1959) defines a thrill as having three essential elements: (1) The course of action must present some actual danger. (2) One must decide voluntarily to pursue the course of action. (3) There must be a high probability of escape or delivery from the potential negative consequences of the course of action. Thus having unprotected sex not only produces the pleasure of intercourse but also provides a bonus of thrill value for a substantial number of extramarital participants.

It seems that much ingenuity is devoted to getting into dangerous situations knowingly, with the expectation that somehow a rescue will take place. Perhaps these are tests of one's secret omnipotence. Oscar Wilde said in *De Profundis* that illicit sex "was like feasting with panthers. The danger was half the excitement" (quoted in Brown 1996, 247). In his account of his life as a homosexual, Roger Brown entitles one chapter "Lie Down with Panthers" in homage to Wilde:

> I imagine his "panthers" to have been athletic feline young men with muscles rippling beneath velvet skin. And Oscar's panthers would have been working class. It was risky for a pale plumpish middle-class aesthete to lie down with such fellows, and they must often have unsheathed their claws and scratched him painfully. In the end they gave testimony that helped send him to Reading Gaol and into exile, but he never said that he regretted keeping company with them.—I was much older than Oscar and it was risky for me to pay to bring morally dubious panthers to my door. I was scratched many times until at the age of seventy I could take no more. (1996, 247)

The urge to drama and to danger is not always so abject and sad. In her cinematic portrayal of Joan of Arc, Jean Seberg is offered the opportunity of returning home as a hero after her initial military successes. But she doesn't want to go home, for she fears—and more than fears, dreads—the anticipated dullness. So she stays and tries to stir up further activity, with the result that she is burned at the stake—an outcome she chooses over life in prison, again a dreaded prospect because of the potential boredom. The movie suggests that because of her aversion to boredom Joan became a martyred saint.

It is an easy piety to oppose war, disease, and disaster. The United

Nations, the Pope, the National Council of Churches, and all right-thinking men and women denounce these obvious forms of evil. And yet our interest in these evils is undeniable—evident on every newsstand, on every listing of television programs, on radio talk shows, and in college curricula throughout the land. One of the characters in Carlos Fuentes's novel of revolution and war in Mexico, *The Death of Artemio Cruz*, remarks, "Sometimes I think the absence of blood and death throws us into despair. It's as if we feel alive only when we're surrounded by destruction and executions" (1964, 36). We do not want to believe this. But ask yourself whether or not you consider the United Nations, the Pope, and the National Council of Churches to be boring.

The thirst for drama does not automatically lead to bloodlust, as William James argued in his essay "The Moral Equivalent of War" (1910/1984). But it is a mistake to miss the point about the deep perversity of human nature. Something in us continues to want to test boundaries, to see and experience the rare, the exotic, the dangerous. Perhaps I am speaking here of a tendency less biological than cultural—something Hellenic in its origins and not characteristic of the East. All we know of the ancient Greeks are their wars and struggles, adventurous voyages and homecomings. Even the intellectual style of Socrates is confrontational. I imagine that Eastern philosophy might give possible place to permanent peace—a Nirvana where we cease for once and always to be in transit and come to accept ourselves in the permanent present, without lust, without perversity, without the urge to kill, and certainly without the urge to kill time. So let us say that Western human culture—rather than human nature in the universal sense—is never going to be at peace with peace, because peace is too boring. Even so, as James suggests, perhaps we can make do with games and debates, without falling back into fighting.

NOT THE DESTINATION BUT THE JOURNEY

The argument is this: out of quiescence—boredom, peace—we search for engagement in drama. The important term here is "engagement," for in some ways it matters less what the ostensible purpose of our dramatic activity is than that we are engaged in it. Objectives of action are not always what they seem to be. Can it be that the teacher is less interested in what students learn than in performing well as a teacher? Perhaps the priest is less interested in leading his flock to God than in saying the Mass, singing the hymns, reciting the prayers. Are not those prayers meant more for the living and present congregation than for the omniscient God, for whom the prayers are probably pretty redundant? The fledgling actor burns to act—any play will do, and if not an actual play, well then perhaps television commercials or modeling.

Artists like to produce art. Scientists devote their lives to conducting research. Athletes want to be in the game. The life of a scholar is meaningful only if the scholar is engaged in the production of something that can be displayed or published. We do, of course, have museums and archives and libraries where some of the results of the labors of artists, scientists, and scholars are displayed and stored. But the joy of a creative act, like the joy of sex and the joy of eating, lies in the doing of it, not in the contemplation of its products.

The psychologist Mihaly Csikszentmihalyi (1988) has studied chess players, rock climbers, dancers, surgeons, and artists with a view to describing the ways these activities contribute to the lives of the people who perform them. The overwhelming conclusion to emerge from this work is that the joy is in the doing. His book is entitled *Beyond Boredom and Anxiety: The Experience of Play in Work and Games,* and the subtitle carries the major message of his research. Over and over again, he found that work can be deeply pleasurable—ludic activity, play, done for the intrinsic joy of it, or to use Csikszentmihalyi's term, "autotelic."[6] Artists, he found, were interesting in making art, and only secondarily in art itself:

> One thing struck me as especially intriguing. Despite the fact that almost no one can make either a reputation or a living from painting, the artists studied were almost fanatically devoted to their work; they were at it night and day, and nothing else seemed to matter so much in their lives. Yet as soon as they finished a painting or a sculpture, they seemed to lose all interest in it. Nor were they interested much in each other's paintings or in great masterpieces. Most artists did not go to museums, did not decorate their homes with art, and seemed to be

generally bored or baffled by talk about the aesthetic qualities of the works they or their friends produced. (1988, xi–xii)

Csikszentmihalyi employs the term "flow" to describe an ideal kind of activity, wherein the challenge presented by the task is roughly equal to the ability of the person engaged in it, and where the activity seems unforced, in a groove, moving along progressively with complete absorption in the task, without worry and self-consciousness. Basketball players describe themselves as being "in the zone" in certain games, when the challenge is great and the performance seems naturally to match the challenge. Csikszentmihalyi find that this experience, this inner state, is characteristic of people in many walks of life. What appears to be the objective of the activity—a theorem proved, a painting produced, a composition completed—is not really the objective: "On a closer look, these goals lose their substance and reveal themselves as mere tokens that justify the activity by giving it direction and determining rules of action. But the doing is the thing" (1988, 37).

Often the fantasy of doing is the thing, and this creates contradictions. I live near the mouth of the Connecticut River. It is picturesque to see so many expensive boats—sailboats and cruisers—*at their moorings.* One occasionally sees boats on the river and on Long Island Sound, to be sure, but it is safe to say that most pleasure craft spend at least 98 percent of their lives not sailing but moored or dry-docked. (I have checked this impression with three marina managers, and they think it conservative.) With some extra time and some extra money, one dreams of sailing—it looks so perfect, so sublime. One buys a boat, but then discovers that one doesn't have a whole lot of time to spend sailing. Per hour on the water, most boat owners pay an appalling cost for the actualization of their sailor's dreams.

But sometimes, of course, ambitious and adventurous sailing excursions take place. A fine example is provided by David and Daniel Hays, a father and son whose book *My Old Man and the Sea* (1995) recounts the story of their voyage from New London, Connecticut, through the Panama Canal, down the west coast of South America, around Cape Horn, back up the east coast of South America, and finally back to New

London after almost a year at sea. They accomplished all this in a twenty-five-foot sailing vessel, which they had fitted out and provisioned with meticulous care.

The sailors encounter hardships, violent storms, seasickness, the grinding boredom of sameness, sameness, problems with the mechanisms of navigation and steering on the boat. Young Daniel is moved to reflections like this in his journal: "What the hell am I doing here? . . . I'd like to be home balled up on the couch watching a movie about this and eating Chinese food" (40). At another point, Daniel muses about why it is that one spends years dreaming about being at sea and then bends all one's efforts toward speeding to the destination. It does seem puzzling.

But viewed as an instance of the drama of everyday life, this is really no mystery. The Hays voyage fits all of Balint's criteria for thrill—a willing entry into danger with a high probability of recovery. This creation of drama is an intensification of life—resulting in dramatic transformations of several kinds. Boy becomes Man, becomes Captain of the ship; Father blesses Son and recedes to the supporting role of Crew. David Hays is the founder of the National Theater of the Deaf—and he knows a good story when he sees one. But he testifies that rarely in his highly eventful life has he had such an authentic and joyful experience as this self-imposed travail conducted jointly with his son. And, of course, the writing of the book and its rise to bestseller status are significant parts of the adventure. C. S. Lewis said, "Our joy is incomplete unless it is shared." Sharing the story of the voyage truly completes the circle.

The Brazilian novelist Paulo Coelho (1993), in *The Alchemist,* provides a fable of a young man following a dream. The pilgrim's story, it turns out, is in the pilgrimage, and not in some sort of consummation to be achieved at its destination. A Muslim merchant who feels the imperative of a pilgrimage to Mecca is asked why he has not completed the trip: "Because it is the *thought* of Mecca that keeps me alive . . . I'm afraid that if my dream is realized, I'll have no reason to go on living.—I just want to dream about Mecca. I've already imagined a thousand times crossing the desert, arriving at the Plaza of the Sacred Stone, the seven times I walk around it before allowing myself to touch it . . . But I'm afraid that it would all be a disappointment, so I prefer just to dream about it" (1993, 57).

A lot of men in our society feel this way about retirement. They like to dream about it. Sleeping in and fishing and idling about, fiddling around in the workshop, taking up gardening and woodworking, watching the stock market and planning vacations to Bermuda with the wife— it all seems pretty good as a dream. But when given the opportunity, many men would prefer to go on working—not because they need the financial security, but because retirement takes them out of the only sustaining drama they really know—the drama of the workplace. This may be purely an American phenomenon, where men are so workbound as to dread retirement as they would dread being shoved off a lifeboat into the wild sea. The Frenchman, it is said, approaches retirement with equanimity and even enthusiasm, envisaging renewed engagement in the world of politics, culture, and the enriched, metropolitan drama of everyday life that his occupational drudgery has kept him from pursuing. But whatever the cross-cultural reality, the principle that stands is this: retirement is forbidding only if its prospect is one of the lack of drama.

Life is not a destination. It is a journey.

THE FABRICATION OF NEWS

Journey. Journal. Every day, the newspaper must be published, television news programs produced, newsmagazines churned out, with such material, rich or poor, bounteous or lean, as the world has to present to the desks of editors. I think of the news media as a machine with an inexorable, insatiable hunger. It is like the threshing machine I remember from my youth—clattering away menacingly when no sheaves of grain were forked into its ravenous maw, only quieting down and running smoothly when steadily fed new sheaves. When it is running empty, without continuous feeding, one has the impression that the whole huge machine will fly apart. So it is with the news machine. Without its daily charge of fresh material, it is likely to turn ugly and self-destruct.

My claim is that the function of news is to enrich the content of the drama of everyday life. Items in the news give people a spectator's view of large and small dramas unfolding elsewhere, and they give people something to talk about. "Have you heard about the big accident on Route 40?" This sort of thing is far less important than other events that happen in the world. In 1996 a nuclear-test-ban agreement was signed by the world's major powers under the auspices of the United Nations, but the event was scarcely noted in the press. It is not something that Everyman and Everywoman can get excited about. Attending to the news is like looking out the window. The voyeur's appetite is endless, but not everything that is seen will claim interest. Difficulties and temptations will claim interest over more pleasant and safer targets. The rule of attention is the same as the rule of consciousness: troubles first.

The absence of danger is not exciting news. The thrill is to approach danger and to flirt with evil. Dante's *Inferno* is far more popular than the *Purgatorio* or the *Paradiso*. Milton's *Paradise Lost* is his lasting claim to fame. Fifteen editions of it are currently in print. *Paradise Regained* is not in print, not much noted, and to get a copy of it you will have to go to a major library. Good story and good drama deal necessarily with troubles. The emptiness of the news is certainly a kind of trouble, but not a kind that the media are likely to trumpet (see Lubenow 1997, 17). The front page of any newspaper or the content of the nightly television news will have content more appropriate for the *Inferno* than for the *Paradiso*. We say we want Heaven, but could we bear the boredom? Ambrose Bierce's remark "Heaven for the climate, Hell for the company" is impious, but reflects some understanding of what commands human interest.

HUGE PUBLIC PROJECTS

The dramatic potential of trouble as a relief from boredom is also illustrated by the kinds of stories that are used to provide the impetus for large public projects. Pharaohs of ancient Egypt did not require much justification or rationale for the public support required to erect the pyramids. Rule by absolute force is trouble enough for the hapless population required to quarry and heft those massive stones. But in our era some kind of story must be told to persuade the populace to accede to the taxation and effort required for major public projects. It is not enough to say that we will be better off if we have an extensive system of interstate highways, or that curiosity drives us to find out what the Moon is made of or to explore the surface of Mars. To be sure, roadways are built and explorations are conducted for their own sake. But vast projects often require vast stories to justify them.

The German autobahn system was constructed during the Hitler years to facilitate the rapid transportation of troops and war equipment throughout the country, making the Blitzkrieg possible. After the war American officials, duly impressed with the quality and effectiveness of the autobahn system, recommended installation of such a system in the United States. Fortuitously or not, the Supreme Commander of Allied Forces in Europe, General Eisenhower, became President in 1952. The most important public works project of the twentieth century was initiated under his leadership—the construction of the interstate highway system. This endeavor has had massive consequences for all facets of life in the United States—the unique importance of the automobile, the decline of railroads, the decay of urban centers, and the demographic shifts of population to suburbia. But the consequences actually have little to do with the major justification for the undertaking offered in the Congress in the 1950s, when it faced strong opposition from railroads and urban centers. The argument was that an interstate highway system was necessary for national defense. Having just emerged from World War II, Americans were conscious of the potential for a World War III, and the Soviet Union posed a credible threat. President Eisenhower urged the speedy authorization of this Pharaoh-like project on the grounds of national defense. The idea was not to prepare for a Blitzkrieg but to enable the mobilization of our population to defend itself and counterattack against an alien invasion. It hardly seems credible today. You had to be there. The drama was real.[7]

Similarly, our ambitious space program was not initiated out of pure scientific curiosity. The Russian launch of Sputnik in October 1957—during Eisenhower's last term—was the starting gun for the Space Race. It resulted in the 1961 pledge by the newly elected John Kennedy to place a man on the Moon within the 1960s—a pledge made good in 1969. As Tom Wolfe (1983) makes abundantly clear in his description of our manned space effort, *The Right Stuff* (1983), the promotion of manned spacecraft was a dramatic necessity and not a scientific one. Virtually all of the knowledge and technical information about outer space, the Moon, and other planets could have been obtained without ever sending human beings into space. Early astronauts groused about not actually flying or controlling their space capsules but being mainly passive passengers—they wanted a more active role in the drama. Against the background of competition with Russia, the "space race" received enormous public support, with major spin-offs for scientific and technical education in the United States as well as the development of technologies having an impact well beyond the imaginations of those who initiated the program. Wolfe describes the massive public relations effort designed to make celebrities of astronauts, to glamorize space exploration, and to conceal its nether side of greed and personal ambition.

In 1995 the space probe *Magellan* crashed into the atmosphere of Venus after a long and highly productive cruise. The television program *Nova* (October 18, 1995) reported that the scientists involved in the project cried at this predictable ending, for they felt they had lost a friend. The point was made that funding for such projects would be more difficult to find now that the Cold War was over and the need for this sort of prestige competition had diminished. Scientists dramatized the 1997 landing of a mobile rover on the Pathfinder expedition to Mars—naming the rocks (Yogi, Shaggy, Poptart, and so on), providing high-resolution color photographs of the terrain, telling stories about those who designed the rover. In short, every effort was made to exploit the news value of space exploration, trying always to dramatize, to claim interest from a dozing summer population, with the hope of justifying the claims of space explorers for public funding. Everything depends upon the story that is told.

Some attempts have been made to construct a psychometric scale to access individual differences in the proneness to boredom. Richard Farmer and Norman Sundberg (1986) have produced such a scale, and have shown that it has satisfactory reliability and some validity. They have found that students scoring high on proneness to boredom are also more likely to judge a given lecture as having boring content. Sundberg and Herb Bisno (1983) have suggested that boredom is particularly characteristic of individuals in adolescence and old age, periods of life when conventional occupational demands reduce meaningful engagement in the drama of everyday life. Cynthia Lightfoot (1997) provides a convincing argument that the reason for a high level of risk taking among adolescents has to do with their attempts to provide some strong narrative sense of their lives—that is, to reduce their boredom. Sundberg and colleagues (1991) report the interesting finding that young men are generally more bored than young women, and that this is true across cultures. The authors suggest that men are generally more concerned with "doing" than with "being" and that this leads them to be more impatient with situations that do not engage them. James (1890) remarked: "All the qualities of a man acquire dignity when he knows that the service of the collectivity that owns him needs them." It seems that men have a harder time knowing that their qualities are needed than do women.

These observations about individual differences in the tendency to be bored can be enriched by reference to the importance of dramatic context. The same scene can be excruciatingly boring to one person and exciting to another.

A woman I know who does not play or know much about tennis was a guest in a luxury box at a recent U.S. Open match—and was present there for eight solid hours. She found the experience grueling beyond belief. The same woman was enthralled by a two-week boat trip through the Grand Canyon. The generalized potential to be bored is perhaps a stable personality characteristic, but surely qualification by situation is part of the story.

Fishing provides an interesting test case for boredom. To one who is not a fisherman, it seems incomprehensible and utterly perverse to spend hours in a small boat, enduring hunger and privation, in search of an elusive prey that could be won far more easily and cheaply at the local fish market. A fisherman I know says it hardly matters if he catches any fish; it is being out on the water that he loves. But I have a doubt: he never goes out on the water without his fishing gear. I imagine a dramatic cycle. The unknown fish is beneath the waves. To pursue the fish, whether he catches it or not, is drama. Again, the doing is much more important than the realized product of the doing. Similarly, the hunter enters the forest with a sense of excitement, made palpable and real by the loaded weapon he carries. He is traveling on the edge, in pursuit of unseen prey. The hunter and the fisherman are keen on their pursuits—they are not bored. Their spouses and companions, not identified with the drama of pursuit, are quickly sated and wonder at the reserves of energy of their Nimrods.[8]

Hunting and fishing are dramas that one can pursue alone. Not so for many other games. I am a player of squash racquets. Occasionally I have shown up at a squash court without an opponent. Hitting a squash ball alone in a court can be quite satisfying for a time. One gets to hit twice as often as when playing with a partner. There is no danger, and things are completely in one's control. But this activity quickly becomes boring. It is difficult to continue for so long as half an hour. A game with a partner, in contrast, even a game without significance for tournament or standing, is rarely boring, and I can play for more than an hour with total interest—to the point of physical exhaustion. Some dramatic cycles require the participation of the other. Without the other, the selfsame activity is boring.

The evaluative cast I have given to boredom in these pages has been predominantly negative—as something to be escaped or eliminated, as a negative motivational principle resulting in the construction of drama. But I have also hinted, after Brodsky, that there is value in the embracing of boredom, in learning the lessons of humility and finitude that boredom alone can teach us. The psychoanalyst Adam Phillips offers a similar reflection in his essay "On Being Bored":

> That boredom is actually a precarious process in which the child is, as it were, both waiting for something and looking for something, in which hope is being secretly negotiated; and in this sense boredom is akin to free-floating attention. In the muffled, sometimes irritable confusion of boredom the child is reaching to a recurrent sense of emptiness out of which his real desire can crystallize. But to begin with, of course, the child needs the adult to hold, and hold to, the experience—that is, to recognize it as such, rather than to sabotage it by distraction. The child's boredom starts as a regular crisis in the child's developing capacity to be alone in the presence of the mother. In other words, the capacity to be bored can be a developmental achievement for the child. (1993, 69)

Just so. If drama and boredom are related, it is as different parts of a human cycle. Let us say that the human animal is uniquely capable of an existential angst, because we are animals capable of self-reflection. The process Phillips describes is the beginning of awareness that one is a Self, held and nurtured by a Mother, to be sure, but a lonely Self for all of the holding and support.

Great minds, it bears noting, have not been immune to boredom's cousin, depression. Jung, out of his depression, said: "The meaning of my existence is that life has addressed a question to me. Or conversely, I am myself a question which is addressed to the world, and I must communicate my answer, for otherwise, I am dependent upon the world's answer. That is a suprapersonal life task, which I accomplish only by effort and with difficulty" (1965, 318). I wonder if, in an age when many look at the world through Prozac-filtered eyes, it is likely that anyone could develop such a preposterous existential pretension. Or whether the enormous intellectual production that is product of this pretension could ever come to exist. Boredom is part of the dramatic cycle of life. Without it, there is no realization of the boundaries of the self, and without that realization, there is no joy in becoming engaged in the drama of everyday life.

COSMETICS AND COSTUMES

Our cosmetics and our costumes are so familiar to us that it is difficult to see the singular strangeness in the ways we make ourselves up. We emerge, all of us, out of our little night chambers, wherein we have temporarily lost our bearings in uncharted sleep, into the light of day, pausing to arrange our faces and clothe our bodies in a way that will naturalize us for the human company we intend to keep. Every day we achieve this dramatic transformation from nakedness into a socially serviceable appearance. Some days require several or even many changes of costume and of face, depending on the roles we are called upon to play.

In all of this we choose and select—grooming our bodies with more or less attention to the art of managing appearances. But our choices are always constrained by the affordances of our closets and cosmetic cabinets. These, in turn, are supplied from the vast but particular cultural wardrobe that is part of the large theater of our secular existence.

Today's clothing seems natural. But look in the attic to glimpse how the mere passage of time produces strangeness—a foreign quality that is immediately apparent in the examination of old photographs. Now at the end of the century, the styles of the 1980s seem oddly jarring—almost but not quite acceptable; the bell-bottom trousers of the 1970s seem amusing; the hippie styles of the 1960s seem both quaint and ugly; the gray flannel suits of the 1950s seem impossibly dull; the people under all those hats in the 1940s are clearly in a different drama altogether.

A cow today looks the same as a cow a century ago. The farmer has changed his garb considerably over this period, though he is the last to be called a slave to fashion. The selection and control of personal appearance are uniquely human problems—to which comparative psychology has nothing at all to contribute.[1] Cosmetics and costumes are unique to our species and are of profound importance in the drama of everyday life. They are the material means for the transformation of the actor.

APPEARANCE AND MOOD

Appearance is intimately connected with the moods and humors of our day-to-day lives—in a circle of cause and consequence. Evidence of the double connection between how we feel and how we look is all around us.

My grandmother said that shining my shoes would make me feel happy. The promise is that a little polishing will yield dividends in enhanced feelings of well-being. Observing the throngs at the mall, we can surmise that the acquisition of new shoes and new suits, new dresses, new potions and lotions is therapeutic in its purpose—not a matter of satisfying physical needs. Over a million cosmetic-surgery operations are performed annually in the United States—not *reconstructive* surgery, where the objective is to repair a missing or damaged feature, but rather *cosmetic* surgery, to improve serviceable but imperfect features of face and body. Exercise programs have proliferated in recent decades—with some attention to advantages for health, to be sure. But the primary sales pitch at the local spa is to sculpt and buff the body toward the models of physical perfection shown in the ads. It is tempting to say that these models present impossible ideals of perfection—but there they are, and existence is testimony to possibility. The images on television and movie screens, and in magazines and newspapers, support the notion of the attainability of ideal physical form. The actual connection between ideal physical form and inner well-being is, of course, tenuous—though research supports the view that cosmetic improvement makes people feel better (see Cash and Pruzinsky 1990). The "look better, feel better" proposition remains compelling, as it has been for many decades. As Emerson remarked, "I have heard with admiring submission the experience of the lady who declared that 'the sense of being perfectly well dressed gives a feeling of inner tranquillity which religion is powerless to bestow'" (1904, 88).

Even in death, the cosmetician is the last to perform services to the body—now surely not intended to improve the defunct one's mood, but rather to convey by complexion and style of dress an impression of inner tranquillity and worldly success. Our faces—quick, dead, or replicated in photograph or drawing—reflect something of our inner being. George Orwell famously said: "At 50, everyone has the face he deserves."[2] He was speaking of permanently etched lines in the countenance, a manifest autobiography. But more transient states register in appearance as well.

"Beauty is skin deep," says the wag, "but ugly goes to the bone." The truth is that superficial appearances, positive and negative, do have deep significance. I contend that our claims to identity are managed through appearances, and that the reflections of our appearances are our major means of acquiring self-knowledge.

The workings of this circular relationship between outer appearance and inner reality are complex and subtle. A wife who carried on an affair under the nose of an unknowing husband said that she took care to bathe and use cosmetics after her sexual encounters in order to avoid "that JBF look." A famous ballet director insisted that his dancers have costumes of fine silk, for while the difference between silk and rayon might be invisible to the audience, it would be obvious to the dancers, and this would have inevitable consequences for the quality of performance. It seems entirely plausible that the conviction one sees in the performances of famous film couples—Tracy and Hepburn, Bogart and Bacall, Gable and Lombard—derives in part from the offscreen reality of their romantic attachment.

While reality and appearance are in the same circle, their relationship is imperfect—sometimes things are as they seem, sometimes just the opposite. Many stage partners are not otherwise attached. Cosmetics and costumes conceal as well as reveal, but even in concealing reveal a truth about human desire. The historical development of the arts of human decoration is instructive, for the ways people arrange themselves say much about the dramatic forces applying to their times.

SOME ADORNMENT HISTORY

Containers for perfumes, unguents, and body paints were among the precious objects left for the imagined future use of Egyptian mummies. The British Museum contains exquisitely carved toilet articles dating from about 3500 B.C. All known civilizations have employed adornments—for both males and females—but the style and intensity of use vary widely. It is surprising that Louis XIV disdained cosmetics, while approving of a wide variety of costume and other decorative arts. Courtly women in Elizabethan England thought it attractive to whiten their faces in a way that would today seem quite ghastly. The Puritans of early New England disapproved of cosmetics and favored a plain appearance. In the first 150 years of American history, the use of rouge and lip coloring was apparently confined to women at the extremes of the social spectrum— aristocrats and prostitutes (Peiss 1990).

In this country, the history of cosmetics and costumes is inextricably bound up with that of gender. Historians of cosmetics and costume in the United States devote almost all of their attention to women, who are the major practitioners of human decorative arts. Katherine Peiss sees the evolution of women's use of cosmetics as a reflection of the tremendous changes in their social identity:

> In the early twentieth century . . . cosmetics took on new meaning in American culture. They became part of an ongoing discourse on femininity that made problematic women's identity in an increasingly commercial, industrial, and urban world. Women linked cosmetics use to an emergent notion of their own modernity, which included wage work, athleticism, leisure, freer sexual expressiveness, and greater individual consumption. At the same time, new forms of mass culture shaped this discourse, as women began to see their faces differently in a number of novel cultural mirrors: in motion pictures, in mass market

women's magazines and advertising, in shop windows, on fashion run-
ways, and across the counters of department stores. (Peiss 1990, 143)[3]

World War I changed the entire drama of Western civilization in
irreversible ways. The war was the greatest demonstration of collective
stupidity that the world had ever seen. That so many people could be
engaged in deadly struggle with so many others for no clear reason was
an everlasting lesson about the bankruptcy of the old moral order and an
invitation to experiment with new forms and styles. Freud was forced to
concede the existence of a destructive instinct in human beings—a coun-
terforce to the surging life-force of Eros.

Among the changes produced by the war was a vast liberation of
experimentation with the forms of personal adornment—particularly for
women. The woman suffrage movement achieved the vote in 1919, and
in 1921 the first Miss America pageant was held in Atlantic City. Thereafter in the twentieth century, women were to be taken more seriously
and at the same time allowed and encouraged to be objectified as beau-
ties. If these seem contradictory trends, the common element is women's
new opportunity and even obligation to diversify the roles they might be
called upon to play.

Since World War I, women have needed larger closets and larger
arrays of cosmetics on their vanity tables. Their cosmetic requirements
have vastly exceeded those of men. At the same time, and without
paradox, women have moved much closer to men in occupational status,
earning power, athletic prowess, and influence in politics and business. I
say without paradox—for I suggest that the same forces that kept women
from making up their faces also kept them from escaping the domains of
church, children, and kitchen. These parallel presentational and social-
psychological changes are in contrast to what is called "the great masculine renunciation" of late-eighteenth-century Europe and America—
wherein serious men gave up elaborate foppery and finery in favor of a
more somber uniform, in keeping with the newly emerging notion that
work was not to be despised, and the realization that work could not
easily be done in the elaborate masculine costumes of the aristocratic
Old Regime (see Kuchta 1996).

CONTROLLING THE UNCONTROLLABLE

Whereas in the nineteenth century women were advised to pursue the ideal of physical beauty by moral exercises and pure habits of living, the twentieth century has produced a plethora of instrumental shortcuts. In recent decades particular emphasis has been given to the "cult of thinness"—again, applying primarily to women. Weight control is an active concern of well over half the female population. It is common for girls to become concerned about their weight before they reach puberty. A major consequence of the growing power of the ideal of thinness is the growing incidence of psychopathology connected with eating. The number of women who fit the diagnostic criteria for eating disorders more than doubled between 1970 and the mid-1990s (see Smolak, Levine, and Striegel-Moore 1996). In 1972, 23 percent of women reported dissatisfaction with their body image; this figure more than doubled to 48 percent in 1995 (Cash 1995). Nancy Friday (1996) and Naomi Wolf (1991) are among the many feminist critics who at once admit and decry the tyranny of the demand for thinness, even as they describe the gap between ideal and reality as growing ever larger.

If the fight against fat bodies has been discouraging, some remarkable cosmetic victories have been achieved as well. The profession of orthodontics is a product of the twentieth century.[4] Nineteenth-century photographs of men and women rarely show toothy smiles. After the widespread use of toothpaste, tooth powder, and toothbrushes began with the turn of the century, smiles with teeth showing became the norm, but crooked teeth were still an embarrassment. Some malocclusion is found in about 90 percent of the population, and severe malocclusion, now thought to require treatment, is present in about 50 percent of the population. In most urban areas of the United States, at least 50 percent of children receive some form of orthodontic treatment. Most people now show their teeth when they smile. Straight and perfect teeth have become the norm, but not without effort and expense.

Medical and surgical interventions now make possible cosmetic improvements that once were simply out of the question. Liposuction can remove unwanted fat. Ears and eyes and noses and mouths can be amended toward an ideal symmetry and form. Chins can be strengthened, wrinkles removed, neck wattles eliminated. Breast implants and breast reductions are now supplemented by tummy tucks and buttock adjustments. Michael Jackson is unsentimental about discarding his formerly defective appearance, as is Cher. Now anyone who can afford it can potentially look beautiful. A comely appearance was once a matter of the gifts you were given. No more.

The vast majority of those who choose to have cosmetic surgery are women.[5] An interview study of the rationales offered for cosmetic surgery revealed that surgeons have a pronounced bias against performing these procedures on men: "Throughout our interviews with surgeons and former patients, we found implicit claims that what was 'normal' or 'natural' for a woman was *not* normal or natural for a man" (Dull and West 1991, 64). The manifestation of gender is not so much given by nature as accomplished by the purposeful manipulation of appearances—a manipulation that both men and women contrive to support.

The problems with this new capacity are ethical, aesthetic, and deeply psychological. Susan Bordo (1990), writing of the "material girl," claims that the possibility of this new plasticity has profoundly changed the way women think about themselves. It is, for one thing, homogenizing: "That we are surrounded by homogenizing and normalizing images—images whose content is far from arbitrary, but instead suffused with the dominance of gendered, racial, class, and other cultural iconography—seems so obvious as to be almost embarrassing to be arguing here" (657). The elimination of consistency of character as a moral criterion seems to be a major feature of what is called postmodernism. Thus, Madonna emerges as an icon for the ideal woman of our era. She can have sex whenever and with whomever she pleases—can have a child, marry or not marry, play the porno house at night and regain her androgynous innocence by day.

THE DRAMATIC RANGES OF MEN AND WOMEN

My wife has more clothing than I have. Much more. I would guess that the difference is about an order of magnitude. And in this respect we are not an unusual couple. I have made inquiries from time to time of many other couples, and most often the woman has more clothes than the man. Moreover, simple observations on any street or auditorium or marketplace will quickly provide testimony that women dress more variably than do men. They employ the full palette of colors, whereas men are likely to display only blues, browns, blacks, and whites. Women can wear skirts as well as pants. Men, in our culture, cannot wear skirts without being silly.

With respect to makeup, again women are more variable than men. Women can and often do these days appear "without their face on"—with no makeup at all. (And some women, of course, never use makeup.) Most men do not use any facial makeup—a splash of aftershave is about as far as it goes. In an exercise in the course I call The Dramaturgical Approach to Psychology (see Chapter 12), a female student went through the routine she normally follows prior to going out for a big night—equipped with all of her cosmetic props. As she described the steps of preparation, the male students in the class gaped in disbelief. Her routine—by no means excessive according to the other women in the class—took her at least an hour and a half, and made use of cosmetic preparations costing over $150. A male student who described his routine was ready for the dance in fifteen minutes, and his tools consisted of razor, comb, and aftershave. My point is not that women always take longer to get themselves ready than do men, but rather that women are much more variable than men in their preparation time. In the matter of rolling out of bed and into a morning class, from the looks of things, male and female students are quite alike in their prep time.

Think of shoes. Women and men wear the same sneakers and loafers and running shoes. But many women also wear shoes with high heels of various elevations—something that is entirely alien to men. The British design critic Stephen Bayley offers a plausible speculation on what makes high-heeled shoes so fascinating, even though they are utterly impractical:

> In terms of static mechanics they induce a sort of insecurity which some find titillating. If a woman wears a high-heeled shoe it changes the apparent musculature of the leg so that you get an effect of twanging sinew, of tension needing to be released. Her bottom sticks out like

an offering. At the same time, the lofty perch is an expression of vulnerability. She is effectively hobbled and unable to escape. There is something arousing about this declaration that she is prepared to sacrifice function for form. (1992, 145)

Who knows whether women's intention in wearing high-heeled shoes is even remotely akin to Bayley's reading of effect? The point is that, once again, men are more uniform than women. Some short men wear elevator shoes, to be sure—but if they do so, they are likely to do so all the time. A woman can, to a certain extent, control how tall she wishes to be on different occasions. And if Bayley is to be believed, she can immediately increase the sexiness of her appearance thereby.

The differences in dramatic range for men and women in our culture extend to the world of work. While women's participation in the labor force has grown substantially in the last generation, still a larger proportion of women than of men do not work outside the home. According to government statistics, in the mid-1990s some 71 percent of women of working age were employed, compared with 87 percent of men of working age.[6] This is in part a reflection of continuing differences in the structure of incentives for women and for men in the world of work. Most high-paying executive positions are still occupied by men, and women's pay for the same work is still not equal to that of men for many occupations. But whether it is because of differences in opportunities or differences in personal preferences, women are more variable in their involvement with jobs and careers than are men.

This differential in the dramatic range of males and females extends even to the giving of names. A study of first names of students at Wesleyan revealed that the most common first names are given to boys.[7] David, Michael, and Matthew were the most common male names; Sarah, Jennifer, and Elizabeth were most common female names. But the three most common male names applied to 11 percent of all male students, while the three most common female names applied to only 7 percent of all female students. Fully 30 percent of the women in the student body, but only 24 percent of the men, had unique first names. (Because of the large numbers involved, these percentage differences are highly significant.) In this nominal way, women are more variable among themselves than are men. In addition, I would argue that Sarah is more variable in the way she presents herself than is David.

Women in our culture are called upon to perform more different roles, to satisfy a wider range of dramatic requirements, than are men. Men are expected to be students and athletes and to earn a living. Women have all of these expectations, but they are also expected to be beautiful, to have primary responsibility for raising children, to be domestic engineers, and to be responsible for such matters as entertaining, buying presents for family and friends, and nurturing their husbands.

Some might argue that women are by nature more variable—that their menstrual cycles and accompanying hormonal changes predispose them away from consistency and toward change. However, the dramatic requirements of being a woman are by no means fixed by nature, but rather are dependent upon the differential evolution of gender roles in our society. (It is worth remembering that women were excluded from enacting dramatic roles in classical Greek theater as well as in Elizabethan theater.) Women of the nineteenth century were far less variable, far more uniform in their dramatic range than their late-twentieth-century counterparts. Middle-class women were expected to mind the home and the children and not to think of getting a job—and certainly not to go into show business. The last thirty years, in particular, have seen a tremendous explosion in the roles played by women.

An extensive amount of effort and equipment is required to maintain this range. Women in the world of work are vulnerable to a pervasive bias against being overweight or unattractive. Rita Freedman (1986) refers to this bias as "lookism": "a form of social control that influences how people see themselves and how they are seen by others" (4). She cites many cases of women who assert that maintaining their looks is not an option but essential to their effective job performance—as contrasted with men, who are allowed to look pretty much as they please. The demand to be physically attractive imposes a burden on women of which men are scarcely aware.

One consequence of women's heightened awareness of the requirements of being attractive is that they are much more attentive to changing styles and fashions than are men. Marketing researchers, aware of this difference between men and women, arrange shopping environments accordingly. For example, in men's clothing stores, shirts are usually displayed with matching ties—on the reasonable supposition that most men have not the foggiest notion of what goes with what. Women's clothing stores, by contrast, are arranged to take advantage of the greater amount of time and attention women give to the selection of clothing. Accessories are, in general, not displayed with dresses and blouses, but are arrayed nearby—relying upon women's ability to discern the elements of an ensemble.[8]

The reluctance of men to shop is another piece of evidence for the restriction of their dramatic range in our society. I confess that I am typical of my sex. Here is a note I wrote upon visiting a nearby mall. Most men, I expect, will recognize the elements:

> I enter the shopping mall and am overcome by a sense of cultural nausea. The parking lots are jammed. The racks of clothing seem endless. I worry that no one will ever buy this stuff—it seems so wasteful. People, mostly women, are in motion—moving along the marble corridors in search of a better appearance, a new appliance. I stop at a cosmetic store. Hundreds of varieties of eyeshade, of lipstick, of creams and powders and foundations and lotions and mascara compete for attention. The air is impossibly sweet. Made-up attendants smile mechanically and advise the clients seeking improvement. It is a place for dramatic transformation. Thinking about it, the mall is mostly given over to costumes and cosmetics. Clothing stores abound—some specialized for feet, some for intimate apparel, some for casual wear, some for the formal world of business, some offer customized fittings. I think the customers are only half-conscious of what they are doing here.

THE POWER OF DRAMATIC ILLUSIONS

But it is facile to take a superior attitude about the ways other people manage their appearance. Would we wish people to give up the effort of maintaining and improving their appearance? The prospect of carrying on our daily rounds among people wholly without decorative interest is more horrid to contemplate than the ambulating, half-conscious hordes in the malls. We are, truth to tell, much more comfortable in a world of our illusions than we are when face to face with unadorned reality.

The power of illusions is truly impressive. Just a half-mask can change the appearance of a well-known friend so completely that one scarcely knows what to say. The experience of meeting a troop of actors or dancers backstage, after they have removed their makeup and costumes, can be unsettling: what appeared so glorious, so superlatively beautiful, now appears—well, so ordinary. Thomas Mann's (1955) fictional Felix Krull was a master of disguise, a master of appearing to be something that he was not, until he actually *became* that which he was not. He is an exemplar of the advisory phrase "Fake it until you make it." The first time I administered hypnosis to a subject in a research study, my mentor advised: "Don't let him know that it is your first time." Sound advice.

Jorge Luis Borges wrote an essay about Shakespeare entitled "Everything and Nothing." Shakespeare, by Borges's account, had a secret awareness of his inner emptiness, and found a suitable way of covering that emptiness by becoming an actor, a playwright, and an impresario:

> His playacting taught him a singular happiness, perhaps the first he had known; but when the last line was applauded and the last corpse removed from the stage, the hated sense of unreality came over him again . . . He became a nobody . . . The story goes that, before or after he died, he found himself before God and he said, "I who have been so many men in vain, want to be one man: myself." The voice of God responded from a whirlwind: "Neither am I one self; I dreamed the world as you dreamed your work, my Shakespeare, and among the shapes of my dream are you, who, like me, are many persons—and none." (1964, 46–47)

Cosmetics and costumes, not to be despised, are essential tools for the realization of vital illusions. We must appear somehow to one another, and ever since Adam and Eve we have not been able to bear our nakedness. Blessings upon Eve for eating the fruit of the Tree of Knowledge of Good and Evil. Without this first dramatic transformation and the invention of costume, we would have known no others.

FEAR AND GREED

In the drama of everyday life, we often take palpable fictions as real. Through the willing or unwilling suspension of disbelief, we can be absorbed by made-up worlds. Such an enthralling world, I contend, is provided by the stock market. The structure of the stock market is not given in nature, but is a cultural creation that has come to be an essential background condition of our daily lives. In this dramatic world, fear and greed play leading parts as alternating and complementary motivating forces controlling the players caught up in the action.

One general fiction is that the purchaser of a share of stock becomes a partial owner of a company. While it is true the ownership of stock has *something* to do with company ownership, the vast majority of people who own stock (now over half of the adult population of the United States) have absolutely nothing to do with the normal tasks of ownership—management and control of resources. People buy stocks because they expect the values of these securities will increase (greed), and they sell stocks because they are concerned that the values of the securities they hold will decrease (fear). If one has the stakes to play, the game provided by the stock market can be as absorbing as hypnosis or any work of fiction. The values of securities do go up and down with scintillating unpredictability, providing not just suspense but watchful excitement loaded with positive and negative payoffs for the participant.

Stock market investing is like casino gambling (see Chapter 10), with two important differences. First, the odds of making money are much better for the individual investor in the stock market than for the player at the casino. Second, the stock market is connected, if in complex and often tenuous ways, to the real world of production and consumption. All of the economic sectors—banks, governments, corporations, research and development units, agriculture, and service industries—that are concerned with production and consumption have an influence on the market, as does the grand public, with its vicissitudes of confidence in tomorrow. Outcomes in the market are determined by multiple and arcane forces, far less simple than the spin of a wheel or a throw of dice. But it is an important part of the game to know that if I invest in a cracker company there really are crackers somewhere out there with intrinsic value for consumption. The stock market theater is a liminal world located somewhere between the hard reality of farm and factory on the one hand and the evanescent cloud space of the casino on the other.

Another of the prime fictions supporting the stock market theater is money—the medium for gauging and measuring the values of securities as well as all manner of commodity and service. Money is valuable only if it is believed to be valuable—it has no intrinsic worth apart from the social consensus of confidence. Numismatics is the discipline devoted to the appreciation of legal currency or tokens of economic exchange. I pull out a bill from my wallet. On the face side it reads: "This note is legal tender for all debts, public and private." On the obverse this legend appears: "In God we trust." The promise is secular, but the backing premise is sacred. We permanently suspend our disbelief, and go about acting for all the world as if money and the securities they purchase have real value—a sacred fiction. Numismatics can tell us about the magic of transforming ordinary material into the sacred stuff called money—material stamped with symbols that vouch for seriousness and authenticity.

An episode illustrating the fictive character of money involved my older son, David, then eight years old. Like many good Americans, we introduced our children to the basic exercise of fear and greed in the marketplace by playing the game of Monopoly. One Sunday afternoon, after hours of play, David landed as a guest on a high-class property sporting several hotels. He paused, looked at his piece, looked at his money, and his gentle, dark eyes filled with tears. "I am ruined," he said, and began to cry.

"No, no, you are not ruined. This is just a game. Monopoly money is not real. Let's all quit." I said something to this effect, and we did, in fact, emerge from the drama. While his tears soon dried, David's somber mood lasted for quite a time. This incident made me ponder: What is the fundamental difference between our tiny world of Monopoly and the big world of real investment, real money? I concluded that there is no essential difference, unless one counts the mere matter of scale as essential. In both worlds, one has printed money. One has a group of people who are willing to consider it to be legal tender, *pro tempore.* The supply is limited. With money one buys advantages and property. Property can yield more money. When the game is over, or outside the context of the game, the money has no intrinsic value whatever.

Once the *Titanic's* lifeboats were away, those left on the ship might have been rich as Croesus, but the change in circumstance rendered their money useless. Rich and poor alike did drown. Hyperinflation is an approximation of this condition of useless money, and is inevitably the consequence of the decay of confidence in the government institutions that stamp money with credibility. Fear that leads to disbelief can make value disappear into thin air—a dramatic transformation.

PSYCHOLOGY IS NOT PHYSICS

The laws of conservation of mass and of energy in physics provide enormous reassurance to science. If some object appears to be missing, one may be assured that it is not truly gone but is merely transformed or hiding in another place. This is not the case with economic systems, for all such systems are based on a psychology of beliefs and values. In this domain the laws of conservation do not apply. If the market loses over 20 percent of its value, as it did on October 19, 1987, this does not mean that hundreds of billions of dollars of wealth just moved from one place to another. In fact, the wealth simply disappeared—a consequence of fear, or lack of confidence. Fear made the prospect of holding on to securities seem riskier to millions of investors than selling them in a wildly declining market. It took about two years for little steps of greed to resynthesize the wealth that had been dissipated in just a couple of days in October. After the stock market crash of October 1929, it took until November 1954 for the market to regain the value it had suddenly lost.[1]

But even so, after every major and even cataclysmic loss in the stock market, recovery has eventually occurred. Over the long run, the wealth represented by the stock market has grown on the average by just over two hundredths of a percentage point per day. While the quantity of mass and energy in the universe may be constant over eons, the wealth of nations has, in fact, steadily increased over the past century. This is because wealth is a creative product of human imagination—at once dramatic and psychological. Apart from being perceived as valuable, no mere object is a part of wealth. Physical reality does not have this nice contingent quality. Creating fairies by clapping your hands is an outrage to physics, but is compatible with the drama of everyday life.

THE ASYMMETRY OF FEAR AND GREED

I argue here on a priori grounds (then later with evidence) that the extremes of fear are greater than the extremes of greed. Hell is bad and Heaven is good; but Hell is worse than Heaven is better. Dante's *Inferno* contains graded degrees of misery and affliction; Paradise has its thrones and cherubim and seraphim, but it is rather more uniform and less extreme than Hell.

Imagine your worst fear. Perhaps it is that you will be stricken with a painful and fatal disease. Perhaps it is that someone close to you, a family member or friend, will be killed. Perhaps it is that all of your worldly possessions will be destroyed by fire or flood. Death probably figures somewhere in the sketches of fearful imagination. One thinks of holocaust.

Now imagine your greatest hope for personal gain. Perhaps it is of winning a $100 million lottery. Perhaps it is of winning a Nobel Prize or an Academy Award. Perhaps it includes enjoying perfect health until a very old age. Perhaps the dream is of great fame and personal power. Perhaps it is the hope of being loved, idolized, even worshipped. One may hope for Peace on Earth, even while worrying that it might be boring.

The test comes in a subjective comparison of the two imaginative exercises. Which is the greater departure from the status quo? Evidence and argument point to loss being more fearsome than gain is pleasing. As Amos Tversky has put it: "You probably imagine things could be slightly better but infinitely worse. We have probably evolved to be very sensitive to losses and much less sensitive to gains" (1995, 3).

One empirical demonstration of this asymmetry of valuation is the phenomenon of risk aversion. Most people choose to accept a sure award of $100 over a 50 percent chance of winning $200, even though the expected values of these choices are identical. Taking a risk entails the fear of not winning, so risk itself is negatively valued. Thus analysts assume that people must be enticed to take risks by enjoying the prospect of greater returns on an uncertain investment.[2]

Tversky and Kahneman (1986) have extended this principle to show that risk on the loss side of the status quo is differently valued than risk for gain. Their findings are represented in the function portrayed in Figure 6.1. The domain of this function shows losses and gains relative to the status quo—not some final position of wealth. The function illustrates the differential valuation of losses and gains. Obviously, the function is monotonic, so that the greater the loss, the greater the pain, and the greater the gain, the greater the pleasure. However, the loss side of the function is much steeper than the gain side, illustrating the psychological fact of asymmetry. For a given magnitude of loss, the pain is greater than the pleasure associated with the same magnitude of gain. The loss of $1,000 hurts more than gaining $1,000 pleases. Finally, the shape of the function is concave in its gain region and convex in its loss region. This reflects the economic equivalent of Weber's Law for perceptual dimensions—that just-noticeable differences in magnitude are an increasing function of quantity—so that, as psychologically experienced, the difference between a loss or gain of $100 and a loss or gain of $200 is much greater than the difference between a loss or gain of $5,000 and a loss or gain of $5,100.

The history of changes in the value of the stock market illustrates

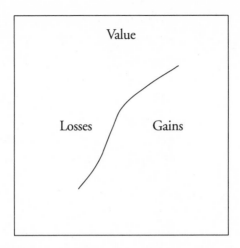

FIGURE 6.1. A hypothetical value function. *Source:* Amos Tversky, based on data from Tversky and Kahneman (1986).

another empirical consequence of the asymmetry of fear and greed. Suppose we calculate the percentage change in the Dow Jones Industrial Average (DJIA) for each day in its history of more than 27,000 days. The mean change for the distribution of daily changes in the DJIA is +.024 percent.[3] But the median change (+.045 percent)—the midpoint of the distribution—is higher than the mean. While well over 50 percent of daily changes are positive, the most extreme daily changes are negative, and the effect of these extreme losses is to pull down the mean, not the median. In fact, the skewness index for the frequency distributions of all major indexes (the DJIA plus the S&P 500, the NYSE, and the NASDAQ) is negative for their entire histories. Figure 6.2 displays these functions.

These figures are almost, but not quite, beautifully normal. They are all negatively skewed. A careful eye will see that they all have a peak slightly above the breakeven point of 0 percent. But the tails on the left are more extended than the tails on the right. For the DJIA, the greatest single loss is −23.52 percent, compared with the maximum gain of 16.83 percent (outside the domains shown on the graphs). The extremes are

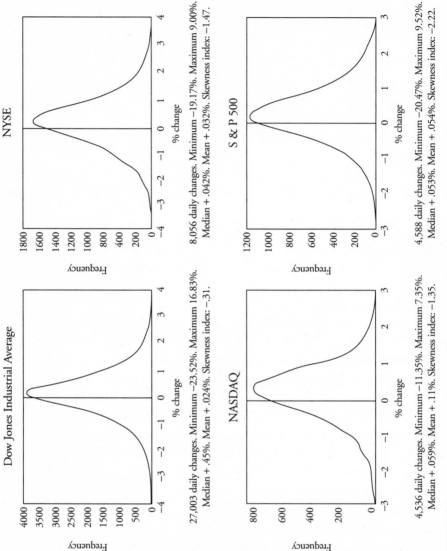

FIGURE 6.2. Daily percentage changes of four major market indexes, with extreme values trimmed.

roughly the same for the other three indexes as well. In all cases, the greatest losses exceed the greatest gains. The extremes of fear are greater than the extremes of greed.

Greed is manifest in many small steps of growth. Nothing succeeds like success, and as the market grows, more and more investors are attracted to the prospect of gain, cautiously but consistently investing their available funds, causing the market to rise still further. The bull market investors are enjoying as I write, dating from August 1982, is the longest period of continual growth in the history of the stock market. Over this period, the value of shares has grown twelvefold—an unprecedented gain. But this period has also seen the largest one-day losses in the history of the stock market.

It is as if fear lurks in the background even as greed has its way. As the market grows and grows, investors start thinking of bubbles. They remember the tulip mania in Holland in the seventeenth century. They imagine castles in the air. The Great Depression looms large in their consciousness. They invoke the example of Japan—where the stock market has still not recovered from its eight-year-old slide. Still the market continues to grow, as more and more cash pours in from eager investors. Then, one day, something happens. Perhaps there are rumors of a rise in interest rates. Perhaps a currency crisis occurs in some country in the Far East. Suddenly investors rush to sell their portfolios. The Roadrunner, having run off a cliff and out into the open air, suddenly looks down, screams, and then plummets like a stone into the sea—this is not physics, it is dramatic psychology. The latent fear has become manifest and has turned to panic—where panic is defined as everyone rushing to the door because everyone is rushing to the door. Portfolio managers are tested for their "vomit index"—that point in a falling market when they involuntarily throw up their holdings.

Because of the tendency for panic selling to run out of control, the stock exchanges have instituted "circuit breakers," which automatically halt trading when losses exceed certain limits. The hope is that the pause in trading will allow heads to cool and fears to subside. But the paradoxical effect of circuit breakers can be just the opposite, given a sufficient load of fear. The interruption in trading can serve as a conspicuous and unmistakable sign that the authorities are worried. And if they are worried, the individual investor is going to be worried in spades.

Recovery usually begins a few days after a major selloff. As the supply of fear is exhausted, it dawns upon investors that the fall in prices is an opportunity to acquire some major bargains, and greed begins to assert itself again, initially in great gains, later as more cautious advances. This has been the pattern for the past sixteen years. This pattern has occurred with a population of investors who have heard about, but not experienced, the Great Depression. The cold chill of that fear lasted for decades but now exists only as an abstract point of reference. The way markets behave is a function of the collective psychology of the actors in the theater of the investing universe.

NOBODY KNOWS

A friend who owns a pension management firm once observed to me after a long discussion of the stock market: "Nobody understands what causes the market to move." He explained that the possible sources of influence are so numerous, and their interactions so difficult to understand, that no one can credibly claim to comprehend what makes the market go up or down. But this does not stop commentators and money managers from offering instant analyses of what caused a particular change.

On April 28, 1998, the *Hartford Courant* business section had this headline: "Dow Takes 146-Point Pounding." The subheading declared an explanation: "Stocks Hurt by Fears about Interest Rates." Within a week the paper announced that the loss was entirely erased, because of an "easing of fears," completing a tight circle of logic.

Sometimes the string of logic will run something like this: The most recently released unemployment figures show a decline—good news! But the rise in employment may cause inflationary pressure—bad news. Inflationary pressure, in turn, may cause interest rates to rise—bad news, again. Rising interest rates make the yield of stocks seem less attractive, bad news again, and the stock market tumbles. But on another day the entire set of connections may be stimulated again by a favorable employment report. Only this time the investors ignore the potential effect on the market and a substantial gain occurs. As Fats Waller said, "One never knows, do one?"

Among other closely watched signals for the market's behavior are trade deficits, Gross Domestic Product, indexes of corporate profits, productivity rates, orders for durable goods, retail sales figures, product inventories, the consumer confidence index, put-call ratios, odd-lot sales, and federal budget trade deficits or surpluses, with accompanying tax initiatives. Sometimes these indicators predict what the market will do; often they do not. But they are all on the shelf to be used as needed. They stand ready for invocation to account for any day's market change.

John Maynard Keynes likened the ability to pick winners in the stock market to a particular kind of beauty contest—where the task was not to pick the most beautiful contestant but rather to choose the girl who would be picked as the most beautiful contestant by others. This requires a particularly delicate form of empathy, where one puts oneself in the position of other judges, to judge how they would judge others to judge qualities of beauty. After the third remove in this regress, the ordinary mind becomes dizzy with the possibilities, with no hope of sorting it all out.

I return to the blunt assertion of my pension-manager friend. No one knows how the market works. Chaos theory, which came into vogue ten years ago, is perhaps the best way to characterize the inner dynamics of the market. It's like a fractal: sometimes you get big waves, sometimes little ones. You never can tell where they come from. And like fractals as well, the movement of the market makes a fascinating display.

A young friend of mine, a recent college graduate, landed a job with a large brokerage firm in New York. Within a year, he had major responsibility for recommending investments for funds with billions of dollars in assets. He privately admits that he has no idea whatever about how to predict the movement of the market in his areas of responsibility—utilities and defense industries. So he is careful to watch what other people are recommending, and he goes with the flow, hoping against hope that he will not end up in disaster. So far, things have gone well for him. A rising tide floats all boats. But he has a strong fear of being found out by his bosses. My hunch is that if he makes it for another year or so he will develop the quality that is essential for success—a capacity to make others believe he understands what is going on. And, of course, he dresses the part and is careful to show his face in the office both early and late.

WHY NOT JUST INDEX?

My young friend has a lot of company, of course, but few are willing to be so candid, and in time he will become more reserved as well. The world of money management is full of people who have a strong interest in not revealing a fearsome and central secret of their lives: that, just as in theater, the ostensible purpose of their professional lives is not its true purpose. Everyone is interested in making money—true enough. And the world of money management is fiercely competitive, with everyone trying to best everyone else. However, the fact is that in any given year about 75 percent of portfolio managers will fail to beat the indexes; that is, their portfolios will perform less well than the average of securities invested in a representative selection of stocks in the S&P 500 and passively managed with no turnover.

This becomes mathematically intelligible at once: the average of averages must be the average, and if the distribution of performance rates of a set of portfolios is symmetrical, at best 50 percent of them will perform above average. Because portfolios have turnover rates (the proportion of their assets that are bought and sold in a given year) of around 50 percent and some as high as 250 percent, it follows that subtracting transaction costs (commissions) will result in poorer-than-average performance for a majority of the portfolios—so the average performance of actively managed funds is bound to be significantly less than the average of a passively managed fund in any year. Hence it is perfectly reasonable that about 75 percent of fund managers perform below the averages.

One might expect, then, that many people would be attracted to the simple and irrefutable mathematical logic of indexing their portfolios. Invest the funds in a representative set of securities and go for long vacations—fishing, at the beach, or in the mountains. But such a strategy has some major disadvantages. The one mathematical disadvantage is related to a psychological one: while one may be assured of performing near the index averages by a passive investment strategy, it is equally certain that one will not beat the averages in this fashion.[4] This lack of opportunity to beat the averages is, for most red-blooded managers, quite intolerable. To quote an advertisement for a state lottery, "You can't win if you don't play." The drive to finish near the top is so great as to create a quite irrational denial that one is likely to finish badly.[5] This is related to a second disadvantage of passive investing: it is boring (see Chapter 4). Frequent buying and selling means frequent complex decision problems, and creates a fresh interest in the largely futile activity of checking the market every few minutes. The third and final disadvantage of passive investing is perhaps the most serious for money managers: the wholesale adoption of passive investing would mean the loss of thousands of well-paying jobs in the financial management industry. Portfolio and mutual fund managers could be replaced by machines run by clerks; the touts and analysts who serve this community would find the reason for their professional roles subverted.[6]

We must see that theater is not reasonable—it is built upon profligacy, waste, and irrationality. And yet its attraction is irresistible. In Chapter 7 I will argue that the accumulation of wealth is not primarily for the accumulation of wealth. Rather, it is about the creation and maintenance of edgy dramas, engaging scenarios about the possibility of enjoying a bonanza. Erich Fromm (1941) said: "Greed is a bottomless pit which exhausts the person in an endless effort to satisfy the need without ever reaching satisfaction" (115). Thank heavens, then, for greed—for a principle that ensures endless effort is dramatically much more interesting than one that runs a straight course toward satiety and boredom. It is in this sense that one might agree with the infamous Ivan Boesky, who said "Greed is good,"[7] and with Keynes, who argued that greed and "the detestable love of money" must continue to rule us until we have grown to the point of eliminating poverty and providing for the satisfaction of all human wants. But I doubt that even Keynes could imagine the psychological and dramatic poverty that could result from satiety and the final removal of fear and greed. Human imagination rather fails on the upside.

NOT A RANDOM WALK

The kind of challenge to the conventional practice of money management that I have just articulated will strike true believers as a dangerous heresy. It is similar to another dangerous heresy that emerged from the barren halls of academe more than twenty-five years ago—namely Burton Malkiel's (1973) claims for an efficient market hypothesis and the related notion that the market meanders along in an essentially unpredictable way, which he called a random walk. I confess that Malkiel's argument had great appeal for me when it was published, and I initially agreed with him (see Scheibe 1979). However, when I and my students performed an elementary empirical analysis of the random walk hypothesis, we found it to be false. There is, in fact, a certain intricacy in the market's dance that belies the impression of random movement.

A random walk process is characterized by an absolute lack of predictability in a series of discrete moves or steps. The efficient market hypothesis is that information relevant to the direction of the market's movements is already discounted and in the market by the time it becomes known—an economic version of precognition. Together, these ideas produce the conclusion that it is a waste of time to try to predict which way the market will turn from day to day, week to week, month to month. Market timers, Elliot Wave enthusiasts, and other prognosticators are no better than blind soothsayers at predicting market movement, according to the random-walk view. Here is a typical Malkiel pronouncement:

> These technical rules have been tested exhaustively by using stock price data on both major exchanges going back as far as the beginning of the twentieth century. The results reveal conclusively that past movements in stock prices cannot be used to foretell future movements. The stock market has no memory. The central proposition in charting is absolutely false, and investors who follow its precepts will accomplish nothing but increasing substantially the brokerage charges they pay. (1973, 120)

Malkiel documents this assertion with a footnote claiming that evidence for it is to be found in the list of references. But my search of the list of references yielded no convincing proof of this null hypothesis, only an odd assortment of failed attempts to find systematic movements in this or that security.

It is one thing to say that no one understands why the market behaves as it does. I believe this to be true. But it is quite another to say that one cannot describe regularities in the market's behavior. This is demonstrably false. Without knowing at all why the market moves up or down, one can still examine the contingencies of movement. Does a movement in one direction on one day yield absolutely no information about the direction and extent of movement on the following day? It is possible to submit this matter to empirical test.

My students and I have used the same daily index values that form the basis for Figure 6.2 in an analysis of conditional probabilities. If the behavior of the stock market is random, then $P(UP|UP) = P(UP|DOWN) = .5$ (that is, the probability of an UP day given a preceding UP day equals the probability of an UP day given a preceding DOWN day, and both are equal to .5 when the UPs and the DOWNs are split at the median). By extension, these conditional probabilities should remain equal to .5 as the length of preceding sequences of events is increased to two, three, four, and so on.

Table 6.1 presents actual data on the conditional probabilities for the first-day and second-day sequences for four major indexes. We computed these conditional probabilities by splitting each distribution of daily percentage change values at the median, then calculating the contingencies just one step or two steps back—considering only whether the previous days were UP or DOWN days. It is easily seen that many of the conditional probabilities are not equal to one another, or to .5.[8] (The statistical significance of the departure of these values from the hypothetical value of .5 is greater than 1 in 1,000 in most cases—those marked with an asterisk.)[9]

Considering only the previous day, each of the indexes shows the same direction of departure from independence—with the probability of an UP day given a preceding UP day being considerably higher than the probability of an UP day given a preceding DOWN day. This prob-

TABLE 6.1   Conditional probabilities for four major market indexes

Period	P(2 | 1)	P(2 | 2)	P(2 | 11)	P(2 | 12)	P(2 | 21)	P(2 | 22)
	Dow Jones Industrial Average					
1st half (1/01/00–7/10/45)	48.3*	51.7*	49.6*	54.2*	46.9*	49.3*
2nd half (7/11/45–4/24/98)	46.0*	54.0*	47.8*	57.1*	43.8*	51.4*
Total (20,003 days)	47.2*	52.8*	48.8*	55.5*	45.4*	50.5*
	New York Stock Exchange					
1st half (1/03/66–12/16/82)	39.9*	60.1*	42.1*	62.8*	36.5*	58.3*
2nd half (1/27/82–12/31/97)	48.3*	51.7*	47.6*	54.0*	49.1*	49.5
Total (8,056 days)	44.0*	56.0*	44.5*	58.2*	43.3*	54.3*
	NASDAQ					
1st half (3/17/80)–3/3/89)	10.4*	59.7*	39.1*	60.7*	42.2*	59.0*
2nd half (3/6/89–2/24/98)	42.0*	58.1	43.1*	61.7*	40.5*	55.5*
Total (4,536 days)	41.1*	58.9*	41.2*	60.6*	41.0*	57.7*
	Standard and Poor's 500					
1st half (1/02/80–12/4/89)	48.0*	52.1*	47.6*	53.8*	48.3*	50.5*
2nd half (1/25/89–2/24/98)	49.9	50.1	50.0	52.7	49.7	47.5
Total (4,588 days)	48.9	51.1	48.7*	53.3*	49.0	49.0

*p < .001.

ability ranges from 59 percent for the NASDAQ index to 51 percent for the S&P 500. While these departures from .5 may seem small, they are overwhelmingly significant.

In order to demonstrate the reliability of these data, we split each distribution of index data in half by calendar date. (We ended up with one DJIA distribution from January 1, 1900, to July 10, 1945, and one from July 11, 1945, to April 24, 1998; the other distributions were split at their halfway points as well). We then recalculated the conditional probabilities for both the early and late halves of each distribution. These split-half data replicate quite closely over the early and late periods, as Table 6.1 shows. These effects are not due to chance.

Our findings indicate strong non-independence of move sequences. The market shows a "positive recency effect"—the tendency for a trend to continue. We continued the analysis of conditional probabilities up through trends involving as many as eight previous days. The resulting conditional probabilities for first-half and second-half samples are strongly related to each other.[10]

These data are sufficient to refute the random walk hypothesis for the stock market. The existence of reliable conditional probabilities for changes that depart from .5 for median-split distributions of sequenced changes means that there is at least some amount of useful information in data on daily market changes. The universe of market investors does have a memory—the dance is not random.

The practical application of this non-randomness to making money in the stock market is another matter. Malkiel raises the challenge in his book: "If you are so smart," he says to the market timer, "then why aren't you rich?" But some market timers are, in fact, quite rich. One of them, Gil Blake, has employed a strategy of trading that was initially a direct application of the principles I have just described. He moved money into a fund when it went up, and moved it out when it went down. (By using mutual funds as his investment instruments, he was able to avoid transaction costs, since many mutual funds allowed unlimited and cost-free transfers of money.) "In the twelve years since he began trading, he has averaged a 45 percent annual return" (Schwager 1992, 230). This is an astonishing level of performance. While Blake has had to modify the rules of market timing as conditions in the market have changed (and when he was no longer allowed free fund transfers), his principle remains simply that of capitalizing on regular and replicable contingencies in the upward and downward movement of certain stocks and funds. He is a market timer. Jack Schwager (1992) reports dozens of other market-timing analysts who manage to beat the market consistently. So the refutation of Malkiel's random walk hypothesis is not just a matter of theory. Practical demonstrations of its falseness are in hand.

The psychological and dramatic interest of these findings should be clear. These regularities in market movement are entirely psychological. They do not depend upon GDP, budget deficits, interest rates, or any other external indicator. Rather, they reflect a psychological trend for those who invest in the market to be encouraged or discouraged by the experience of a given day, and to translate this encouragement or discouragement into a decision to add or remove funds from the market on a subsequent day. People believe in the market being hot or cold, and because they believe this, the market does in fact get hot and cold. What happens on the stage is controlled by the actors in the audience.

Investors are moved to action by the complementary yin and yang of fear and greed. Both are constant presences in investors' minds, like different strains of bacteria in the digestive tract. A rational and safe strategy of investing would be to buy and hold a representative variety of securities for long-term gain. But the daily action of more than a billion shares is testimony to the reactivity of investors to the fear and greed of the day.

Greed is active on more days than is fear, but when fear hits, its effects are more extreme. The existence of systematic regularities in the day-to-day movement of the market is testimony to the power of momentum for investors as a collective entity. People have a demonstrable tendency to believe that the market will continue to move in the direction in which it is moving. No one understands why the market moves as it does. But by a willing suspension of disbelief, one might endeavor to learn to dance in step with the market's gyrations. The stock market is theater for the masses in contemporary capitalist society. Its movement is captivating, entrancing, hypnotic in its effect.

TOO MUCH PLENTY

Allegro ma non troppo.

—Tempo indication

Ours is a culture based on excess, on over-
production; the result is a steady loss of
sharpness in our sensory experience. All
the conditions of modern life—its material plenitude, its sheer crowdedness—
conjoin to dull our sensory faculties.

—Susan Sontag

Jane Goodall, in her early observational work on chimpanzees in the
Gombe Stream Reserve in eastern Africa, employed a technique of attracting the animals to her by placing bananas in bait boxes. The chimps
would come to the boxes, take the bananas, and sit around enjoying the
offering. As an experiment, Goodall decided to see what would happen if
she increased the quantity of bananas in the boxes to well beyond the
one-time eating capacity of visiting chimps. The result was chaos.
Chimps began to load themselves with more bananas than they could
carry, and to fight with one another for access to the extra bananas.
Goodall's film shows chimps dropping bananas, trying to pick them up,
warding off competitors with snarls and growls, finally dropping all of
the bananas and fighting in earnest.[1] This is an example of too much
plenty—of a degeneration of conduct brought about by excess.

In examining the effects of excess on the drama of everyday life, I
will limit my attention to the excess of things that are normally considered to be good: wealth, information, friends, knowledge, fame, progress, beauty. Psychological research has little to say about excess—but
much to say about deprivation. The ages have taught us how to live with
deprivation. The number of fat people in the United States is brute
testimony that we do not deal well with excess.[2]

The premise that more is better pervades our thinking and our lives.

Through the ages, scarcity of resources has been a common condition, a common enemy, providing an unquestioned premise for the human drama. But attempts to accumulate more goods can lead to peculiar consequences—as when a wasp whose abdomen has been severed drinks incessantly from a saucer of sugared water only to have the nutrient dribble uselessly out of its thorax. The habit of acquiring more becomes detached from the value of having more.

One might not imagine that enriching a field by fertilizing it could lead to anything bad. But it is possible to place more nutrients in soil than is good for growing plants. Overfertilized fields can lead to a plant condition known as "burn." There are secondary consequences as well. The runoff from an overfertilized field can cause the wild growth of algae in ponds and lakes, creating a condition known as eutrophication. Think of a pond covered with a thick and putrid green scum, creating oxygen-deficient water wherein no fish can survive.

The profession of academic psychology provides an analogous case. We are drowning in a tide of psychological research, but still the main criterion for judging the worth of a psychologist or a psychological theory is how much research is produced. *Psychological Abstracts* now catalogs about 50,000 published articles and papers every year—not including books or presentations made at conventions. The senses are dulled. One begins to perceive that the game is not what it seems. Production is dramatically required. Stasis is death. We are rather like the wasp with the severed abdomen, for we do not pause to digest and apply such truths as are discovered. Rather, we race on to produce another study.

Because of dulling of the senses, we hardly notice the oddities pro-duced by the difference between cover stories and underlying dramatic function. I watched and heard the following sequence on the morning news on television. A male-female team of anchors is giving the local news in typical talking-head fashion—alternating from one speaker to the other. As a final item, the woman reports a murder that happened yesterday. A young man gave his friend $100 to buy some marijuana. When the friend failed to deliver, the young man bludgeoned him to death by repeated blows to the head with a plumber's wrench. The anchorwoman comes to the end of the story, pauses for just a beat, and then, attempting to fill time with spontaneous chat, turns to her partner and asks, with sunshine in her voice, "Have you been out to pick apples yet?" He responds, "Yes, I have." "Oh, you've done that already. I am so envious." Cut to the weather.

Wait a minute! A horrible murder has just been reported. A young man, somebody's son, perhaps somebody's lover, has just been the victim of the senseless rage of a supposed friend. Do we need any time to assimilate this information, to think about it, perhaps to generate a feeling, a sympathetic reaction or one of revulsion? No time is allowed. It is obvious that the anchorwoman herself cannot have been thinking about what she was just saying. Rather, she invites us to an image of those lovely apples hanging on trees, and how fine it would be to go out and pick some. But even this is not really what is going on. The anchor is filling empty time—dead air is considered unprofessional. This is not a special incident but a common occurrence. Senses are dulled. The peculiarity is not just in the performance. No one stops to notice such dramatic incongruities, such senseless insincerity. No one will call the station in outrage. To borrow a term from an older psychology, we are conditioned not to react with horror to horror. We have come to accept the theater of the absurd without recognizing its absurdity.

A eutrophy of the senses can result from too much information. Roger Shattuck, in *Forbidden Knowledge: From Prometheus to Pornography* (1996) defends the illiberal thesis that there are some things we are better off not knowing.[3] Knowledge is not intrinsically harmful, but we cannot cope with complete knowledge. We can be told of the hordes of dust mites crawling over our furniture, clothing, and skin, but enlarged knowledge of the microscopic only makes us feel creepy. The making of politics, like the making of sausage, it is said, is something that the general public is better off not observing. Shattuck argues that the works of the Marquis de Sade and other forms of pornography are a knowable domain and full of fascination. But exploration of this domain can have evil consequences: murder, rape, and torture can and do result. Science has claimed an exemption from those who would warn of too much knowledge. Even so, after the development of the atomic bomb, J. Robert Oppenheimer observed: "In some sort of crude sense . . . the physicists have known sin." It is difficult for any scholar or scientist to

admit to the possibility of too much knowledge, for to do so is tanta-
mount to denying the legitimacy of the purpose that animates our
dramatic actions. Telling the scholar that it is possible to know too much
is like telling the capitalist that it is possible to be too rich: it will seem an
attempt to rob life of legitimate purpose.

AMBIGUITIES OF EXCESS

The ancient Greek myth of Midas, king of Phrygia, is a lesson on the
ambiguities of wealth. When everything he touches turns to gold because
of Dionysus's didactic joke, the king is led to see the value of the
ordinary and to plead for the return of wine he can drink and food he
can eat. Lucretius posed this question: "Why dost thou not retire like a
guest sated with the banquet of life, and with calm mind embrace, thou
fool, a rest that knows no care?" The lesson of moderation is one that
will not be learned, for moderation in practice tends to produce boredom (see Chapter 4)—as Oscar Wilde understood when he said, "Moderation is a fatal thing . . . Nothing succeeds like excess." One may
preach against the evils of excess and point to countless examples of the
corrupting effects of wealth and power as object lessons—Louis XIV,
Henry VIII—but this will not stop people from lusting after wealth,
power, beauty, money, fame, and the more the better!

Of course, perverse purposes develop in reaction to the dominant
theme. Not all young people will want to play the game of accumulating
more wealth, for the children of affluence are in a good position to see
the futility of the games in which their parents are so earnestly engaged.
I remember walking on campus with a wealthy Wesleyan trustee in
1972, and hearing him lament about his semi-wayward son, then a
Wesleyan student. The son was rather slovenly in manner and dress and
given to interests in West African drumming rather than economics.
"This is the first generation of students who seem to be willingly down-
wardly mobile," he said. "I don't understand it." Of course, it is hard to
understand this paradoxical behavior if you accept the universality of the
principle that more is better, and if you use this premise as the purpose of
your life drama. The trustee's son, and many of the son's generation,
sought a more authentic drama, without necessarily finding it.

John Kenneth Galbraith, in *The Affluent Society* (1984), articulated a central theme about the insidious and character-eroding properties of our economic system. We are completely dependent on an ever-accelerating cycle of production and consumption—of producing goods and services, then creating a need to consume those goods and services, with growth the only acceptable index of progress. The lessons of the emptiness of material success are all around us, but few are those who shut down their lives to a minimum of material simplicity and live a more authentic purpose.

Money is profoundly ambiguous, as the philosopher Jacob Needleman points out in *Money and the Meaning of Life* (1991). The love of money, he observes, is the root of all evil, and yet money is the principal driving force of our capitalist economy. The Christian church, while denouncing avarice and usury, has not hesitated to amass great wealth itself. Nor has the mantle of religion been sufficient to hide the corrupting effects of excess. As a friend of mine said when he first saw St. Peter's in Rome, the splendiferous center of Roman Catholicism, "Jesus would cry." Freud recognized the ambiguity—money and human excrement were for him symbolic equivalents.

The ambiguity of excess extends well beyond money. A classic claim in the sociology of suicide is that those in upper social classes are more likely to kill themselves than those who have lower social position and less leisure.[4] A client of mine who was a jet-setting beauty in the France of her youth said, as she approached fifty, "I had a lot of fun, but I wasn't happy."

Recognition of the ambiguities of success moved the acclaimed Emerson to assert that he was "now as happy as it is safe to be" (in Richardson 1995, 88). Jung is said to have told someone who had just received a promotion: "I'm very sorry to hear that; but if we all stick together, I think we will get through it." Jung also greeted a friend who had just been fired from his job with joy, suggesting that they open a bottle of wine in celebration (see Bly 1990, 71).

What is the relationship between apparent success and ultimate benefit? Formulaic or pat answers to this question are not satisfactory. Lord Acton's assertion "Power tends to corrupt and absolute power corrupts absolutely" is, I suspect, false as often as it is true. Great wealth, great beauty, and great intelligence can have self-defeating consequences, but not necessarily so. The common belief is that anyone who wins millions in the lottery soon becomes a miserable wretch—languishing alone in a cold garret, abandoned, sick, and in despair. But a careful examination of the actual lives of sudden winners reveals that while some are, in fact, destroyed by their new wealth, many handle it quite well.[5] The former cases have greater dramatic appeal. Again it is a case of troubles first.

UNFORESEEN CONSEQUENCES

A young woman told me that as a little girl she had prayed fervently to God that she be given beauty—and that if she were given beauty she would ask for nothing else in life. Indeed, she became beautiful as an adult. But she also encountered a host of unanticipated problems in her relationships with others and with her own depression. Some of the problems may have been effects of her endowed beauty, for it was as if no one could get beyond her outward identity to her inner self. She felt admired and even loved, but never understood.

Her story illustrates the difference between decision utility and experienced utility, or between the way things are valued when a choice is made and the way outcomes are actually experienced. For example, people are not good at predicting whether repeated exposure to a piece of music or a kind of food will make them like it more or less (Kahneman and Snell 1992). Just about everyone enters into marriage with the expectation that things will turn out well—that the chosen spouse is the best of possible choices. Alas, in about 50 percent of cases in the United States, the actual pleasure derived from the marriage not only is less than anticipated but is such a severe punishment that the pain of divorce is preferable to continuation. Perhaps this principle should be named "It Seemed Like a Good Idea at the Time." Those who have trouble controlling their appetites for more—more food, more drugs, more sex, more toys, more clothes—often end up in a condition of lamentable excess. Experience, in these cases, is no teacher at all.

Surely if Howard Hughes had had an opportunity to see an image of the form his life would take in its final phase—isolated, paranoid, compulsively afraid of germs, sickly, and weak—he might not have opted for the series of financial successes that brought him to this culmination. After J. Paul Getty died, one of his closest associates and confidants described him this way:

> He was a lecher, a miser, a womanizer whose private life was often bizarre beyond belief. He never conquered his fear of death and he tried in vain to stay the ravages of time by frequent face lifts. He was secretly contemptuous of the sycophants who surrounded him, particularly the members of his "harem" and it was his firm belief that anyone who approached him was simply trying to muscle in on his millions . . . He lacked affection yet he yearned to be loved. (Mark Goulden, in Miller 1985, 303)

For Getty, the enjoyment of great wealth was considerably less than the anticipation of that enjoyment before he acquired the wealth. If the Ghost of Christmas Future had appeared to Getty in a Dickens-like dream, would he have chosen the course of life that brought him to such a dismal end? Getty enjoyed getting rich—but he hardly enjoyed being rich.

Donald Trump is a more recent example of the value of the quest for wealth as opposed to the enjoyment of wealth. He says in *Trump: The Art of the Deal*, "I don't do it for the money. I've got enough, much more than I'll ever need. I do it to do it. Deals are my art form. Other people paint beautifully on canvas or write wonderful poetry. I like making deals, preferably big deals. That's how I get my kicks" (1987, 3). Trump, by his own testimony, is never bored. He is involved in the drama of making deals—of making things happen. His co-players are the rich, the famous, the powerful. He testifies to making hundreds of telephone calls every day, participating in dozens of meetings, none lasting more than fifteen minutes. What seems to irritate him is stability—when things don't move, when nothing seems to happen. It is small wonder that his relationships with women have been tempestuous and not enduring. Who could satisfy his taste for novelty? Failed relationships, like failed deals, do not seem to bother Trump for very long. He invokes "It Seemed

Like a Good Idea at the Time" to account for what are, in retrospect, bad choices, but he doesn't dwell on the past. He's moving on: new engagements, new deals, new prospects—renewed drama.

A person makes a decision and thereby expresses a value in a particular setting, at a particular time, in the presence of particular others. The purpose that is expressed is a property not only of the person but of the entire dramatic setting. It is ephemeral, of the moment. Later on, consequences of the expressed decision are realized—sometimes in a way that is congruent with the initial purpose, sometimes not. But the setting itself will change over time and with it the way events are experienced. People are not very accurate in anticipating the actual quality of the experience that will follow from a given course of action. When the alcoholic has been dry, enlivening the evening with a couple of drinks seems like a good idea. Later, a prayer uttered over the toilet bowl will express an entirely different valuation. However, once the body has recuperated, this scene can be forgotten, and another opportunity for indulgence can be seriously considered. Recovery can become an ongoing drama, if the person can sustain a self-definition as an at-risk alcoholic, often with a supportive cast of fellow AA members. Memory of the chastening effects of experience is partial and incomplete, and often falls victim to the dramatic sense of the moment.

FROM PLAY TO THE RAT RACE

B. F. Skinner and William Morse (1958) found that something happens when you begin to reward rats for an activity that they normally perform spontaneously. Rats will run in an exercise wheel on their own, apparently just for the fun of it. But when food rewards are introduced as an incentive for running, the rats seem to lose interest in running in the wheel except to earn the rewards. Similarly, it has been shown that children lose interest in a task if they have been specifically rewarded for performing that task (Lepper, Greene, and Nisbett 1973). This effect has been explained by the "overjustification" hypothesis—the idea that an activity conducted for extrinsic rewards becomes less intrinsically valuable, because the extrinsic reward becomes a sufficient reason for performing the act.

The title of this chapter came to me during the major league baseball strike of 1994. During that season—the first in almost a century that did not end in a World Series—loyal baseball fans were treated to the sorry spectacle of baseball players, whose average salary was $1,168,000 per year, going on strike in order to force the owners to give them more benefits. While it was hard to be sympathetic to the players—after all, they were being paid huge sums of money to play a game that many American boys would pay to play—it was even harder to be sympathetic to the owners, who comported themselves during this conflict like a bunch of greedy, fat cats, with little evident sense of the harm they were imposing on an institution that many people regard, rightly or wrongly, as almost sacred.

Canceling the second half of a baseball season, including the World Series, is certainly worse than canceling the Fourth of July. It was a severe blow to the dramatic order of things. Alas, it was also an illustration of the overjustification hypothesis—for here was proof that baseball, the National Pastime, had become a grim business, rather like mining coal or running a railroad. Too much plenty spoils the game. The game is transformed from play to work. Ernie Banks, with his joyful plea— "There's sunshine, fresh air, and the team's behind us. Let's play two!"— is held up to ridicule as an atavism, a throwback to the naiveté of youth when baseball was fun. It is a case of eutrophication again: too much nourishment produces a stinking mess.

THE DIFFICULTIES OF GREAT FORTUNES

Great fortunes are visited upon a few, and in our society that few is growing. From 1979 to 1993 the number of U.S. households reporting *incomes* in excess of $1 million increased about fivefold. Currently there are more than 65,000. In 1992 there were about 3,200,000 U.S. households with *assets* of over $1 million (Hacker 1997). But even while the wealthy class is expanding, the gap between rich and poor is getting wider. As a consequence, more than 20 percent of all household income is received by the wealthiest 5 percent of families. Despite this growing disparity in the distribution of wealth, no hue and cry is discernible to soak the rich with taxes. Some may resent Bill Gates's reported net worth (in 1998) of $50 billion, but envy outweighs resentment. Perhaps even social critics in our time are so well-off that their critical force is dulled.

Even so, our century has seen some remarkable cases of personal disaster at the end of wealthy lives. I have already mentioned J. Paul Getty, reputedly the richest man in the world when he died in 1976 and, according to most accounts, one of the most unhappy (see Lenzner 1985). I have also mentioned the super-rich Howard Hughes, who lived out his last years in a miserable way (see Drosnin 1985). Armand Hammer, the petroleum king and self-appointed ambassador between the United States and the Soviet Union, managed to maintain a more positive public image until after his death, but his life story turned out to have much in common with those of Hughes and Getty. Married three times, he was involved in ugly family disputes over money, and behind his facade of respectability he was a master manipulator in the domains of politics and finance and supremely paranoid about his personal fortune (see Weinberg 1989). Ted Turner, still among the living, has been criticized for his ruthless ambition, his drinking, and his romantic affairs (see Goldberg 1995). In Turner's case, middle age and perhaps his marriage to Jane Fonda have brought some sobriety, some mellowing—and his donation of $1 billion to the United Nations would seem to put him in a philanthropic class of his own. But it is still possible to observe an association between massive wealth and weirdness.

While Lee Iacocca is hardly in the same class of wealth as those mentioned above, the story of his retirement is directly relevant to my thesis about the impact of wealth in our culture on the drama of everyday life. In 1993 Iacocca retired from his forty-seven-year career in the automobile business. The former CEO of Chrysler was one of the most successful executives of the century. When he retired, he moved to California with his young and pretty wife and tried to live out of the public eye. A few years later, however, he was divorced, still living in California, and forced to admit that he had "flunked retirement." He didn't have, as they say, a life:

I'm alone too much. It's difficult. You can't go out looking for partners, you've got to go out looking for friends. If you happen to run into somebody you want to get romantic with or spend time with, it's tough. I'll take some girl out for dinner and she'll say, "People coming up to the table and all that stuff, you have to put up with this all the time?" It is not conducive to a nice atmosphere. But you make your own bed. You write a book, you go on TV, you turn around a company, your privacy goes to hell. In Detroit you couldn't get a conversation going on religion or politics. Everyone wanted to talk cars. Out here, it's worse: you can only talk movies—the fantasy business. If you get away from movies, you might as well be a dunce. (Taylor 1996, 42)

The life of a successful businessman is full of appointments, telephone calls to make and return, meetings with bankers and creditors, critical decisions about personnel and policy, and talk about the stuff of the business—the oil business for Getty and Hammer, the aircraft industry for Hughes, real estate and casinos for Trump, entertainment and sports teams for Turner, automobiles for Iacocca. The result is the development of an extremely strong identity—but an identity that is dependent upon continued commerce with ratifying others. Like the beautiful girl who feels loved in the form of admiration but does not feel understood, the rich businessman is never sure that those who appear to admire him are not meretricious sycophants. In terms of the distinction between self and identity set forth in Chapter 1, the difficulty here might be called hollow identity (see Sarbin and Scheibe 1980), in which the public persona is hypertrophied and the self is unexpressed, mismatched with identity—lonely and sad.

Iacocca is an example of men who have had full and enriching careers over the course of decades, who have amassed considerable personal fortunes. Such men do not go into retirement easily. Take a player from one setting where he is a giant, place him in an alien setting where his game is not the topic of talk, and he becomes irrelevant, disengaged. A brilliant auto executive like Iacocca feels like a dunce where the conversation is all about movies. Appraised and self-appraised intelligence is subject to dramatic constraints—a person can feel like an idiot when separated from an audience that can appreciate his performance.[6]

SEX AND SUCCESS

Removal from the work setting is particularly damaging for men, for men are more dependent on work than are women in our society and more driven to amass great fortunes. Of those earning $500,000 or more annually in United States, 89 percent are men. Among the wealthiest individuals in the nation, men are clearly dominant. Using the *Forbes* annual list of the 400 wealthiest Americans as a gauge, Andrew Hacker notes: "Of the more than one thousand Americans who have been on the successive lists, five have been women who founded enterprises of their own" (1997, 93). Only five.

I do not believe that women are inherently less able than men to make extraordinary incomes or to accumulate assets. But I think it plausible to assert that women are less dependent on occupations for their identities and also less interested in accumulating More. Sociobiologists have argued that men and women are attracted by different features of prospective mates. For example, Cunningham (1986) and Cunningham, Barbee, and Pike (1990) have produced evidence that men are more attracted to clear skin and smooth and regular features in women, while women are more attracted to strong or dominant features in men. Whatever the origins in biology, our culture presents a clear picture of different base values in what men and women choose to do with excess.

It may seem outrageous to claim that men are interested in sex while women are interested in success. With full awareness of the exceptions to such a simplification, I believe the evidence supports such a bifurcation of interest. If men are interested in sex, then women, knowing this and wishing to be attractive to men, should use their excess in acquiring clothing, cosmetics, and jewelry—adornments that will enhance their physical attractiveness. Men, meanwhile, knowing that women are attracted to the security that success brings, should want to become wealthy and powerful—more interested in accumulation and in conspicuous displays of wealth in cars, appliances, and palaces than in spending their wealth on personal apparel. I think it facile to account for this difference by referring to the survival-driven interest of men in spreading their seed as widely as possible among available women, and the converse survival-driven interest of women in attracting men who are powerful enough to ward off predators and competent enough as hunters to provide for the family. I say this is facile as an explanation, for it is simply a story that is roughly coincident with Darwinian principles of evolution. It has great dramatic appeal, but it is essentially useless as a scientific proposition, for no means could ever be found to prove it false. Whatever the origins of these differences in genes or in culture, women do not accumulate as much money as men, and men do not accumulate as many clothes. No male counterpart can be found for Imelda Marcos's collection of 3,000 pairs of shoes.

PATHETIC ENTERTAINMENT

The Greek root of pathos is the same as that of pathology and pathetic—pathos means suffering. In our affluent society, a society of unprecedented abundance, senses are dulled, lives dramatically impoverished by the very quantity of material wealth and substance we produce and consume. Identities are rich and quite fat, while selves are miserable and blinded by too much plenty. As a consequence we need desperately to be entertained—to participate vicariously and indirectly in games and dramas not of our own making. We seem to want to watch movies without end—almost as if anything would be better than the stultifying and deadening lack of drama in our own lives. Consider the following advertisement for DIRECTTV:

> If you like movies you're in for a treat, because now you can take advantage of one of the largest selections of movie programming in America. With DIRECTTV programming, you can enjoy up to 55 different pay-per-view movies every night with DIRECT TICKET—with the latest hits starting as often as every half hour. Plus you can get great movie channels like American Movie Classics, Turner Classic Movies and Bravo. Enjoy 7 channels of Encore!, movies from the 60s, 70s, and 80s—with entire channels devoted to love stories, mysteries, westerns, action, true stories, drama and more. All this plus our favorites like CNN, TBA, USA, A&E and the Discovery Channel. Choose from 7 family-oriented Film Channels, and more.
>
> And if that wasn't enough, you can also get 31 channels that just

play music. Commercial-free music ranging from rock, to country, to classical, to jazz—dependent on which channel you select. Enjoy household chores, entertain guests or sit back, relax and enjoy the concert. All adding up to the most incredible variety of entertainment ever offered. And it's all right inside your home. Right in front of your favorite chair.

Starting with the notion that I might dip into as many as fifty-five movies every night, my soul feels imperiled. A double feature at the most, and then I gasp for light, fresh air, a relief from the mental confinement of having the retina and the cochlea tuned steadily to reproduced images and sounds. My imagination is controlled entirely from the outside—by someone else's will. What liberty have I to think thoughts of my own manufacture? None. And the agony of neglect! Think of all those love stories, and true stories as well. I must see more, more! All of this wonder is right inside my home, in front of my favorite chair. Shall I ever dare to leave it?

So forget the movies and instead go to a live party, with real people talking about real events, eating real food and drinking real drink. Let's imagine a Hollywood party—beautiful people and the best of catering. Fortunately, we don't have to attend, for John Updike offers this priceless portrait of the world of too much plenty:

> . . . and then going to the parties in somebody or other's absent par-
> ents' house with everybody a different flavor of stoned it seemed and
> the water in the swimming pool lit from underneath like a piece of sky
> upside down by wobbly golden bulbs and the pet Russian wolfhound
> lying out on the terrace watching with a worried look and wanting to
> play with the chewed yellow tennis ball between his long white paws
> but nobody playful, everyone too wasted and self-absorbed and care-
> fully moussed and pinned together to go entertain a dog, all this
> arduously attained and Mex-trimmed multi-million-dollar home being
> turned into the shit of boring chatter going nowhere, not even to bed,
> people too strung-out and scared of or tired of the idea of love, the
> moviemakers had DONE love, the songwriters had done it, what was
> left were the jagged images, one after another, mocking, slicing in

MTV like sharks mouths in a feeding frenzy in that documentary about the Great Barrier Reef. (1996, 411–412)

Perhaps this seems a bit infantile, as if meant for the burned-out younger set only. Another capsule version of an evening out in the entertainment capital of the world is provided by Lee Iacocca, in his description of his flunked retirement in Los Angeles, this time at a party for grown-ups:

> The social life out here isn't much either. If you go to somebody's house for dinner, everybody looks at each other's clothes. Then you sit down. No, you don't sit down, you have a buffet; you eat standing up. There are a lot of guys you never heard of with all these young girls, and it's showtime. After you eat, you go in to see a movie. All these houses have private theaters that seat 20 or 30 people. Instantly, when the movie is over, everybody gets up to shake hands, trade a little gossip, get in their cars and go home. Why not just go to the movies? (Taylor 1996, 42)

The entertainment industry is the most rapidly growing segment of business in the United States. People have time and money for diversion. As we will see in Chapter 10, gambling provides a powerful redirection of serious attention and money. Pathos, our own suffering of emptiness, drives us to the movies, or perhaps if we are really lucky, to some behind-the-scenes parties where movies are made, so that we may have the sophistication of insiders. But pathos is there as well it seems, at those end-of-the-world fantasias. It is pathetic.

Those enamored of plenty are missing the show. Viewing everyday life from a dramatic perspective at least allows us to see the doubleness of the proceedings surrounding us. Those not aware of this doubleness— that entertainment is business, that business is entertainment, that wealth is its own purpose as well as a means to an end, that being sick has compensations that being well lacks, that beauty can be a barrier as well as an advantage, that outward success can mask inner failure, that a stage kiss is still a kiss and a real kiss is stylized, that games become work and work becomes a game—are simply sleepwalking. The serious and unrelenting pursuit of plenty can result in dullness and a reduction of the drama of everyday life.

EATING AND SEX

Eroticism is the most intense of passions
while Gastronomy is the most extended.

—Octavio Paz

No one has hitherto tried to investigate in
a serious and thorough manner the "erotic
theater."

—Nicolas Evreinoff

Eating and sex have enormous importance in human psychology. But
the character of this importance has been largely misconceived. Freud
considered the base of all psychic energy to be sexual—the secret source
for the development of civilizations. The behaviorists later considered
eating to be the quintessential form of human motivation. Tissue deficits
lead to hunger, and hunger serves as the source of secondary and derived
drives and hence the *fons et origo* of all that we do. Both eating and sex
have obvious significance for the survival of species, including the human species. This has encouraged the advocacy of a somewhat different
form of reductionism by sociobiologists, who have attempted to account
for varieties of nutritional and sexual practices under the banner of
Darwinian natural selection (see Wilson 1975; Diamond 1997; Wright
1994). Here the need to be safely scientific has outrun the requirements
of understanding; for while it is true that human genetic material has not
changed in any substantial way in the last millennium, our manners
around eating and sex show a profligate variety within the space of a few
years. These manners furnish material for a vast quantity of stories—stories that both compel and challenge human imagination. We are far
more easily sated in our bodily appetites than we are by images and tales
of romance and banquet. The major psychological truth about human
beings is not that they are driven by needs for food and for sex, but
rather that human imagination has transfigured eating into gastronomy

and sex into eroticism. Gastronomy and eroticism, in turn, are the stuff of rites, of ceremony, of theater.

DRAMATIC TRANSFORMATIONS

Children play at tea parties and enjoy games like "doctor" and "house." But the teacups and platters are empty. The consummations of "doctor" and "house" are only vaguely imagined, but surely have to do with the mysteries of sex. Dolls will do for guests and partners at these games as well as or even better than other children; for the play is a workout for the child's imagination—a step on the way to becoming a master dramatist. I have watched a four-year-old child conversing easily with the seated rag dolls invited to tea—admonishing them to mind their manners, not to drop imaginary crumbs on the floor. Similarly, Barbie and Ken are dressed and matched in various settings—perhaps in a doctor's office, perhaps in the bedroom. No real food. No real sex. It scarcely matters. The drama is the thing, and it will continue to be, overwhelming the mere activities of feeding and breeding.

Eating and sex are at the center of so many human dramas because of the power and the importance of the transformations they entail. As with children in their earnest play, much of our daily drama revolves around eating and sex. But also as with the children, our dramas easily become autonomous and detached from the actual consummations of ingestion and coupling.

Holy Communion is ingenious and effective theater—a major reason for the success of the longest-lived social institution ever created by human beings—the Roman Catholic Church. Transubstantiation is accomplished by an impressive display of Latin words and stylized gestures—the wine becomes blood and the bread becomes flesh, and by eating what is the putative body and blood of the Lord, members of the congregation become as one. The act of communion is fundamental to human bonding—in the church and in all other institutions. The casting of the Church as the Bride of Christ, the exclusion of women from the priesthood, the wearing of cassocks by male priests, the prominence of the Virgin Mary, and the emphasis given to sexual prohibition makes the church a place for the flourishing of erotic imagination as well. Actual eating and actual sex in the physical church are practically nonexistent. But the symbolic and imaginative elaborations of these two forms are huge in ecclesiastical significance.

Our fantasies swirl about the delectable and exciting possibilities afforded by table and bed. We devote special attention to presentational images on the pathways to these destination points. Getting there is almost all the fun. Actual arrival can lead to heartburn and heartache.[1] Like the wine taster who never swallows, the hunter who shoots cameras rather than guns, and the fisherman who throws the catch back, the gastronome and the erotophile find pleasure mainly in the pursuit. Consummation is optional, for it exposes one to danger, to sadness, to feeling stuffed or drained.[2]

BREAD AND HUMILITY

The drama of food is illustrated by the history of a loaf of bread. Wheat grains are planted in bare fields in the fall. By spring a grassy field appears—the first transformation. Throughout early summer the grass grows tall, heads out, and by midsummer the field turns golden, with weighty heads atop the stalks—the second transformation. Now the harvesters come, cutting the grain, threshing out the wheat, producing bins of wheat and rows of golden straw—the third transformation. Now the wheat is milled and ground and separated from husk and bran—yet another transformation. Salt and water and yeast are added, making dough—another transformation—and this is baked in an oven, making something solid, brown, fragrant, and pleasing to the taste, yet another transformation. This is both an end and a beginning, for now the bread, the product of so many miraculous transformations, can enter in consort with hundreds of other foods—butter, jams, cheeses, spreads, soups, viands of every type—to form harmonic ensembles of endless variety. For feeding purposes, we could do with one kind of bread. But human imagination has created hundreds of varieties around this basic theme, each one a dramatic culinary achievement, not often appreciated by those who merely grab a loaf of white bread off the supermarket shelf.

To top it all off, bread is for eating, not just admiration. Placing a morsel of bread in the mouth triggers another transformation: as soon as saliva moistens the bread, the enzyme amylase begins to change starch into sugar, so that one has a sensation of sweetness as the digestive process begins. Eating is the final link in a dramatic circle, an act that is at once destructive (of the bread) and nourishing (of the body).

One of my first vivid memories of bread is from when I was three years old. My grandmother instructed me to eat two pieces of white bread just after she discovered with some alarm that I had swallowed a penny. The bread was to help the passage of the penny through my body, a prospect I did not initially grasp. But lo! the next day, the very same copper penny appeared with the stool in my potty. Easily washed, it was not transformed. But I could see no trace of the bread. What I did see and smell was what, I concluded, had become of it. This was a powerful lesson about transformation.

This fundamental transition from food to feces has a larger social meaning. For the act of ingesting food is always and everywhere an occasion for social gatherings, for prayers and ritual, where music and candlelight enhance the occasion, where people laugh and talk and tell stories, where deals are made, where birthdays, anniversaries, engagements, deaths, graduations and promotions are commemorated and celebrated with toasts and the expression of noble sentiments. The varieties of food are beyond description and multiply daily. However, on the other end of the transition, the act of defecation is almost always solitary. Every effort is made to conceal the waste product from sight and smell. And while the foods consumed are delightfully variable, the waste product of human digestion has an apparent uniformity and is also universally regarded with loathing.

Humility has the same etymological root as humus, the soil from whence bread comes and to which it returns. Every day, in secret, every human being has this reminder of humility, no matter how grand the banquet of yesterday. This is an essential but rarely acknowledged constituent of the drama of everyday life. Bowel movements remind us of our finitude, our inexorable ties to the soil, even though as philosophers we may pretend to eat only clouds.

PARALLELS AND SYNCRETISMS

The frequency of the use of gastronomic terms to describe erotic attraction is striking. The biblical Song of Solomon is entirely a gastro-erotic duet, in which she describes his kisses as better than wine and he describes her lips as a honeycomb, her tongue as honey and milk, and her entire being as a garden of delights, flowing with spices. Honey and sweetheart are terms of endearment, as are pudding, dumpling, pumpkin, lamb chop, sweetie pie. The apple of my eye is surely not an apple. A tart is either a small pie or a sexually promiscuous woman. Cheesecake and beefcake refer to female and male erotica. And so on.

The obverse borrowing is perhaps less common, but still frequent. A feast can be described as an orgy. A rich dessert may be praised, among familiars, as an orgasmic delight. The film version of Henry Fielding's novel *Tom Jones* contains a bawdy seduction scene in which eating seems indistinguishable from sex. Films wherein sex and food are strongly intertwined are so common as to compose a genre—*Babette's Feast; The Cook, the Thief, His Wife, and Her Lover; Like Water for Chocolate; Big Night.* In all of these cases the erotic is suffused with the gastronomic, the gastronomic with the erotic. It is remarkable that these entertainments are served up in a mode that is entirely aural and visual—not a molecule of substance is exchanged with members of the audience—yet the experience is gustatory.

The mouth is the focal point of the syncretism between eating and sex, while the anus plays a similar role but more secretly. In Brazil, to "eat" someone is to have sexual intercourse. In the United States, to "eat" someone is to have oral sex. The mouth is at once a place for the ingestion of food and an erogenous zone. The anus is at once the place for elimination of waste and for illicit sexual activity—sodomy.

But more broadly, eating often serves as part of the ceremonial buildup to sexual activity.[3] In contemporary urban society, asking a woman out to dinner is often construed as a prelude to asking her for sex—a kind of reciprocal food-for-favor exchange. In many societies, the giving of a food gift by a suitor to a girl is a part of engagement ceremonies (see Harré 1981.)

THE WEDDING AS DRAMA

"The world, in truth, is a wedding," said Erving Goffman (1959, 36). And a wedding is not a wedding without the feast—the ceremonial extension of celebration to the community, where the meal laid on is not just a feeding but an elaborate and extravagant bacchanal, accompanied by much drinking and the offering of public toasts. Nor is a wedding a wedding without the intensity of sexual consummation in the nuptial bed. Most couples these days are well experienced at sexual intercourse by the time they reach their wedding day.[4] Even so, they do not neglect that special act of coupling on their wedding night, even though they may be tired from dancing and smiling and talking with friends. Here ceremony finally reaches the flesh.

A wedding is a deeply serious drama. All of the feasting and the invocation of sacred and secular authorities is meant to provide weight to the transformation that is being accomplished—no less than the binding of two previously unrelated individuals into a permanent covenant of unity. At the level of biology or chemistry, nothing at all happens to ratify a wedding as the union it pretends to be. Even though in our day and in our country some 50 percent of these unions fail, it is still testimony to the power of serious human drama that marriage remains an effective and highly respected social institution. Among other things, a marriage is a commitment to eat at the same table and sleep in the same bed for the rest of life—to focus and confine gastronomic and erotic life. Even so, as Octavio Paz has said, gastronomic life is extensive, in that it includes other people, includes children and the old, and is required for the sustenance of life. Erotic life is intensive: it is not normally social, excludes the very young and the very old, and becomes optional. It follows that, within the family, gastronomic drama is open and public, while erotic drama is secret and private.

HUMILIATIONS OF EATING AND SEX

Suffering about matters of eating and sex is different for men and for women. While men can be just as obese as women, diagnosed eating disorders such as bulimia and anorexia are far more common for women than for men (see Smolak, Levine, and Striegel-Moore 1996). But sexual pathologies—pedophilia, fetishism, satyriasis—are far more common among men than among women (see Allgeier and Allgeier 1984, esp. ch. 20). Sexual appetites are more difficult to control for men than for women, while appetites for food cause more problems for women than for men.

The person who is addicted to food feels quite powerless to control eating behavior. A plate of chocolate brownies proceeds into the stomach as inevitably as a rock falling off a cliff. Daily reminders of this power- lessness are a constant source of humiliation. For the sex addict, things are no better. Men who have been in jail for rape or for assaulting children have a high rate of recidivism. They know they will misbehave again, even though they also know that they are marked by the authori- ties for quick arrest and prosecution when the inevitable occurs.[5] Sex addicts incur enormous risks of humiliation in order that their appetites may be temporarily satisfied. They seem to accept Oscar Wilde's epi- gram: "The only way to get rid of a temptation is to give in to it." Wilde was in a position to know the risks, for he suffered the consequences of his own sexual appetites in a society that was not prepared to tolerate them.

Part of the drama of sexuality that we share with other primates is that men strive to be powerful while women strive to be attractive (see Chapters 5 and 7). While male chimpanzees in the wild prate and posture and growl and scream at each other to determine who will be the alpha male, men compete on athletic fields and in boardrooms for essen- tially the same position. Women, in general, are less interested in domi- nation than in being noticed. This asymmetry leads to the different importance that men and women give to eating and sex in the dramas of their lives.

For a man it is a great humiliation to be impotent. The word has the double meaning of failing to achieve an erection and of being powerless. For a man, sex is, in the words of John Updike (1996, 313), "an enter- taining smooth chute into the dark-red bliss of things," but it is a ride one cannot take unless one's device is inflated. Lacking that dramatic transformation, an attempt at sexual relations becomes a humiliating slide into the deep-yellow torture of things, from which the recent development of Viagra becomes a hope for redemption.

For a woman, impotence is not so great a problem, in either sense of the term. Rather, the greatest humiliation for a woman is to feel rejected, to feel that she is unattractive, not noticed. As a consequence, eating takes on a significance for women that is strange to men. As the prevailing culture presents thinner and thinner figures as the ideal type, women are driven to diet. Failing to achieve the desired result, they may go to the other extreme, giving themselves over to the sensual pleasures of eating, of enjoying the texture, taste, and feel of food in the mouth. Coupled with the conflicting desire to remain thin, this can lead to bulimia—a pattern of binge eating combined with purging by means of vomiting or the overuse of laxatives. Often excessive eating leads to obesity, with the effect of taking a woman out of play sexually, and thus relieving the psychological pain of rejection. But a different kind of psychological pain is incurred: depression, self-hatred, feelings of worthlessness become internalized as a psychological backdrop for the conduct of daily life.

For men, sex is an exercise in power. Therefore, it has a different psychological significance than it has for women. The British novelist Carol Clewlow has said: "For men, sex is a gender underliner, they need it for their egos. We [women] don't need sex to make us feel we are the person we need to be."[6] This seems true, but women also have needs for their egos. While it is easier for a woman than for a man to lead an asexual life, it is more difficult for a woman to become indifferent about her own appearance, and hence to ignore struggles about food.

The reason that sexual politics is so tumultuous is that the ultimate interests of the two parties are often mutually unintelligible. Freud was perplexed about what women want, not because what they want is so terribly complex, but because what men want is, in Freud's view, so terribly simple. Deborah Tannen (*You Just Don't Understand,* 1990) and John Gray (*Men Are from Mars, Women Are from Venus,* 1992) concur in the generalization that men and women differ in fundamental ways—in terms of communication style, the need to resolve problems as opposed

to understanding issues, and the requirements for their egos for support or domination. Part of this difference, I contend, lies in the ways
the typical erotic and gastronomic imaginations work for men and
women.

A major manifestation of the differences in female and male erotic
imagination can be found in the commercial theater of sexual exhibi-
tionism. The Internet yields the information that 2,582 strip clubs are
operating currently in the United States. These clubs are only those
exhibiting female exotic dancers. A search for male exotic dancers yielded
relatively meager results—the major one being a site for viewing male
strippers in various postures of bondage being dominated by females, a
site meant primarily for female viewing. In the professions of exotic
dancers, pornography performers, and prostitution, women reign supreme, with some representation on the masculine side. Such men as are
represented in these professions suffer humiliation, lesser pay, and relative anonymity. Commercial sex is illicit because it is explicitly based on
money, not love. Within its confines, men are no longer dominant,
except insofar as they bring offerings of money. The dominatrix provides
a feminine revenge on the standard domination of men.[7]

Professional sex workers and sexual exhibitionists display the deeply
ingrained motivational significance of power for men and attractiveness
for women in the drama of everyday life. Men fuel this industry with
their money, and this is their source of power. It is ironic that they are
willing to accept domination and control by women within the confines
of the brief social contracts of illicit sex. The purchase by older and richer
men of erotic stimulation by young and attractive women is also represented in the phenomenon of May-September marriages and liaisons, of
the J. Paul Getty, Donald Trump, and Hugh Hefner variety.

With full recognition of all sorts of exceptional cases and overlap-
ping distributions, I believe that the differences I have described are
general for our species and likely to remain that way. Here I believe that
sociobiologists such as Robert Wright (1994) have made some contribution to our understanding. Even so, we are the only animals who speak,
and we need not remain locked out of a reasonably full understanding of
the mind of the other.

COMPARISONS AND CONTRASTS

Sex and eating have seemed to provide a firm foundation for the problem of motivation within psychology. But matters are not so simple, for the dramas woven about erotic and gastronomic themes are so various and so compelling as to shift attention away from the mere facts of breeding and feeding. The drama itself is of greater motivational significance. We see theaters for food—restaurants, kitchens, dining rooms, grocery stores, and a vast market for guidebooks-cookbooks that pander to the gastronomic imagination. We see erotic theaters as well—nightclubs and bars, bedrooms and sex clubs, a dominatrix hired to beat and humiliate rich old men, a thriving market in erotic film and literature, not to mention romantic novels, a staple for hundreds of years for the exploration of inner life.

The festivals of Dionysus, god of wine and fertility, are the origins of Greek theater, and Greek theater is the beginning of the Western theatrical tradition that continues to this day. Both gluttony and sexual dissipation are among the seven deadly sins—sins we are now likely to call addictive behaviors, but no less deadly for all that. Eating and sex are pervasive parts of the human adventure—sources of continual surprise, satisfaction, anticipation, and memory.

Eating and sex are sources of risk as well, for they are two of the major ways of contracting disease. Poisons and contagion are constant risks. Sex entails other risks—of unwanted pregnancy, of being detected in violation of the most serious laws and customs of propriety. Both eating to excess and engaging in sex to excess are likely to earn one the label "animal." While one may live a life of complete sexual celibacy, one cannot live without food—so food addiction is the only case in which complete abstention cannot be prescribed. Both sex and eating can become secretive activities, comprising for many individuals both thoughts that cannot be shared and activities that cannot be exposed to public view.

I know a woman who, as a child, suffered both physical and sexual abuse. Her foster mother made her eat dog food and swallow her own vomit. She was sexually abused by her father and by the son of her foster mother. Her adolescence and early adult life were characterized by wild swings of sexual promiscuity, bulimia, obesity, drug and alcohol addiction, and physical abuse by her husband. She developed into a classic case of dissociative identity disorder—a fragmentation of self into several distinct personae, some nice, some rather wicked. Her life is full of ambiguities and contradictions, many of them revolving around food and sex. She seems to have lost the fragile membrane that maintains the self as an integral unit as it absorbs the contradictory demands of different social situations. She is now in therapy, which seems to have become a stabilizing element in her life. While her gastronomic and erotic fantasies have filled many notebooks, her actual conduct for both eating and sex is very much under control.

The motif from William Saroyan's (1939) play *The Time of Your Life* seems apt: "No foundation, all the way up and down the line." Psychology does not have the motivational foundation it once imagined in eating and sex. Simple reductive models do not work—and, more, they are not needed. Eating and sex deserve our respectful attention because they are central dramatic themes for all human life and especially for an understanding of our troubles. Some of these troubles are particular to our times.

The United States is so obsessed with work as to have produced some frightful reductions in the play of gastronomic and erotic imagination. Think of fast food and fast sex. The penchant for franchised efficiency has produced food that might as well be injected directly into the stomach as eaten—diet milk shakes, Happy Meals, cheeseburgers made with processed American cheese. And on the sexual side we have the "quickie," no longer an exclusive offering of the professional sex trade where efficiency has its reasons, but a staple of what passes for a sex life for many married couples, as husband and wife, with their dual careers and children in the next room, find very little time left over for fooling around. The French are to be admired for the care and time they commit to eating and to sex. You may be sure that if you go to a Parisian restaurant in the evening you will be the only party booked at that table for the night, while an American restaurant will plan on having three or four seatings at a given table in an evening. I can only surmise that the French are more patient in bed as well.

But all is not trouble. One of the most widely sold books of the twentieth century is *The Joy of Cooking*, now in its seventh edition after having been continuously in print since 1931 (Rombauer 1931/1997). More recently, the *Joy of Sex* was published (Comfort 1972) in a frankly imitative format. (Its subtitle is "A Gourmet Guide to Lovemaking.") Perhaps both books are testimony to our having lost contact with the secrets of our tribes. We no longer have our savants and earth mothers to inform us of the secret arts of cooking and making love. But then again, perhaps we are doing both better than in the past. Octavio Paz (1972) has said that progress in love is as ludicrous as progress in art.[8] I am not so sure on either count. But I am sure that skill in the arts of cooking and in the arts of love can be a genuine source of human pride. A gentle touch, a sensitivity to beauty, a capacity to give pleasure to the other and thereby to increase the pleasure one enjoys—these are common to the pride of gastronomy and the pride of erotic skill. Passion and desire are ultimately positive life forces in the drama of everyday life. What a joyless drama it would be if gastronomy and eroticism were reduced to feeding and breeding.

WHILE WE WERE DANCING

Friendship is evanescent in every man's experience, and remembered like heat light-
ning in past summers.
—Henry David Thoreau

The grand points of human nature are the
same today [as] they were a thousand
years ago. The only variability in them is
in expression, not in feature.
—Herman Melville

The Senior Prom is not a universal human experience, but in the United
States it is nearly so. In classes, I have often asked students to tell the
story of their high school prom. Everyone has something to tell—even if
it is a story of not being asked by anyone, or of being rebellious and not
attending, or of the high cost of rented limousines and the awkwardness
of crinolines. At the time of its staging, the high school prom often serves
as a point of culmination for one stage of life and beginning for another;
it is a time of first and last experiences. It is all about the pairing of young
men and young women. Students typically evince a great deal of anxiety
about this pairing. Sometimes they are happy with the result—often they
are disappointed. It is rare for the relationship between the two dancing
partners at a senior prom to continue much beyond graduation. By the
time I talk with college seniors about their high school proms, it is all a
distant memory—the intensity and sincerity of the moment have dissipated. While they were dancing it was a scene. But when the scene was
over, so was the dance, so was the connection, so was the temporary
mutual ownership and accountability. It is on to what is next; everyone is
looking for a new partner.

In the drama of everyday life, human relationships are commonly
bounded by contexts and particular social framings—while individuals
often suffer the illusion that their relationships are permanent and tran-

scendent. Othello and Desdemona are not merely two lovers *sub specie aeternitatis,* but a general and the daughter of a senator in Renaissance Venice in a time of troubles. As the scene of the play shifts from Venice to Cyprus, the new marriage undergoes a transformation as well. Gone are the easy confidence and clarity of Venice. In Cyprus Iago's poisonous contrivances do their work—all is miasma, desperate jealousy, and credulity. The marriage is destroyed; its partners die miserably. What seemed permanent and well-bonded love turns out, with some change in circumstance and the passage of a little time, to be quite temporary, corruptible, no match for Iago's destructive cunning.

In the last generation the institution of marriage has suffered a remarkable weakening. In a given year in the United States, one divorce occurs for every two marriages. The age of first marriage is rising (the median is currently twenty-four for women and twenty-six for men). Thirty-one percent of all babies are now born out of wedlock. The proportion of men and women aged eighteen and older who are married has dropped from 71 percent in 1960 to 57 percent in 1995 (Whitehead 1997). An uncounted but large number of young people live together without benefit of marriage. The frequency of breakups within this cohort is unrecorded—a good thing for our divorce statistics. It is still customary for marriage vows to contain the phrase "until death do us part." But it is even money that the parting will occur well before the death, leading such thoughtful types as Donald Trump (1997) to insist that every marriage should include a prenuptial agreement, to avoid those expensive lawsuits—foreseen if not foretold, and let us not think of the contradiction.

"The grand points of human nature," Melville (1887/1984, 71) said, "do not change." However, the natures of our invented institutions most assuredly change—let us not now judge whether for better or for worse. The point of interest is to see how our little dramas unfold in this changing context. We dance many dances with many partners—some of them brief, some lasting a lifetime, some mendacious, some sincere, some having only momentary magic, some yielding enduring enchantment.

SALABLE CARE

That we dance is a universal of humanity. *What* we dance is a product of our particular cultural moment. In his "Guidelines for Living," G. K. Chesterton included dance among the things a normal person ought normally to do: "to dance, however clumsily, at least some of the dances of his native land" (1912, preface). About a century ago Freud invented a new form of dance. Adam Phillips describes this as "a curious solitude *à deux* called the analytic situation" (1993, 29). The starting posture has the patient recumbent on a couch, the analyst sitting behind the patient's head—out of sight but strongly present. The analytic dance is truly curious, for in its prototypical form the leader asks the follower for complete trust, and then asks the follower to lead by hazarding free associations—steps not yet taken, surprising revelations of moves not recognized as within one's competency. And then the leader proffers interpretations of these moves—attempting to weave sense and the security of understanding out of the inchoate strands of memory, fear, dream, and fantasy. The therapist comes to be a kind of surrogate parent for the patient, with versions of attachment typical of that earlier dance applying now, often with considerable intensity. Transference and counter-transference are the code words developed for the affections and loathings thus created. Of course, this dance is also a commercial transaction.

From this initial form, a thousand variants have developed. I have participated in this dance with hundreds of patient others. In my preferred form, I sit in a comfortable chair facing my partner, who is also comfortably seated. We talk for fifty minutes, more or less. I sometimes take notes on the pad on my lap. The room has two clocks—one in the line of sight of each. It is a privileged form of conversation. I ask questions, inducing the clients to speak of their troubles from a variety of perspectives. I offer interpretations, sometimes explanations, sometimes advice and suggestions. Often I just listen—trying to be alert and sympathetic. I have learned that it is good to have an agenda for a session of therapy, but it is an agenda that works as a kind of backup, in case what the client wants to talk about loses its force. While I do not use the theoretical structure of psychoanalysis or its particular therapeutic practices, I do notice that the emotional accompaniments of repeated therapy sessions have much in common with what the psychoanalysts describe.

This dance is conducted within the context of the culture that supports it—including financial support. Classical psychoanalysis, with its prescribed intensity and duration, is virtually impracticable in the current climate of support—few have the time or money. I see clients once a week, or once every two weeks, perhaps once a month—for as few as one session or as many as several hundred sessions over a period of years. My double privilege is that of hearing stories of struggles, sorrows, and troubles—intimate stories—and then being paid for my time and attention. This double privilege carries real dangers—for being trusted so openly by so many others can lead to an inflated sense of self-importance, while being paid can and does generate doubts about sincerity. Am I sincere and authentic in this relationship, or am I only pretending to be in order to earn my fee? The parallels between psychotherapy and the oldest profession are too obvious not to note.

This suggests something to be said in favor of prostitution.[1] One dishonors psychotherapy by calling it a form of prostitution. One might as well honor prostitution by calling it a form of therapy. Surely the issues here are complex and almost unspeakable, for prostitution is in common understanding the most degraded and degrading of occupations, while no one is particularly ashamed of confessing to the practice of psychotherapy. I would certainly not like to be understood as suggesting a perfect parallel between these two cases. However, the "while we were dancing" characterization applies to both—intense, intimate, and time-limited relationships—in these cases between a professional and a client, with a fee for service.

The moral advantage commonly attributed to psychotherapy hinges on such issues as:

1. *Seriousness:* The psychotherapist is a learned professional who attained the status through a program of extended training and certification procedures. The prostitute can turn professional on a whim and a dime, and is not thought to be seriously committed to the profession.

2. *Indifference:* The psychotherapist professes genuinely to care

about the welfare of clients, while the prostitute is thought to be indifferent to the beneficent effects of services rendered.

3. *Authenticity of identity:* The psychotherapist is assumed in name, qualifications, and background to be congruent with the identity presented. The prostitute is assumed likely to practice under an alias and to be incongruent with such storied background as might be presented.

4. *Authenticity of self:* The psychotherapist is thought to be acting in a way that is consistent with the moral requirements of inner being, including qualities of decency, fidelity to principle, and other silently attributed pieties. The prostitute is considered to be engaging in activities that are deeply in conflict with the requirements of inner being—decency, fidelity to principle, and other pieties are compelled to silence.

5. *Legitimacy of dramatic framing:* The practice of psychotherapy is recognized as legitimate by statute, by society at large, and by insurance companies. The practice of prostitution is not normally recognized as legitimate by any of these.

6. *Sexual expression:* Ethical psychotherapy is not characterized by sexual expression, while prostitution is.

By these six criteria the two professions are quite distinct—and thus perhaps the moral advantage accorded to psychotherapy is quite justified. However, I invite the reader to imagine possible exceptions or inversions for each of these criteria—as, for example, when the psychotherapist is practicing under false credentials and the prostitute is using a real name and telling a true story. With the exception of the final criterion—that of sexual expression—all of these tests admit the possibility of reversal. The other five criteria are dramatistic in that they involve matters of self-presentation, proper staging, public acceptance, matters of social convention. If one takes the bold step of suggesting that sexual expression might conceivably be a proper form of human caring, then it becomes clear that one ought to be cautious in giving unwitting assent to the idea that the psychotherapist is more worthy than the prostitute. The whore with a heart of gold may be a literary contrivance and a masculine fantasy, but one ought not to deny the possibility of Good Works being done in this poorly regarded setting. It is not hard to envisage the obverse case of meretricious labor being performed in the more respectable setting of psychotherapy.

Other relationships are instances of "while we were dancing." A lawyer and a client, a minister and a parishioner, an employer and an employee, friends, romantic partners, neighbors, professional colleagues—all seem to fit the criteria of sharp, lively, mutual, and honest attention during the time of exchange, and then an ending to the encounter (see Goffman 1971).

The lists and instances above are by no means exhaustive. But the question now arises: What are the causes and consequences of permanence or brevity in human relationships?

DEVICES OF BONDING

Weddings are the main exhibit for idealized performances, or performances of social idealization. Weddings are characterized by fine dress, fine food, formal music, and arch ceremony, by people acting somewhat above their class and station, and by the pronouncement of solemn vows, under the auspices of state and usually of church, that affirm pious principles and expectations about the future life of two people. They are preeminently social occasions—the extended family and witnesses are essential features of the drama. For without an audience you don't have much of a show.

As a child watching many weddings in my father's church, I knew that there was magic in the occasion. The ritual kiss at the end of the ceremony, I imagined, was what culminated in the birth of a baby. I was on the right track—and to this day there is *some* degree of association between the performance of wedding ceremonies and the birth of babies. Goffman might say that a wedding represents a ceremonial enactment of the moral values of the community, and that the expressive biases of the occasion are accepted as reality. I knew weddings as magical, and I still think of them that way.

For a wedding is a ceremony wherein two temporary partners take vows to become partners for life, and not just for a brief dance. It is the prototype for all rites of sanctification for relationships. The whole business is a social construction, as we say—but let no one deny the power of social constructions to work the magic of transformation. This ritual sanctification of a relationship is accomplished by the invocation of blessings from above (the State or God or both) in the company of Society, viewing the union here on Earth. The wonder is that, despite all the failures and institutional weakenings, marriage still does work—and works precisely in the sense of creating a permanent partnership out of what was once transitory.

Looking at rites of sanctification more broadly, a class of ceremonial occasions can be seen as attempts to create permanence in relationships. In the Old Testament story, God chose Abraham to be partner to an eternal covenant, and his seed, the Jewish people, are still partners to this covenant—represented by such markers as circumcision and the celebration of Passover. The Catholic Church is the Bride of Christ, and its baptism ceremonies are meant to consecrate new members to their permanent identity as Christians. Nuns and priests taking vows of their orders utilize imagery and rituals of separation and rebirth, including the taking of new names, and often, for nuns, bridal finery, as a way of assuring that their dance with the Holy Church will not soon come to an end.[2]

Famous friendships—Damon and Pythias, David and Jonathan, Thelma and Louise, Butch Cassidy and the Sundance Kid—are not necessarily marked by public rites of sanctification, though it is implicit that something like the exchange of vows takes place to transform mere friendships into epic examples. In all of the cases here cited, the friendships are famously remembered because of their association with death or the threat of death. Death is the ultimate seal of seriousness. Witness the New Testament assertion: "Greater love has no man than this, that a man lay down his life for his friends" (John 15:13).

Sometimes the process of becoming permanent partners works in a reverse fashion; the permanence comes first, and then one notices that the relationship is bonded. I am still friends with several of my college roommates—and we were thrown together quite by chance. Brothers and sisters are close to one another not by choice and not through ceremony. They discover after spending years together that they have a special bond. The psychological literature on interpersonal attraction strongly supports the importance of proximity, along with similarity and familiarity, for the formation of lasting relationships (see Bersheid 1985).[3]

I think of the special bond that forms between owners and their pets as a result of permanence, not its cause. Recently a famous psychiatrist came to my university to give a lecture. He noticed on the board in my office a photograph of my son with our pet springer spaniel. He became choked with emotion as he told me that he and his wife had just lost their pet dog. This friend had been in the family for more than twelve years, and they were both deeply saddened, in mourning. He was serious. I sympathize. My wife and I suffered a similar loss. We think of our pet and talk of her frequently, with the sadness of loss of a true friend. We are not generally sentimental about the death of animals, but this was no mere animal—this was Jessie, our faithful companion for more than fifteen years. She was a pretty good dancer.

Rites of sanctification are no guarantee that bonds will be formed—their success is irregular and dependent upon cultural context. When I was in college, pledges in my fraternity were obliged to learn some songs as part of an extended rite of sanctification for brotherhood. Here are some lines, from memory, of one of those songs:

> Our strong bonds cannot be broken, formed in Theta Xi.
> Far surpassing wealth unspoken, sealed with friendship's tie.
> *Amici usque ad aras,*[4] deep graven on each heart,
> Shall be found unwavering, true, as we from life shall part.

Well, not quite. In fact, I have no contact with my former fraternity brothers, and no residual loyalty to the fraternity itself—with one notable exception: I married the sister of one of my fraternity brothers, and my brother-in-law and I remain good friends. At the time, the bonds with my fraternity brothers seemed fairly close, and I would have predicted retaining friendships with them over the years. But our pathways diverged so radically that I have had little natural contact with any of them but my brother-in-law, and he and I think and talk precious little of our old fraternity. Most relationships do not survive the scene of their formation.

STYLES OF RELATIONSHIP

One of the limitations of a purely sociological way of looking at relation-ships is that it can offer no account of individual differences in styles and modes of attachment. Yet distinctiveness of style is a prime fact of life. Some people are easier to dance with than others; some prefer to sit it out; some are crazy to dance. One speaks metaphorically of the chemis-try between partners as something that is surprising, not strictly replica-ble, mysterious. It is a challenge for poetry to do justice to this phenome-non; science is much slower than poetry, less adequate to the task.

Every pairing of human beings produces a dyadic unit with unique properties. Once I witnessed a boxing match that had to be stopped because the two boxers—both middleweights, one right-handed, the other left-handed—could not avoid clinching because of the unique combination of their respective styles. They clinched within seconds of the beginning of the fight, then clinched again within seconds of being separated, and so on throughout the entire first round, with scarcely a punch being thrown. The same futile struggle continued in the second round, despite repeated instructions from the referee, shouted advice from the corners, and the booing of the crowd. Finally, in the third round, the referee mercifully brought this sorry dance to a halt and called the fight a draw.

Who can predict or describe the qualities of a particular human pairing? With some, we are never bored; with others, tedium begins with the hello. Some conversational partners seem to draw us out to unex-pected delights; with others we can't dance a step. Emerson exults in "great happiness when two good minds meet, both cultivated, and with such differences of learning as to excite each other's curiosity, and such similarity as to understand each other's allusions in the touch-and-go of conversation" (in Richardson 1995, 191). Another mind, used to such stimulation, might suffer a profound depression at finding no suitable partner. Edmund Wilson, spending a year at Wesleyan, lamented its dullness, its grim monotony, the difficulty of finding people to talk to—and this from a learned critic about a place that some have found just too stimulating for words (see Wilson 1993). It is a formidable challenge for psychology to develop some understanding of the peculiar chemistry of human pairings.

The most fruitful line of theory on styles of relationship within psychology derives from the writings of John Bowlby on attachment and loss (see, for example, Bowlby 1988). Bowlby suggested that children develop either positive or negative models of the self as a relationship object, and similarly develop either positive or negative models of the other as a potential partner. Mary Ainsworth used Bowlby's theoretical conceptions to describe several distinct pathways of infant development. These pathways were operationalized and illustrated in her "Strange Situation" test, wherein toddlers were observed to react in distinctive ways in the presence of a strange caretaker in a strange situation. In contemporary social-psychological literature these patterns have come to be called attachment styles. The major attachment styles are *secure, anxious-ambivalent, and avoidant;* a fourth style, *disoriented-disorganized,* has recently joined the list.

The fundamental principle underlying this approach to the study of attachment is that children develop expectations about themselves and others through repeated experiences with the proximity, attentiveness, and responsiveness of others. If parents are near, attentive, and responsive, then the child develops a positive model of both self and other, comes to be trusting and *secure* in relationships. If parents are remote, inattentive, and not responsive, then children tend to become *avoidant*—having a negative model of the other. If the parents are inconsistent—sometimes present, attentive, and responsive—then the children become *anxious-ambivalent,* with a negative model of self, and a positive model of the other, and with behaviors that are clinging and rather pathetic. Patricia Crittenden (1985) observed that particularly abusive and cruel mothers tend to have infants who are *disoriented-disorganized*—exhibiting a combination of avoidant and anxious-ambivalent behaviors that is more destructive than the other types. These children have negative models both of self and of other.

Philip Shaver and his colleagues have explored the applicability of these patterns to typical adult romantic relationships, with the general finding that the styles remain consistent for individuals and influence their experiences in human relationships. Using a simple paper-and-pencil assessment technique, Shaver and Cindy Hazen (1993) have shown that about 55 percent of adults are secure, 25 percent are avoidant, and 20 percent are anxious-ambivalent. (They did not employ the disoriented-disorganized style in their initial research.)

Secure individuals tend to form lasting human relationships, have lower divorce rates, tend to have many friends, and are more likely than the other types to believe in God. *Avoidant* people are less interested in developing intimacy than are the other types, and tend not to grieve when a relationship ends—they move on. They are more likely to be agnostic or atheistic, and tend not to be trusting of others. *Anxious-ambivalent* types tend to be argumentative, intrusive, and overcontrolling. They tend to break up and get back together with the same partner more often than the other two types. They tend to engage in extreme forms of religious behavior, such as speaking in tongues, more frequently than the other types (see Shaver and Clark 1996). Research by Kim Bartholomew (1990) suggests that individuals of the fourth type, *disoriented-disorganized,* tend to be fearful of intimacy and anxiously avoidant in relationships, rather than merely dismissive like the avoidant type.

Shaver and his colleagues are careful not to claim that these attachment styles are immutable. Indeed, psychotherapy might succeed in the establishment of an attachment style that is secure and trusting, with the therapist serving, perhaps for the first time in a patient's life, as an adult figure who is available, attentive, and responsive. A prolonged experience with the theater of selfishness, exploitation, and indifference produces cruel effects on developing actors. Psychotherapy can be the theater of redemption if it can help transform their models of self and of other from negative to positive.

Another line of research casts light on the ways relationships change in significance for older people. It is well known that social contact declines with advancing age—young folks tend to go to the dances. Some theorists assert that this disengagement is a result of an emotional apathy that accompanies aging, or perhaps is a result of the inactivity brought about by withdrawal from occupational roles. Laura Carstensen

(1993) has proposed a different interpretation. Analyzing findings from several longitudinal studies, she has shown that older people are as emotionally close in their relationships as are younger people, but that they are far more selective than younger people in the kinds of relationships they choose to pursue. A young person may be interested in making new friends because they may provide stimulation, display novel possibilities, or help in the advancement of career or interests. Older people tend not to be interested in making new friends—for these or other purposes. But they remain quite strongly committed to existing relationships that have strong emotional significance for them. "Thus, it appears that in old age, day-to-day choices are made with the conscious or unconscious awareness that time is limited, and choices are based on the affective potential of social interactions more than future-oriented goals" (Carstensen 1995, 154).

Over the life span, what one seeks in a dancing partner varies. In the beginning one is interested in someone who can advance one's career or interests, enrich one's understanding, or provide diversion. Later, all one wants is a kind friend.

INCONSISTENCIES AND INCONGRUITIES

As helpful as these generalizations from psychological theory and research are in understanding the broad outlines of individual differences in human relationships, they still must be counted as inadequate. The richness and variety of experienced connections between people are beyond the scope of current psychological theory. For at base these ambitious attempts to account for the peculiarities in our experiences of pairing assume a rough consistency of personal style or a regularity of progression. Psychologists, like novelists and biographers, strive for consistency in the stories they tell about people. The only truly consistent characters are the artificial contrivances of these professionals. As Melville put it, "If reason be judge, no writer has produced such inconsistent characters as nature herself has" (1887/1984, 70).[5]

Naturalists are said to have at first denied the possibility of a duck-billed platypus, on the grounds of its inconsistency with the known taxonomic order. Among human beings, analogues to egg-laying mammals with duck-like beaks abound. Viewing everyday life from a dramatic perspective helps us to understand these inconsistencies, even to see some regularity in the incongruities. I list some cases:

1. Cyrano was such a fool! He loved Roxanne with all his heart. And yet his fearful pride prohibited him from ever professing his love for her or confessing that he was the author of the eloquence she so admired. He preferred pathos to fulfillment, carried his secret love to his grave, acting always so as to preserve his precious suffering rather than risk the consequences of revelation.

2. A client of mine suffered long in a marriage to a woman who must have been of the disorganized-disoriented type. She treated him in a way that was alternately punishing and humiliating. It took him two full years after moving out of their house to consummate the divorce, such was his residual loyalty to her and her children. At the same time, he developed a fulfilling relationship with another woman, this one remarkably secure. But even after the divorce he could not bring himself to marry her, even though he was convinced he loved her and wanted very much to marry her. He had changed scenes, but he was still not psychologically detached from the previous marriage.

3. A seventy-two-year-old man returned to his native village in Germany after sixty-one years of absence—and was greeted by former school chums with a hearty "Johann, you've come home!" After much to-do in the village during his visit of two weeks, everyone cried copious tears at the moment of the new departure. When his son expressed concern, Johann was reassuring. "Never mind," he said. "We know that we will never see each other again. But the pain will soon pass. The tears will dry as soon as we leave." His did. So, probably, did theirs.

4. A young man had a date for his senior prom with the girl of his dreams—a girl who was available only because her boyfriend had graduated in the previous year and she needed an escort. He danced the evening away in great happiness, and she ap-

peared to be happy as well. After graduation she married her
boyfriend, and her prom partner moved away and never saw
her again. But thirty years later he confessed to thinking about
her virtually every day, despite having had absolutely no contact
with her, pursued a successful career and marriage, and raised a
large and flourishing family. As with Cyrano, this is a case of
the voluptuousness of misery.

5. One of the world's experts on the theory of equity and exchange
   in social psychology, Roger Brown, expresses in his memoir an
   utter naiveté about the norm of reciprocity in practice. He tells
   of giving a sizable fund of money to a young lover who is starting a business, with the understanding that there will be "no
   strings attached." Later, when the young man begins to ignore
   him, Brown becomes enraged at this display of ingratitude.
   Later Brown describes knowing that a relationship is over even
   while pretending that it is not: "Far wiser to deny any change
   and let the realization grow so slowly that when it becomes
   definite, one has already habituated to the pain" (1996, 206).
   And yet when confronted by the possibility that one of his former lovers has a new boyfriend, he becomes angry: "Now could
   I drink hot blood."

6. Willy Loman, in Arthur Miller's *Death of a Salesman,* professes
   his love for his wife, Linda, and pretends that he has mastered
   the secret of success as a salesman. Yet his son finds him in a ho-
   tel with another woman—he gives this woman nylons while
   Linda darns her hose at home. Willy is sincere and pathetically
   self-deceived. And he is a slice of life.

Some of these examples are from the theater, some from the drama
of everyday life. All exhibit the poignant reality of shifting perspectives
on human relationships. Emerson opined that "All lives, all friendships
are momentary. *Do you love me?* means at last, *Do you see the same truth I
see?*" (in Richardson 1995, 330). When the scene changes and new truth
emerges, then the separation is accomplished and it seems unnatural to
cling together, though some will try and some out of tenacity will
succeed. Inconsistencies and incongruities occur in the drama of every-

day life because personal engagement in stories is layered and multiple, and often a scene is not over when it seems to be over. And often one continues in secret to imagine involvements long since lapsed.

Happy and fluid and continual dances do occur. Of them, we need not speak but only rejoice in their secure and blessed condition. But mistakes and troubles deserve attention, as always.

TIMING AND FALSE MOMENTS

A friend told me this story of a relationship that failed to form, perhaps because of a momentary lapse in timing: It was a Saturday evening on the campus of a graceful woman's college in New England in the early 1960s. The protagonist was a young man from a nearby men's college, fixed up by his roommate with a most attractive partner for the evening. After attending a few parties and dancing, they took a leisurely stroll on the woman's campus, all alone in the moonlight, with an hour to spare before her curfew. The late spring evening was warm, the moon was full, and they reached a promontory on their walk where before them a meadow glowed in mysterious light. She turned her face to his, they paused in their conversation. He looked into her eyes, then awkwardly looked away, and continued walking. Not ten paces later he turned to her again and tried to kiss her. She refused to return his kiss, saying, with both sadness and kindness, "The moment has passed." Alas, he recognized that she was right. Later she allowed him to kiss her goodbye, but there was no ardor in the kiss, and it was indeed, goodbye.[6]

Not all relationships have such a delicate critical period. However, all relationships have a characteristic periodicity, and a gesture or merely a presence at any time takes its meaning from that periodicity. Consider some false moments:

Showing up back in the neighborhood just a few days after a huge farewell party for one's departure to China.
Asking for the next dance after being refused for the last one.
Stalking one's ex-wife.

Making a career of reliving one's misery at the treachery of one's
former husband.

Blithely promising to "do lunch" with a former friend or colleague
one meets accidentally at an airport.

Timing is paramount in the dance of personal relationships. If the
right steps are executed at the right time, the relationship itself can
endure. Poor timing and bad steps result in false moments—and a
disagreeable sense of imposition or of stepping on toes.

DISENGAGING FROM THE DANCE

The self is profoundly alone, and yet escapes for long moments the
experience of being alone by acts of communion with others. The communion is always limited in time, while the self's experience is continual
and without temporal delimitation.

I have an image. It is of the self in a crowd of people—some with
distinct and caring faces, some indistinct. Now the self draws apart from
the crowd, and all the faces become blurred and commingled. The story
that was to be told can no longer be told, and so it ceases to matter. The
drifting continues, without will or direction, away from the crowd. What
was the crowd is now just a pinpoint in the distance. Soon even the
pinpoint is gone and all is undifferentiated—neither light nor dark.

The dance is over. One is grateful for the memories.

In the words of the poet John Ciardi: "It is something—and more
than something, much—to realize that we do not matter—except to
each other. For then we can matter mightily—if only for a while."[7]

GAMBLING

But any gambler will tell you that a man
may spend as much as twenty-four hours
at cards, glued to his seat and without ever
taking his eyes off the game.

—Fyodor Dostoevsky

Here is the Calvinist solution to life: Once
the individual divides his daily activities
into ones that have no effect and others
having a small contributive consequence,
nothing can really go wrong.

—Erving Goffman

Since the Foxwoods casino opened in Ledyard, Connecticut, in February
1992, its doors have not closed. It has operated continuously, day and
night, year after year. Now it bills itself as the largest casino in the world.
Cars stream into its massive parking lots and garages day and night. Over
40,000 customers file through its doors—weekends, weekdays, every
day. They leave each day several millions of dollars in net earnings for the
casino—a tribute to the collective need for action.[1] New England was
settled by people who were strongly committed to Calvinist principles—
Puritans who had no use for sport and gaming. Perhaps the repressive
force of these principles created, over the centuries, an enormous potential for cathartic release. Now this release is occurring and the results are
stunning. The Foxwoods casino produced about $1 billion in revenue in
1997—just five years after its opening.

What is it that moves many thousands of people to come from all
over the northeastern United States to a rather desolate spot in rural
Connecticut to leave, on average, $50 to $100 per person, in exchange
for nothing but the uncertain and perhaps titillating manner of making
the deposit? No one is coercing these people to tax themselves. To be
sure, some may come to see performances by big-name stars. Theatrical
stars are used as a hook for the real theater—that of gambling. The
challenge is to understand the attraction of gambling for the masses of
people. How can an activity that is so regularly and certainly punishing,

in a material sense, come to be so fascinating, so full of charm and wonder, as to produce such a spectacle as the Foxwoods casino? The answer lies in the complex spinning of drama around the act of gambling.

Place yourself imaginatively in one of the massive slot machine salons at Foxwoods. The room is carpeted and decorated with subdued colors. Each of the hundreds of electronic slot machines is fitted with a cylindrical light at its top, which lights up on the occasion of a payoff so that the collective effect is that of random fireflies flashing their signals throughout the entire expanse. The sound level in the room is rather high, just short of cacophony—a sound composed of the clatter of coins, the ringing of bells from machines where the coin discharge is especially high, and an indistinct background of music. The sound could be described as eerie—continual, rhythmic, undulating—rather like the Carnatic music of South India, but without words and not as soothing.

It is midafternoon on a Tuesday—not a peak time—and only about 85 percent of the machines are in use. Each player sits on a cushioned stool that is fixed securely to the floor. The players are about 80 percent women and the average age appears to be the mid-fifties. Dress is casual. There is little conversation among players in the room, though it is evident that most of the players are part of a "with," to use Goffman's term. Players commonly keep their coins (usually quarters, sometimes dollar tokens) in large plastic cups. From these they feed the machines up to three coins per play (additional coins increase the payoff values). Put in the coins, press the button, the three electronically simulated wheels spin and stop—blip, blip, blip—in order, left to right, the payoff (if any) is registered, and the next play begins.[2] When coins are delivered into the large payoff trays, the accompanying clatter is loud, for the stainless steel trays are made like sounding boards to amplify the reinforcing effect of winning. This entire sequence takes less than five seconds. The player, scarcely pausing to note wins and losses, proceeds to feed the machine for the next play. In one minute, ten to twenty plays are completed, and the typical player continues at this rate for several hours. On some machines one may dispense with the delaying effect of inserting and delivering actual coins. On these machines an initial mass feeding (say by a $20 bill) produces a credit, indicated by an illuminated number. There-

after, each press of the button diminishes this number by one, and wins
cause the number to increase, according to the symbols on the payout
line. This method of play is also cleaner, for those inserting and retriev-
ing actual coins quickly get dirty hands; dedicated players and money-
changers protect their hands with light cotton gloves.

Patrons generally believe that the payout ratios of machines are not
constant but vary from machine to machine. Managers and industry
officials concede that rates vary, but will not, in general, say what the
rates are or how they vary. In New Jersey, the machines may not legally
retain more than 12.5 percent of the amount bet, so those machines
must return at least 87.5 percent. (Working out the mathematics, this
would mean that a typical 25-cent slot might return about $1 per
minute to the house.) In Connecticut and Nevada there are no statutory
limits on machine payoffs. The return rate may be as high as 95 percent
on some machines. Management is not generous with this kind of
information.

A food court and adjacent restrooms are indicated by large neon
signs. Uniformed attendants stand by to answer questions, provide directions, keep out minors and alcoholic beverages, and maintain order.
Other attendants push coin exchange carts to players at the machines, to
facilitate the exchange of bills for coins. In this room there are no
windows or clocks.

As a dramatic setting, the slot machine salon is ethereal, but for the
nonparticipant it quickly becomes tedious. Players are intensely involved
with their machines and show little affect—either joy or sadness. One
sees signs of fatigue but not ennui. The little units composed of the
players and their machines have an intensity about them that seems to
exclude attention to much else. Players do not object to casual over-the-
shoulder onlookers. No one seems to notice. And yet the dramatic feel of
the player-machine unit is vastly different in the isolated setting of a slot
machine in a grocery store or a gas station in Nevada, where players tend
to drop by, play a coin or two, then move on. A slot machine room with
400 machines running simultaneously produces a continual music of
clattering coins, jackpot signals, and human droning. It also creates a
sense of informal and unratified fraternity with a host of other players, all
of them involved in the same, prolonged quest for flashes of luck, all

willing to defy the certain mathematical odds against them, all willing to spend their time and risk their money in their search for favor. Everyone in this room has a role—player, attendant, moneychanger—and they play these roles with unflagging zeal for their full shifts. To the out-of-role observer, as I have said, the setting is tedious and it is difficult to spend an hour there.

The dramatic opposite of tedium is illustrated in this description of a payoff celebration for a big jackpot winner at Harrah's casino in Las Vegas: "When someone hits big on a slot machine, 'win committees' converge like cheery commandos, toting a boom box that plays Kool and the Gang's 'Celebration.' Glittery 'lucky dust' is sprinkled over the area—a salt lick to draw slot hogs foraging for a hot machine" (Hirschey 1994, 50).

HYPNOSIS AS SOCIAL CONTRACT

I have often conducted demonstrations of group hypnosis for classes of students, using the Harvard Group Susceptibility Scale—either reading the induction text or using the recorded version, it makes little difference. In performing this exercise with a class of approximately one hundred students, I always take the precaution of having student teaching assistants stand by as attendants and observers—to distribute and collect response booklets, to accommodate latecomers to the class, or to meet any other exigencies of the moment. Responses of students to the Group Scale vary from profound to nil—reliably demonstrating individual differences in hypnotic susceptibility. But the responses of my attendant-observers never vary. They do not shut their eyes in response to the suggestions and instructions to do so. They do not extend their arms, clasp their hands in front of them, or comply with any of the other instructions. Cast in a different role, these people would show the same differential response to hypnotic suggestions as do the student subjects. But casting makes all the difference. Out of role, they are immune to the hypnotic suggestions that seem to have such a profound effect on so many of their classmates. The hypnotic role is like a brief social contract. Once the role and contract are accepted, the effects can be quite compelling.

BEING CAST AS A GAMBLER

Casting makes all the difference in the world of gambling as well. The players in the slot machine room are constitutionally no different from the attendants or the occasional observers. It is not surprising that studies attempting to differentiate gamblers from nongamblers in terms of personality variables such as "locus of control" or "impulsivity" or "extroversion" have consistently yielded disappointing results.[3]

This is not to say that the self-casting process that leads to gambling is not in some ways systematic. Reuven Brenner and Gabrielle Brenner (1990) have shown that older and poorer people buy more lottery tickets than younger and wealthier people. They suggest that the poor and the old have come to realize that the only way they will become rich is to win the lottery. This provides an account for the demographically unrepresentative sample of people found in the slot machine rooms. These are people who over the years have become discouraged about obtaining the smiles of good fortune. They are older people who have some time and a little money on their hands. They are willing to cast themselves in the role of slot players as a way of exchanging time and money for the possibility—not the probability—of favor. Many with the same psychological, social, and economic characteristics do not make this choice. But once the gambling whim is honored and the room is entered, one is carried along by the atmosphere of common quest, supported by the flashing lights, the sound of frequent cascades of money into someone's else's bin, and the curiously compelling music of possibility. Like hypnosis, gambling on the slots is a brief social contract. As it happens, more women than men prefer this particular form of gambling exercise, but at the poker and dice tables the opposite is observed, with men predominating. At the roulette wheels women and men are found in about equal numbers.

The patrons of the casino do not really need to be anywhere else. I had a client who was a recovering heroin addict. Through Narcotics Anonymous, individual therapy, and his dedication to an educational career, he has been free from heroin for over ten years. He had also been helped in the initial phases of his recovery by an intense romantic relationship with a divorced woman who had two children. This small family moved in with him and he became a dedicated father to the children. But after four years he and the woman broke up and he was reduced to living alone. Now with time on his hands he began to feel lonely and depressed. He began to frequent the poker tables at the Foxwoods casino.

He realized that his gambling was costly and not a rational response to his situation, but he was powerless to stop, though he did keep it within bounds. He became a skillful poker player, and would sometimes leave the casino with winnings of $300–$500 for an evening's play. But more frequently he lost. I urged him to keep a careful and detailed record of his wins and losses, together with a log of the actual number of hours he spent gambling. We discovered that week in, week out, he was spending about $10 per hour for the diversion of playing poker. His poker playing continued at a more or less steady rate for several years, with monthly losses averaging about $500. He broke off therapy, but he did not revert to drug abuse and he continued his educational program. It is interesting that $500 was about the limit of discretionary cash in his budget.

While he said he would have preferred to save the money or to spend it for more worthwhile projects, he was not able to carry out these intentions until a major change occurred in his life. He got married, to a woman who, like his previous companion, had two daughters. During the courtship, he continued his gambling—initially surreptitiously, later more openly. Gambling was never an activity he and his fiancée shared. After the wedding the gambling stopped completely. Now living with his new family, he found he was needed elsewhere and no longer had time for the casino. He has, at least temporarily, retired from his gambling career. The success of his abstinence from gambling will depend upon the success of his marriage.

GAMBLING AS DRAMATIC ENRICHMENT

Gambling is a means of achieving drama in one's life. Gambling, like theater in general, is transformative. The soil out of which gambling grows is tedium, boredom, a life of confining domesticity, a life without realistic hope for a better future. Of course, many solutions exist for transforming dullness into interest—and they are all, in a sense, theatrical.

Religion is a traditional solution to the problem of human loneliness, isolation, and despair. Religion gives an individual significance in the eyes of the great other, provides a sense of duty, obligation, and moral purpose. By participating in a religious community, a person may gain identity with a supportive collectivity. Religion, however, requires something like faith—a belief in the unseen, an acceptance of truth that lies beyond the evidence of the senses. Ours is a secular age, and while religious theater certainly exists and flourishes, its requirements of faith and practice make it unappealing to large segments of humanity and thus insufficient as a way to redeem life from a default condition of nullity.

Kenneth Burke, the literary critic who used dramatism as a means of understanding human motivation, recognized the commonalities of religion and gambling. He mused, "If they cannot have religion, they should have lotteries" (1964a, 58). What is common between religion and gambling? Both have temples—casinos, horse and dog tracks, off-track betting parlors, poker and bingo rooms, corresponding to churches, synagogues, mosques, and prayer rooms. Both have strictly codified rules of conduct—highly ritualized and exactly specified procedures for the activities of gambling or worshiping. As many scholars have noted, the origins of gambling have much in common with those of religion. Soothsayers often used dice and the drawing of lots as well as other auguries to discern the will of the Gods (see Burnham 1993; Cohen 1960; Cohen 1973). Viewing the entrails of birds and spinning coconuts are not practices of modern casinos or churches, but both have been used as means of divination—a set of ancient practices at the common source of both modern religions and modern gambling: "Divination by lot or riddle was never merely a resort to meaningless chance. It was an appeal directed to supernatural powers, as when the Greek heroes cast lots to determine who should fight with Hector. Since it is impossible to predict the fall of a die or the result of casting lots the outcome must presumably be decided by divine intervention" (Cohen 1960, 57).

While a cycle of gambling is completed much more rapidly than a cycle of worship, something quite similar is evidently at stake in a psychological sense. In a typical Christian worship service, a prayer for forgiveness of sins is followed by "words of assurance"—words intended to neutralize or eliminate the sense of guilt resulting from sinful thoughts and acts. Rituals of absolution regularly follow confessions. I recently watched a player at a craps table throwing the bones with the oath, "Come, baby!" Alas, his petition was denied and he lost the dice as he "sevened out." Disappointing. But the worshiper might wonder if the bland and universal words of assurance are really meant for him—for surely the favor of God depends upon the will of God, and this will is perplexing and beyond human knowing. So while the gambler may lose, and often does, at least the outcome is clear and unambiguous. More-over, nothing keeps the gambler from trying his luck again. A win is an unambiguous affirmation. You can believe it. Even so, praying and throwing dice have something in common. Each includes a period of uncertainty—a period when outcomes are determined not by human agency but by the forces of destiny.

The economist Peter Bernstein has published an intriguing book entitled *Against the Gods: The Remarkable Story of Risk* (1996). Noting the common origins of gambling and religious soothsaying, he proceeds to argue that bringing risk under control is the central feature distinguishing modern times from the distant past. Now insurance actuaries are able to estimate risk with great accuracy, enabling the collectivization of risk. Now statistical techniques can be used to provide remarkably precise predictions for the aggregate outcomes of a variety of manufacturing and economic processes. But after describing the successes of the past three centuries in bringing risk under control, Bernstein not only admits the existence of residual insecurity but concedes that "discontinuities, irregularities, and volatilities seem to be proliferating rather than diminishing" (1996, 329). The objective of creating a certain and secure world remains unfulfilled.

Psychologically speaking, where there is no uncertainty there is no interest. Watching the paint dry or the grass grow is not an activity that will absorb lasting attention. Dostoevsky grasped this point clearly, and understood as well the paradoxically positive appeal of anguish. A man is a creature who chooses. But he does not always choose as reason or interest dictates: "He is a man and not a piano key! If you say that all this, too, can be calculated and tabulated—chaos and darkness and curses, so that the mere possibility of calculating it all beforehand would stop it all, and reason would reassert itself, then man would purposely go mad in order to be rid of reason and gain his point!" (1960, 206).

Perhaps an evolutionary explanation could be offered for this incessant interest in uncertainty and novelty. As prey, living creatures increase their potential for survival if they are able to avoid being entirely predictable. As predator, it helps to be alert to the least perturbation of the surrounding field as a possible indication of one's next meal. But a more satisfactory explanation from a psychological point of view is that the human capacity for self-reflection introduces a compelling fascination with the not-yet-known because of its potential consequences for our very being. George Eliot offers this insight:

> So absolute is our soul's need of something hidden and uncertain for the maintenance of that doubt and hope and effort which are the breath of its life, that if the whole future were laid bare to us today, the interest of all mankind would be bent on the hours that lie between; we should pant after the uncertainties of our one morning and our one afternoon, we should rush fiercely to the exchange for our last possibility of speculation, of success, of disappointment. (1985, 291)

However much we may seek it, the human mind abhors the moral vacuity of certainty. For where certainty exists, there is no room for play, for sport, for dramatic transformation. Where uncertainty exists, there we may have commerce, at least in our fantasy, with unseen forces that enter our world from a different level. God may not play dice with the universe, but we play dice with God. While play may seem a disrespectful way to force him out of his reticence, it is at least interesting—and for the gambler, enthralling.

Observations of contemporary American culture support the proposition that we have more taste for uncertainty than we have for beauty. All-news radio stations supplant those playing classical music. The sports pages and the business pages daily provide their readers with novel numbers—the former related by the curious ties of fandom to the identity of the reader and the latter to the reader's fortune, or imagined fortune. We know how the play or the opera will end, but sporting events, even though they are composed of endlessly repetitive sequences, are attractive only because their outcomes are uncertain. For many years automobile racing has been a most popular spectator event in the United States.[4] The uncertainty around automobile racing is twofold: one doesn't know who will win the race, and one also doesn't know if the race will produce a spectacular and perhaps fatal crash. Without these two kinds of uncertainty one might as well watch the cars passing on the freeway. A horse race is beautiful. But of the total time spent at the track—perhaps four hours for an afternoon's card—only about twenty minutes will be spent in watching the horses. The rest of the time is absorbed in thinking about what might happen in the next race and in getting down bets.

A SPECIAL FORM OF DRAMATIC CYCLE

Goffman (1967, 154–155) described four phases of the gambling cycle. *Squaring off* is the laying of bets or the declaration of an investment. The *determination* phase is when the outcomes become set—the three-second spinning of the slot machine wheels, the running of the horses, the dealing of the cards, the movement of the market. The *disclosure* phase is the period between determination and the informing of participants of the outcome. In slots this is instantaneous. In horse racing there is a pause between the outcome of the race and the official disclosure of payoffs to bettors. In the stock market, modern machinery makes the disclosure phase extremely rapid. The *settlement* phase is devoted to collecting and distributing gains and losses.

The final two phases of this cycle are completely determined and routinized for all conventional gambling games and for stock market speculation as well. But variability can and does enter at the first two phases. In the first phase, the bettor must make a choice, place a wager, and certify that wager as backed by actual money. The second phase allows the gods of determination to enter the play. In the stock market, the investor can ordinarily determine the length of this period—making an additional decision about when to cash in, either because the fear of additional loss is too great to bear or because the hope of additional gain is insufficient to remain invested. Similarly, in a hand of poker, the player can choose "when to hold 'em and when to fold 'em"—again as a function of the hopes and fears generated by the action.

Many cycles of dramatic forms can be identified. Kenneth Gergen and Mary Gergen (1983) have described the particular successions of phases characteristic of comedy, tragedy, romantic saga, and melodrama. The slope of the function relating valuation to time is positive for the progressive narrative (things get better and better), is negative for the regressive narrative (things get worse and worse), and curves up and down in identifiable ways for all of the major dramatic forms. Of relevance to the present discussion is Gergen and Gergen's description of suspense:

> A goal is apparent, the protagonist is moving toward it, but any moment a setback may occur—the secret agent may be discovered, a wild beast may leap from an overhead branch, or the lover's seamy past may be revealed. In effect, dramatic engagement in this case is created not by the story itself, but by a potential or anticipated series of events . . . In particular, when the narrative slope can undergo sudden acceleration and/or shift in the opposite direction from its present course, dramatic engagement is accelerated. Thus, any indication that the story line could change rapidly and/or in a different direction adds substantially to the drama. (1983, 30–31)

Suspense is dramatically interesting because of the threat or promise of bad or good events that may happen but are not fully determined up to the moment. Suspense is set up in gambling by the squaring off phase, but it is actually experienced in the determination phase of Goffman's idealized gambling cycle.

But suspense too long endured produces frustration, irritation, and finally despair. Those who make an investment hope for reasonably rapid disclosure of results. The pigeon-drop con game illustrates the prolongation of the disclosure phase. The con asks the mark to hold a bag of phony money while the con makes arrangements for distribution of the funds—the con possessing the mark's earnest deposit of real money as a guarantee. Eventually, when the con does not return, the mark grows bold enough to examine the money in the bag, only to discover that it is shredded newspaper. Many a legitimate investor has been told to wait as a real estate development matures, an import-export scheme takes shape, or a new product is properly marketed—to wait *ad nauseam* and to despair. The suspense phase in gambling cannot be too prolonged, else it loses its affective fizz. This is one major reason why buy-and-hold or indexed investing is no fun (see Chapter 6).

Dramatic cycles can be found in all kinds of human endeavors. The hunter goes hunting and finds and kills game only with the cooperation of forces outside his control, then returns home with his bag and shares it. The farmer plants, cultivates, and hopes—and with luck gathers in the crop for a good payoff at the end of the season. Courtship involves the taking of risks, and the sweetness of love cannot be realized without reciprocation from the other. The return of love is invited but cannot be forced—the determination belongs to the other. The act of procreation can be seen as having the same phases as the gambling cycle—squaring off (intercourse), determination (the chance combination of egg and sperm), disclosure (the revealing of the outcome through birth), and settlement (absorbing the consequences of having a child). To live and to love is to risk.

We can now see that what distinguishes gambling from other dramatic cycles is the nature and duration of the phase of determination. I believe that the particular character of this phase in conventional gambling is what produces the moral ambiguity about gambling—a suggestion of the reason why games of chance have a liminal moral status, between Good and Evil.

THE MORAL AMBIGUITY OF GAMBLING

For the novice, just the act of entering the Foxwoods casino produces a *frisson*. The enterprise is, without question, fully legitimate—licensed, chartered, permitted, and even encouraged by the State of Connecticut, which has managed to cut itself in on a healthy percentage of the slot machine profits. And yet one has the sense of entering into a forbidden and even sinful territory—a realized version of the Pleasure Island described in *Pinocchio,* with perhaps the same potential of turning us all into donkeys. All is orderly—but in the half-light, with the crowd of

strange yet familiar people, with so much visible money and with the
discordant and haunting music of the games, it is both thrilling and
ominous.

In *Ethics,* Aristotle classed gamblers with thieves and plunderers. The
Koran prohibits gambling, as does Talmudic law. Even with these strictures, gambling has been present from antiquity to the present day.
Gambling is clearly something that people have wanted to do, while
established interests have frequently and vigorously opposed it. Today,
church groups are commonly arrayed against the promoters from Las
Vegas and Atlantic City who would propose to install new casino facili-
ties in Hartford or Baltimore or New York.[5] The promoters argue in
favor of economic prosperity—jobs, urban renewal, new construction, a
sense of vitality. The opposition cites the case of Atlantic City, where the
legalization of gambling in 1974 resulted in the creation of massive and
self-contained pleasure palaces, but did not bring general prosperity or
vitality to the surrounding city, which continues to decay (see Sternlieb
and Hughes 1983). Liberal critics point out that gambling is generally
regressive—for the poor spend a disproportionate amount of their income on gambling.

In press clippings describing the controversies over the introduction
of legalized gambling, another theme—not economic, but moral—is
present. Concern is expressed over the connection of the gambling industry to organized crime—the Mob. Prostitution is also feared as a
consequence of the introduction of gambling. Proponents of gambling
are at pains to demonstrate their lack of ties to organized crime and to
express both disdain and caution about prostitution. But popular films
reinforce the stereotypes. *Bugsy* describes the role of the notorious mob-
ster Bugsy Siegel in founding the modern era of gambling in Las Vegas.
It is a portrait of violence and amorality. *Leaving Las Vegas* is a bitter
evocation of end-of-the-world death spasms, drowning in alcohol and
illicit sex. Official investigations about the connections of organized
crime to legalized gambling are constant. The concerns about easy sex are
certainly reinforced by the traditional image of Las Vegas, where call girls
and show girls have been an inextricable part of the scene (see Burnham
1993).

Las Vegas has recently made a major effort to invest in Disney

World–like theme parks, to create an image of healthy hospitality to families, with a corresponding deemphasis on sex as the hook for the gambler. Even so, Nevada is the only state with legalized prostitution. In comparison to Las Vegas or Atlantic City, the Foxwoods casino is quite demure. Cocktail waitresses cruise the floor dressed in skimpy Indian costumes, sporting a long feather or two in their hair—but the overt sexuality of the scene is restrained. Even so, the association of gambling and sex is simply there; it would take an energetic and principled act of denial to ignore it.[6]

The evident association between gambling and sex is somewhat beside the point, or is merely a case in point. The point is that the world of gambling is morally liminal—located at the borders between Heaven and Hell. This is because of the particular character of the dramatic cycle of gambling as opposed to other types of dramatic cycles.

First, if gambling is related historically and ontologically to divination—to finding out the will of God, or finding out one's status with God—then it is, as early critics of lotteries pointed out, disrespectful. For by casting lots or throwing dice, one forces God to respond immediately—the phase of determination is not allowed to be prolonged.

Second, most dramatic cycles do not involve the complete passivity of the agent during the phase of determination. The farmer is supposed to work at cultivation, fertilization, care, and pruning of the growing crop. The hunter and fisher must exercise qualities of patience, perseverance, and willingness to suffer hardship and privation in the phase of determination. Even the market speculator can think of the investment being employed for capital improvement projects and the like for the company in which investment is made, for unlike gambling establishments, most companies make tangible products or provide services.

A third and closely related proposition is that if the ethic of gain implicit in the structure of gambling becomes generalized throughout a society, then the society as a whole will become less productive, less inventive, less progressive. Gambling does become pathological—a self-destructive activity. From the point of view of management, gambling is a business—the idea being to produce a reasonable return on investment while providing entertainment and diversion to the clientele. For the clientele, gambling may start off as a mere diversion, but it is possible to become addicted to gambling—to become a pathological gambler of the sort illustrated in Dostoevsky's famous novel *The Gambler* (1922). While only a small proportion of the people who gamble are pathological gamblers, it is indisputable that the absolute number of individuals afflicted with this problem increases with the legalization of gambling and is considerable at present.[7]

Despite these suggestions that gambling is naturally associated with sin, the concept of sin itself is not faring very well these days, and by extension, gambling can seem pretty innocent. Most states now have state lotteries. Most states now also license and profit from other gambling activities, such as jai alai, horse racing, dog racing, bingo and poker parlors, and casinos. States have abandoned the moral high ground. They cannot oppose gambling without exposing an utter hypocrisy, for they profit hugely from gambling. The involvement of states is shameless for two reasons. First, the payoffs of state lotteries are commonly as low as 50 percent, making them far less attractive gambles than the worst of casino games. Second, states commonly advertise their lotteries in a way that is particularly pernicious: "You can't win if you don't play"; "Don't fight it—it's bigger than you are."

By the measure of state-granted legitimacy, gambling is becoming more and more respectable, less associated with sin, crime, and the underlife. But by its nature, and regardless of the legal and cultural conditions that happen to prevail at the moment, gambling always has had and always will have a liminal position in the moral sense—located on the margins between the world of sunlight and the world of darkness. The general tendency of casinos to lack windows is mute testimony to this twilight status.

GAMBLING AS DRAMA

Because gambling is not quite respectable, because it involves the heady possibility of being identified as among the Chosen or the Lucky Winners, because it is a way of forcing God's hand, and because so much of life is filled with tedium, gambling will always have great dramatic appeal. Not everyone will gamble, of course, because not everyone is bored to begin with, and some may be sufficiently respectful of God or observant of the conservative principles of the Calvinist approach to life as to be immune to gambling's attractions.

But for many, gambling is a way of opening a door of possibility in the confining walls of necessity. Such a door can carry you away. Here is a description from a novel by Tim O'Brien:

> After the first two or three hours [of blackjack] she'd been hooked hard. She loved the flash. She loved the sound of the dice and slot machines, the clatter of mathematics. It wasn't the money that had kept her up all night; rather, in ways she didn't care to fathom, it had to do with the possibility of a prodigious jackpot just out of reach. Possibility itself. The golden future. Everything was *next*—the next roll, the next card, the next hour, the next lucky table. Gaudy and artificial, cheap in the most fundamental sense, the place represented everything she found disgusting in the world, but still she couldn't deny the thrill of a black ace descending like a spaceship on a smiling red queen. It did not matter that her wager was only five dollars. What mattered was the rush in her veins. The pursuit of miracles, the rapture of happy endings. (1994, 223–224)

The purchase of possibility can be a bargain even at a high price. The need for some action depends upon the dramatic context of an individual life. I know of a respectable Bostonian, a widow in her eighties, a woman of Brahmin background, thoroughly, even painfully respectable. But in her elegantly furnished apartment she receives a daily avalanche of mail-order sweepstakes proposals—the kind that scream, "Congratulations! You are a winner! Open this envelope to see how you can receive your One Million Dollars!" What's the deal here? The answer is, by participating in mail sweepstakes, she is placed on the mailing lists for other mail sweepstakes—and there are hundreds of them. Many ask for the purchase of magazines or other small articles—not as a necessity for receiving a prize, but as a way of increasing one's chances. Others ask for a small deposit to be made against a large prize that is, they imply, (almost) sure to be won. A most effective gimmick for this woman is the paid consultant—a friendly, considerate, and well-spoken young man who periodically calls her to provide counsel on how to proceed to collect the huge prizes that are somewhere in escrow. For this service he charges a modest fee—which over the course of a year amounts to thousands of dollars.

This well-educated lady is thrilled with the possibility of surprising her friends and family with a quantity of unexpected money that neither she nor they need. She has been admonished by her financial advisors and by her family that she is being swindled, that she will win no prizes, that she is throwing her money away. But really, something is coming back to her: the daily quantity of mail is in itself gratifying, for no one else ever bothers to write. And there are those telephone calls from that nice young man, the one who takes the time to inquire about her health, her family, and her state of mind. In all, these little in-house diversions cost her perhaps five to eight thousand dollars per year. There is no way to stop it without having her declared incompetent and removing her power to use checks or credit cards. This lady is, in her way, a gambler. To be such requires that she act in a way that is a bit naughty, but apparently the compensations in terms of attention and action make it worthwhile for her. One doesn't want to be, after all, too secure and too proper. What's the fun?

I know of another woman, in quite different circumstances, who in her old age was even more consumed with gambling. She came from a relatively poor background, was highly intelligent, and in her younger years was quite beautiful. She married a minister, somewhat against her better judgment, she always thought, and had four children. The oldest son, at age seventeen, ran away from home and became involved with gambling, mostly horse racing. He introduced his mother to betting on the horses, and for the last forty years of her life she was hooked. She divorced the minister and married a man who was more permissive about her gambling. She moved to California, nearer to the tracks. She became an expert handicapper and enjoyed remarkable successes on some days. More frequently, of course, she lost. But in losing she always had an excuse, a story, a reason why, a lesson learned. This rather punishing habit of gambling and losing became the center of her life and remained so for many years. She referred to her trips to the track as "Going to work." When, late in life, she became too feeble to go to the track, she seemed to lose interest in life. She died shortly thereafter.

Gambling is not really about money. It is about the drama of life.[8]

Fantasies are by definition not realistic—but realism can be confining and dull, while fantasies are the stuff of life. Even though it is commonly expensive to purchase these doors of possibility in the confining wall of necessity, the purchaser often considers it worth it. It is everlastingly important to be chosen, to win, to be favored. The value of this possibility outlasts all other human appetites. At the Last Day, one hopes desperately to be chosen.

THE DISAPPEARANCE OF SCHIZOPHRENIA

Throughout most of the twentieth century, mental hospitals were a powerful and conspicuous feature of our cultural landscape. Schizophrenia was the most prominent and serious form of chronic mental disorder throughout the century; most patients in mental hospitals were classified as schizophrenic. It is difficult to conceive of these given facts as dramatic creations—for the reality of mental hospitals and severe mental illness seemed so ineluctable. Mental hospitals and the schizophrenics they contained seemed to be essential features of the world, essential points of reference for psychology. This is another case of the essential crystallizing out of a set of arbitrary developments. Now mental hospitals are fading as institutional structures. More surprising, schizophrenics are also fading as a class of people. Schizophrenia, I wish to argue, was an enveloping dramatic construction. And now it is a dramatic construction that is demonstrably losing its force.

In the 1960s I conducted research in the major mental hospitals of Connecticut in order to determine the effects of introducing college student volunteers to work on chronic mental wards for a summer program. Our research team found that the program had a considerable impact on the patients, on the wards, and on the one hundred or so students who participated each summer. The chronic patients became more lively and communicative. The wards became more active and had fewer critical incidents of violence. The college students benefited in terms of self-report measures of emotional maturity and the focusing of career plans.[1]

Chronic mental wards seemed intractable to change because they were part of a rigid institutional structure—a structure that had evolved over the course of a century to serve as the place for the custodial care of madness in our society. But by the mid-1960s the winds of change were already blowing—we did not know at the time how strongly. Erving Goffman (1961) had already described the typical mental hospital as a total institution. Thomas Szasz (1961) had had the temerity to assert that mental illness was a myth, implying a flawed premise at the very foundation of "mental hospitals." R. D. Laing (1961) stood at the forefront of an anti-psychiatry movement within psychiatry, suggesting that schizophrenia might be a sane response to an insane society. Theodore Sarbin (1964, 1967a) applied the concepts of social psychology to traditional categories of mental disorder and concluded that traditional labeling and treatment of disturbed individuals was futile and counterproductive. So when our ground troops entered the crowded mental hospitals in the mid-1960s, they were unaware that heavy artillery had already done considerable damage to the structures they were entering. They met some resistance, to be sure—but it was mostly from charge aides and nurses. The field generals already had lost heart.

The research was conducted in the period 1964–1968. At that time I was obliged to visit and observe every major ward for chronic patients in Connecticut. There were men's wards and women's wards, closed wards and open wards. The average census on a ward was forty-one patients. And, of course, the modal diagnosis for the patients on these wards—63 percent of the total—was schizophrenia. The modal length of stay for all patients was over eleven years, and for the schizophrenics it was considerably longer. They didn't seem to be going anywhere, but they were.

Here is a description from one of the student volunteers:

The seven of us arrived on the ward for the first time on the afternoon of June 25. S.T. was tied to her chair asking no one in particular, "What now, what now?" L.N. sat diligently rocking in "her" chair slapping her hand against her knee and muttering assorted profanities.

N.E. lay curled up in an impossible position in a chair, hands laced across her averted face. S.H. stripped off her simple vestments, stood in the middle of the sun porch adamantly demanding that S.E. take note of her female attributes. The remainder of the ladies sat in their "very own seats" lined up along the four walls of the porch staring into space, muttering to unseen friends, flailing at those mysterious nothings which flew at them through the air, and moaning.

During those years, the typical census for all the major state mental hospitals in Connecticut was about 8,500 patients, of whom about 4,700 were classified as schizophrenic. Now the three major hospitals are consolidated into one campus, Connecticut Valley Hospital in Middle-town, and the current average census is below 700 patients—a decrease of more than an order of magnitude—of whom only 35 percent are classified as schizophrenic.

Where have all the schizophrenics gone? If the majority of the patients on the chronic wards were schizophrenics, and if the modal length of stay for these patients was measured in decades, then what accounts for the evident reduction in their numbers in the state mental hospitals? Is schizophrenia disappearing? A careful look at data from Connecticut's mental hospital system reveals that, far from being an ineluctable and substantive condition, schizophrenia is a dramatic label, and one that is losing its essential character.

The data to be presented here are derived from the annual statistical reports of the Connecticut Department of Mental Health. They show substantial reductions in both the incidence and the prevalence of schizophrenia in Connecticut's mental hospital system. The conceptual and methodological issues surrounding these trends are complex—involving consistency in the use of diagnostic criteria, changing modes of treatment of deviancy in our society, and a host of changing political, economic, and ideological circumstances. However, the data do, in a strong sense, cut to the heart of the matter. Were the people on those wards left there for years because they were incurable schizophrenics, or were they left there for years because they were *cast as* incurable schizo-phrenics? If schizophrenia is a disease, perhaps genetically transmitted, perhaps a result of some interactive (stress-diathesis) process, then shouldn't the incidence of this disease, in the absence of a proven cure, remain more or less constant?

Changes in the number of individuals occupying a given class can result from either of two logically distinct processes—one intrinsic and one extrinsic. Examples of intrinsic changes are the population density of lemmings, gypsy moths, dinosaurs, and cases of poliomyelitis. The definitions of class membership remain constant, but numbers decline, increase, cycle, and sometimes disappear altogether. Extrinsic changes are brought about by alterations in the definitions of class membership or in the stringency of the application of those definitions in the diagnostic process. Witchcraft is such a class. Once there were many witches—now there are fewer, because the working criteria for attaining the status of witch or warlock have changed. The same is true for blasphemers. In colonial times, blasphemers was a real class, into which real individuals were cast. The last jailing for blasphemy in the United States occurred in 1838 (and in the seventeenth century the penalty was hanging, not jail; Levy 1993). It is hard to imagine what one would have to do to be charged with blasphemy in our times, but certainly many of us would qualify for inclusion in this class by the standards of two hundred years ago. Blasphemy is not now seriously regarded as a dramatic category. "Classification systems are neither inherently self-evident nor given. On the contrary, they emerge from the crucible of human experience; change and variability, not immutability, are characteristic" (Grob 1991, 421).

The term "schizophrenia" was coined by Eugen Bleuler in 1911 as a refinement of the earlier term "dementia praecox" introduced by Emil Kraepelin in 1896. Theodore Sarbin and James Mancuso (1980) consider schizophrenia to have no more ontological status than the term "unicorn," for no one has been able to say precisely what the "disease" consists of or how it might be definitively diagnosed or cured. Their review of hundreds of published studies of schizophrenia shows that there is no critical feature—behavioral, anatomical, or biochemical— that can be used to identify it. In her careful historical review, Mary Boyle (1990) also concludes that there has never been an unequivocal diagnostic marker for schizophrenia. Diagnosis is based instead on a disjunctive symptom pattern.

Boyle also argues that the symptom pattern identified by Bleuler (and by Kraepelin before him) is no longer seen: "There is some difference between Kraepelin's and Bleuler's population and that called schizophrenic today" (1990, 65). She continues: "There is, in fact, a remarkable similarity between their descriptions of 'cases of dementia praecox/schizophrenia' and later descriptions of people said to be show-ing Parkinsonian sequelae to the . . . viral infection called encephalitis lethargica" (66). One simple hypothesis to emerge from this conjecture is that as individuals suffering from the long-term consequences of en-cephalitis are assigned to neurologists rather than psychiatrists, the inci-dence of schizophrenia will be correspondingly reduced. Either this, or the definitional boundaries of schizophrenia will have to be defined more loosely, so as to accommodate many individuals who would not have had this diagnosis a hundred years ago.

Several studies have presented evidence that incidence rates for schizophrenia have been in decline over the past few decades. New diagnoses of schizophrenia in England and Wales declined by about 50 percent from the mid-1960s to the mid-1980s (Der, Gupta, and Murray 1990; Eagles 1991). Similar declines were observed for Scottish hospitals (Geddes et al. 1993). In Danish hospitals, new admissions for diagnosed schizophrenia declined 50 percent from 1971 to 1987 (Monk-Jorgensen and Mortensen 1992). I have found no comparable studies of changes in the incidence or prevalence of schizophrenia in North America.

Textbooks suggest that the incidence and prevalence of schizophre-nia are more or less constant: annual incidence is variously quoted as between 20 and 35 cases per 100,000, with prevalence at between 110 and 300 per 100,000 (Bromat, Dew, and Eaton 1995). Studies present-ing these figures vary widely in methodology. Some are based on community samples, with lay-administered structured interviews; some rely on psychiatric diagnoses of treated individuals; diagnostic criteria vary, and of course sample size and populations studied vary widely. Epidemiological studies of incidence or prevalence of schizophrenia in the United States have not produced conclusions about time-based trends.

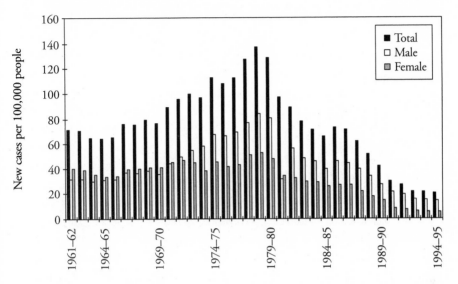

FIGURE 11.1. Rate of incidence of schizophrenia: Connecticut, 1962–1995.

THE CONNECTICUT DATA

Figure 11.1 shows the rate of incidence of new cases of diagnosed schizophrenia in state mental hospitals per 100,000 Connecticut residents. This rate increased steadily from 71 per 100,000 in 1961–62 to 138 per 100,000 in 1977–78. Then it began to drop sharply, and continued to drop until the most recent year reported, 1994–95, when it was 20 per 100,000. The 1994–95 rate of incidence of diagnosed schizophrenia in Connecticut's state mental hospitals was 72 percent lower than the corresponding rate in 1961–62, and 85 percent lower than its peak in 1977–78. Figure 11.1 also shows a breakdown of newly diagnosed cases by sex. More women than men received the diagnosis from 1961–62 to 1970–71; thereafter, men consistently outnumbered women among new cases—in 1994–95 by 78 percent to 22 percent. Women newly diagnosed as schizophrenic in the Connecticut system in 1994–95 numbered 193, or fewer than 6 per 100,000. Schizophrenia among women, it seems, is becoming quite a rare phenomenon.

Figure 11.2 presents data from the end-of-year in-house censuses of Connecticut's state mental hospitals. Note that the shape of this figure

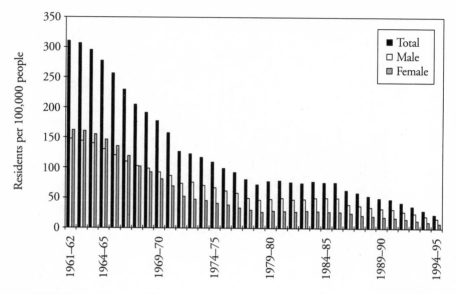

FIGURE 11.2. Prevalence rates for residence in state mental hospitals: Connecticut, 1962–1995.

does not resemble that of Figure 11.1. The number of patients in Connecticut's state mental hospitals began to fall substantially in the 1960s, despite increasing admission rates and, as we have seen, an increasing incidence of schizophrenia until 1977–78. The solution to this conflict lies in reductions in length of stay, beginning in the 1960s and continuing to the present. The average length of stay for all patients was over eleven years in 1961–62. In 1994–95 it was less than six weeks.

It follows that the prevalence rates for schizophrenia must have been tremendously reduced over the period of this study. Indeed, Figure 11.3 reflects the fact that in 1994–95 the average census for schizophrenic patients in the state's mental hospitals was 243—compared with 4,700 in 1961–62. Where have all the schizophrenics gone?

POSSIBLE INTERPRETATIONS

Both intrinsic and extrinsic reasons for this reduction are possible. An example of an intrinsic change that might be responsible for reductions

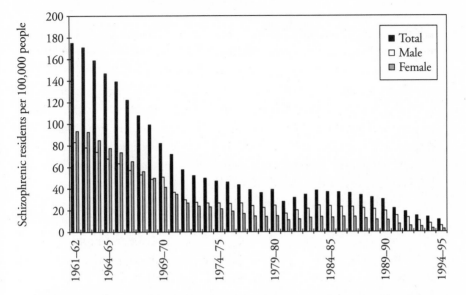

FIGURE 11.3. Prevalence rates for schizophrenia at state mental hospitals: Connecticut, 1962–1995.

in schizophrenia is the use of effective psychotropic (so-called antipsychotic) drugs, such as Haldol and Thorazine—most of which became available in the 1950s. But the timing is not right to account for the changes here described. Other drugs (such as opiates) have been available since the 1850s to control unwanted human conduct (Sarbin and Juhasz 1982). Also, the pattern of reductions in beds for mental patients is highly variable from region to region, whereas drugs are uniformly available. Finally, even though one might argue that schizophrenia is controlled through the use of modern medications, this would account only for decreases in the number of patients needing to be hospitalized (that is, decreases in prevalence), not for decreases in the number of cases diagnosed (that is, decreases in incidence), and as we have seen, the rate of newly diagnosed cases in the state mental hospital system has fallen drastically.

Another possible intrinsic change is that fewer people are schizophrenic these days because the conditions responsible for the development of the disorder—whether genetic or environmental—have been sharply and continuously reduced. But the published literature on schizophrenia reveals no claims or independent evidence for this sort of reduction. Nor does it reveal substantial claims for the discovery of effective means of prevention or cure of schizophrenia.

The currently observed decline in schizophrenia might simply be part of a longer cycle of change, with a resurgence due with the next outbreak of sunspots. But if this were true, then similar cycles should have been observed at earlier periods in history. There is no evidence that severe mental disorders such as schizophrenia undergo such cycles. Herbert Goldhamer and Andrew Marshall (1953), after examining admission rates in Massachusetts and New York mental institutions from 1850 to 1950, concluded: "There has been no long-term increase during the last century in the incidence of the psychoses of early and middle life" (41). While the prevalence of hospitalized psychotics did increase steadily over this century, Goldhamer and Marshall attribute this to the increasing use of mental hospitals as asylums for the aged; as life expectancy increased, the number of old people increased, and many old people were diagnosed as psychotic. No period in their analysis shows a decrease of incidence or prevalence resembling what we have witnessed in the last few decades.

This leads us to examine extrinsic changes in schizophrenia—changes in diagnostic criteria or anything else that may have caused a change in the tendency to apply schizophrenia as a label for a person's condition. Goldhamer and Marshall, while aware of changing definitions and labels, did not believe such changes carry much consequence for the diagnosis of psychosis:

> We are not suggesting . . . that the diagnostic categories of the older period are to be equated with the classifications in use today. But the manifest character of psychotic behavior, such as extreme agitation, excitement, deep depression, delusions, hallucinations, suicidal and homicidal acts, are sufficiently recognizable as insanity, irrespective of the classificatory terminology that is used . . . The contemporary emphasis on the arbitrary character of psychiatric nosology is not unique to our own day. Dr. Woodward writes: "In truth, insanity is as a unit, undefinable, but easily recognized by those who have watched its ever-varying appearance." (1953, 42–43)

So no matter by what name it is called, mad behavior, these authors assert, can be recognized as such by those who have experience in observing and recording these matters—and this has been the special province of psychiatry throughout the twentieth century. However, in recent years some dramatic changes have occurred—calling into question the tranquil acceptance of psychiatric authority on critical diagnostic matters.

While schizophrenia seems to be on the wane, several other categories of mental disorders are decidedly on the increase. Eating disorders are vastly more prevalent now than they were a generation ago (Hoek 1995). The same is true of Attention Deficit Hyperactivity Disorder or ADHD (Safer and Krager 1994). More to the point of the present discussion, Multiple Personality Disorder or MPD, now called Dissociative Identity Disorder, is far more conspicuous today in terms of both incidence and prevalence than it has ever been.

In *Rewriting the Soul* (1995), Ian Hacking notes the conventional textbook distinction between schizophrenia and MPD and cautions against equating them. Yet he observes that MPD (and Janet's concept of dissociation) lost out in the early twentieth century as schizophrenia (and the Freudian notion of repression) gained prominence. Hacking asserts that the symptomatology of the two disorders is quite similar and that some MPD patients have had an earlier diagnosis of schizophrenia. This is a suggestive lead for developing an explanation of what has happened to at least a portion of those individuals who formerly would have been classed as schizophrenics. This possibility is fortified by the fact that the preponderance of cases of MPD are women, while women are among the missing in newly diagnosed cases of schizophrenia. The hypothesis is that a substantial number of women who would formerly have been called schizophrenic are now called cases of MPD. This could be a result of conceptual as well as institutional changes. Conceptually, the notion of dissociation is back in vogue, with therapists now routinely searching for repressed memories of early sexual trauma that might somehow account for the patient's presented symptoms. MPD is not thought to be a disorder that routinely requires inpatient care, but is commonly treated on an outpatient basis, unlike schizophrenia.

This suggests a most obvious solution to the mystery of the drastic reduction in schizophrenia. If one is labeled schizophrenic, then the sequel is institutionalization, for the disorder still carries with it the characteristics of permanence and danger to self and others. But with the dramatic process of deinstitutionalization that has been under way since the 1960s, there are no longer places to put people who are called schizophrenic. On the male side, a colleague has suggested that many cases of "post-traumatic stress disorder" in Veterans Administration hospitals would formerly have been diagnosed as schizophrenic. Others are doubtless called criminals, and incarcerated in prisons rather than in mental hospitals—for the growth in the capacity and inmate population of our prison system is inversely related to the diminution in the capacity and census of our mental hospitals. Others are doubtless street people— the homeless. It is difficult to be precisely quantitative about the proportions of putative schizophrenics who may now be in one or another of these categories or who may simply be tolerated in their homes and communities without official label.

A psychologist who works for the Department of Mental Health suggested to me: "It is no longer politically correct to diagnose someone as schizophrenic." I don't think this is a jest. For most of the twentieth century, diagnosing someone as schizophrenic carried with it an assumption of responsibility by the state to give institutional care to that person for many years, perhaps for the rest of his or her life. But economic, political, and ideological changes have now produced an extreme reluctance on the part of most of our states to assume that kind of liability. We no longer have in place the institutional structures that are the *sine qua non* of maintaining schizophrenia as a disease.

Schizophrenia has been an enveloping dramatic conception for the nine decades of its existence as a class. It is still commonly regarded as the most serious of mental disorders. Throughout most of the twentieth century, most hospitalized mental patients carried this diagnosis. However, the data I have presented suggest that schizophrenia is becoming a hollow class.

The chronic wards on which our college students worked thirty years ago are no longer in existence as social institutions. I think of them as stage settings. They demanded powerful and serious involvement while they were up. But now that the stage settings have been struck, the actors who populated the wards are no longer controlled by the settings' mythical constraints and are now walking on other boards, no longer identified as chronic schizophrenics, no longer treated as such. The social context or framing of madness has changed. Now those in positions of authority are less likely to certify individuals who exhibit bizarre behavior as schizophrenic. And so a dramatic transformation has occurred in the incidence of schizophrenia. What was regarded as essential can now be seen as arbitrary.

DRAMA IN THE CLASSROOM

Then the whining schoolboy, with his
  satchel
And shining morning face, creeping like a
  snail
Unwillingly to school.
—William Shakespeare

Going to school has seemed onerous for centuries. Still today students complain of the drone and the drudge and the pedant. They complete their assignments and exercises more out of duty and obedience than out of joy and eagerness—finally to be certified, after many rounds of suffering and occasional experiences of gratification, as being educated in their subjects. It seems especially unfortunate that this might be so in psychology classes, where one might expect to discover exciting and satisfying truths about one's inner life and one's outer successes and failures. But it has regularly seemed to me, both as student and as teacher, that psychology courses deliver less than they promise: that something better could be done in the way of teaching and learning about human psychology, something that would bring the lessons of the classroom closer to the drama of everyday life.

This critical restlessness led me to develop a course that I call The Dramaturgical Approach to Psychology, which I first presented in 1979. I had just published a book entitled *Mirrors, Masks, Lies and Secrets* (1979), in which I explored the limits of human predictability, argued that such limits exist, and concluded that in order to understand human predictability one must understand first the engaging force of drama. Now it occurred to me to undertake a radical pedagogical experiment— one of taking drama seriously as a point of departure for the enrichment of psychological understanding. The idea was to use the language, techniques, and concepts of theater in the presentation of a seminar exploring a series of psychological topics.

The traditional teaching of traditional psychology courses makes heavy use of experiments, studies, and theories derived from remote sources. The textbook is the object of study. In the best of cases the text is subjected to considerable critical scrutiny, so that the student develops healthy doubts even about what is presented as true. But nowhere in the psychology curriculum is the analogue to a course in gross anatomy, a course in which one might confront directly the messy material of psychological inquiry—touch it, see it, feel it, smell it. Laboratory courses in experimental psychology might qualify, but their content is dictated more by the requirements of scientific tractability than by the need to address significant questions.

Even courses in humanistic and theoretical psychology do not satisfy the need for directness. For in such courses students are led through Dilthey, Maslow, May, Rogers—or more recently, Lacan, object-relations theorists, deconstructionists, postmodernists, Foucault, and other theoretical heavy hitters—with what objective? To be able to participate in a learned way in what is called the contemporary discourse on psychology. Freud spoke of developing and testing his views in the crucible of the clinic. Like William James and Wilhelm Wundt, Freud never took a psychology course—and yet these three are acknowledged as the greatest psychologists who ever lived. The founders of modern psychology were in direct touch with the material of their inquiry. It is tragic if the only way to get in touch with this material now is through these or other remote sources. Modern students should also have the advantage of looking at psychology directly, without the interposition of textbooks.

The Dramaturgical Approach to Psychology was designed to meet this challenge. Texts are used in the course, to be sure. But the texts are not the object of inquiry. Rather, they serve to set and illustrate problems and issues, to pose questions, to facilitate the inquiry in the classroom. Othello is a study in jealousy—but the object is not so much to understand Othello as it is to use the play as a way of understanding jealousy as we see it and know it in our own lives.

The major material for the course is provided by the participants—

students and teacher. If we are to study fear, then let us speak of our fears. If we are to study attachments, then let us examine our own. If we seek to understand the operation of social pressure, then let us see how such pressure operates in our own lives. If we are to appreciate family dynamics, then a serial display of the family dynamics in the experience of class members will be richly instructive. We can examine our cuticles, that part of ourselves hardened by exposure to the dry air of social commerce, and also our hearts, never exposed to air but always supplying the force and sense of our being.

Such a course is intensely personal; those who are inalterably defensive about self-revelation need not apply. But the course is not directed inward with therapeutic intent, but outward toward a developed understanding of psychological principles. An indirect benefit of the course is that of personal development: students commonly testify to having overcome their shyness and to having achieved new self-understandings. The challenge posed to students in the course is to learn from others and from themselves about psychological functioning. The challenge to me as an instructor is to direct this process—providing discipline, structure, and evaluation, while getting out of the way as the source of knowledge. Teaching, I have come to believe, is a matter of providing students with the opportunity to make their own discoveries.

What started as an experiment has grown into an institution. The course has evolved over time and many details have changed, but the basic principles and practices are the same now as they were in the beginning. I believe that something of value about teaching in general can be learned from this pedagogical experiment. The drama of the ordinary classroom is often boring. By contrast, The Dramaturgical Approach to Psychology has been regularly exciting, and I hope to show how and why this is so.

THE CLASS IN PRACTICE

The premise of teaching psychology through drama implies both method and content for the course. The method places a premium on involvement—through role-playing, improvisations, dramatic inventions, actors acting, audiences observing, reacting, interpreting, understanding. The class is limited in size so that everyone gets into the act. As instructor, I recede into a kind of director-producer or playing manager role—taking part in the exercises along with the students, but always retaining the reins of final control, even while delegating the leadership of the class meetings to student teams.

Content consists of a series of psychological topics that can be dramatically conceived, displayed, and explored: hatred, greed, love, jealousy, dependency, anger, transcendence, imagination, fantasy, conflict, charm, betrayal, loneliness, influence. Not a standard set of chapter headings to be sure, but recognizably psychological topics, and about matters likely to have both immediacy and urgency in the lives of students.

The texts assigned for the course consist of a balance of plays and works from social psychology. Certain plays have become fixtures, as have certain psychological texts. The plays include Albee's *Who's Afraid of Virginia Woolf?* Shakespeare's *Othello,* Rostand's *Cyrano de Bergerac,* Shaffer's *Equus,* Arthur Miller's *Death of a Salesman,* and Tony Kushner's *Angels in America.* I have assigned my own book, *Mirrors, Masks, Lies and Secrets,* and commonly assign works by Goffman (1959), Moreno (Fox, 1987), and Sarbin (1977).

Since I have always offered the course in the spring semester, I interview candidates the previous fall. I give preference to senior psychology majors, though I have admitted some juniors and even a few sophomores if they seemed sufficiently mature. I have also reserved several spaces for theater majors, if they have had at least some courses in psychology. The class is strictly limited in size to twenty-one students.

The class meets in a large, square room, equipped with a small movable stage. Simple track lighting with movable flood lamps with a brightness regulator is an alternative to the fluorescent room lights. The room is carpeted and contains twenty-two folding chairs, a collapsible table, and two portable vertical room dividers. A blackboard covers one wall. Another wall is a bulletin board, which fills up over the semester with photographs and other memorabilia from classes.

The course meets for thirteen three-hour sessions, with spring break splitting the first six weeks from the last seven. A typical class meeting consists of the following stages:

1. Brief comments from me, usually about mechanics of course organization, paper requirements, and the like. The leaders are introduced, and the topics and leaders for the next two weeks' meetings are announced.
2. Warm-up exercises, almost always involving movement, often accompanied by music.
3. Exercises directed by the team of student leaders, with three or four students assigned to be leaders each week.
4. A break of fifteen minutes for snacks.
5. Additional exercises directed by the leaders.
6. Final discussion and evaluation of the class.

THE FIRST MEETING

At the first class meeting, students are greeted by a sign on the door instructing them to remove their footwear before entering the room. (Since exercises often involve sitting or lying on the floor, it is important to keep the carpet clean. Also, shoe removal functions as a ritual exercise for moving into the "sacred space" of the course.) When students enter, they find twenty-one chairs set up in a strict pattern of four rows. When they are all seated, without introduction, the lights are turned off and a slide projector is turned on, presenting pictures of last year's class. The slide show is accompanied by recorded instrumental music—commonly Scott Joplin rags.

At the conclusion of the slide show, a photograph is taken of the students in their seats, with the information that the camera will be available throughout the course, and that students may at any time take pictures. Students draw numbers to determine the composition of weekly leadership teams and the schedule of leader assignments for the remainder of the semester. The syllabus is distributed, and students are told of written requirements for the course—a journal of about three hundred words per week, and a term paper.

Students are conducted through a ritual of silent greeting, so that every student makes eye contact and touches right palms with everyone else in the class, including the instructor.[1]

The next exercise is a name game, wherein each person learns everyone else's name. The class is seated on the floor in a circle. The technique for this game is for the first person to give his or her name and some identifying feature, such as a like or dislike, a hobby, or another tag. Each succeeding person gives his or her own name and feature, then repeats in order all those of the preceding speakers. The instructor completes the exercise by repeating the names and features of the entire group. So, for example: "Joe, who likes to play guitar; Sally, who rides horses; Molly, who comes from the Bronx; Matt, who loves opera," and so on.

I have chosen to be called by my last name only by the students in the course. Thus, I introduce myself as Scheibe. For I wish to avoid the false parity of status in the course suggested by mutual use of first names, and yet I also wish to avoid the loftiness and distance of title and last name—Professor, Doctor, or Mister Scheibe. The common solution to a dilemma of this kind is to "no-name"—that is, never to address the problematic other with a proper name—but this is a continual awkwardness. I discovered that students referred to me as Scheibe in their own private conversations, so I simply announced my comfort with the last-name-only usage, and it has worked well.

I provide snacks at the first class meeting—cider, fruit, cheese and crackers, cookies—and we have a break after about an hour and a half to eat and talk. This is an important part of the class, for during the snack time everyone "breaks role," and the discussions are spontaneous, animated, and purposeful. It is the responsibility of the team of leaders at each subsequent class to provide snacks, and they do so faithfully and creatively.

The remainder of the first class is devoted to demonstrating features of the course by means of exercises. Rather than inviting students to ask questions about the course, I might have them write a question on a three-by-five card, deposit the card in a pile in the center of the room, and then choose a different card from the pile. I then go to the stage, turn off the room lights and turn on the stage lights, and sit on a stool. Students then read the questions on the cards they have drawn. The questions elicited in this fashion are more plentiful, more honest, and more probing than they would be without this kind of framing and distancing of author from animator.

One of the main fears students express on entering the course is of "being on"—of being required to perform. At the first class I try to assuage this fear in two ways. First, I attempt to establish an atmosphere of trust and tolerance of failure in the course—letting the students know that the course is experimental in its character, and that to experiment is to risk failure, failure without shame. Second, to reinforce the notion that "we are all in this together," I conduct a "serial improvisation" exercise near the end of the first session. With everyone seated on the floor in a semicircle facing the stage, I begin an improvisation with the first student from the left extreme of the semicircle, whom I invite to join me on stage. I might begin to address her as a doctor to whom I am bringing a complaint of stomach pain. She must pick up on my theme and respond appropriately. After about a minute of this, I leave the stage, and another student goes to the stage, and now the first student improvises another conversation with the new student, with entirely different characters and setting. The serial improvisation continues in this way until everyone has been on stage in both the first and second positions.

The first class closes with questions, comments, and reactions. The atmosphere is always one of excitement, and students often express surprise at the rapidity with which the three-hour period has been consumed.

A TYPICAL CLASS

Let us take as an example a class meeting at which the assigned text is Albee's play *Who's Afraid of Virginia Woolf?* The group of three leaders begins to meet two weeks before the designated class meeting. They are given a set of themes to explore in relation to the play: "insults," "appearance and reality," "secret bonds," "betrayal," "sex and aggression," and "biology and history." The leaders meet with me after they have formulated an initial plan of activities and exercises for the class meeting. We meet for about an hour, discussing how various proposed exercises are likely to work, revising the order of exercises, bringing order to the schedule of activities. The leaders then meet again, as often as they think necessary, and then just prior to the class they check with me again about the final plan.

As I have stated, class periods normally begin with warm-up exercises—aerobics, verbal check-ins, circular shoulder and neck massages, and the like. Students tend to invent novel warm-up exercises as the course progresses. The function of the warm-up is to create a ritual beginning to the functioning of the group, to bring attention to the leaders, to encourage a spirit of cooperation, and to disinhibit class members. A warm-up for the Albee play might be for the class to sing "Who's Afraid of Virginia Woolf?"—perhaps with other vocal improvisations.

A first formal exercise might be created about the theme of insults, deriving from "Fun and Games"—the first act of the play. A scene from the play is read, with volunteers from the class taking the parts. Then individuals are paired off and instructed to trade ritual insults with each other, after the manner illustrated in the play. This is followed by a group discussion of the dynamics of insults—why they are given, what they consist of, how they feel, and their consequences.

Another exercise often used for this class consists of the revelation of personal secrets. Individuals are asked to write down, anonymously, a personal secret on a three-by-five card. (The assignment to think of a secret and write it down is normally given a week ahead of time, and cards are carefully destroyed immediately after the exercise as a further protection of confidentiality.) Cards are deposited in the middle of the room, and then students choose cards, making sure they do not get their own. Room lights are dimmed and the stage is lighted. Class members then proceed to the stage, one by one, to read the secrets on the cards as if they were their own—but of course, they are not. The content elicited in this fashion is extremely powerful. Secrets center on such themes as cheating on exams or papers, family problems such as alcoholism or illegitimacy, illnesses, sexual experiences, and secret passions. The discussion following the revelation of the secrets is always intense and animated. In the end, someone may remember to relate this discussion to a secret in the play: that George and Martha's son is a fiction—a fiction within a fiction. But the major lesson of the exercise is that significant and carefully protected secrets are common to all.

Once the leaders of a class session on the Albee play appeared to get into a major argument, which became a physical fight, over some detail of control of an exercise that was under way. They did this so convincingly that the entire class was taken in. Later the leaders revealed that the fight had been contrived to produce an experience of real conflict, akin to that experienced by Honey and Nick in the play. It took an extended discussion for the class members to assimilate the lesson they had just learned about the fine line between appearance and reality.

GENERAL PROCEDURES

No more than 15 percent of class time is spent in discussion. Exercises involve improvisations, scene readings, work in pairs or in groups of three, four, or five. Small groups are sometimes challenged to invent skits to illustrate certain points or problems. The skits are then serially performed, with the remainder of the class serving as audience.

For the most part, exercises are conducted in the classroom. But after spring break, the weather makes possible the enlargement of the stage. Generally once a year, usually in late April, a class session is conducted in the woods, with students led blindfolded under instructions of silence to vehicles driven by the leaders to a secluded forest, where blindfolds are removed and most of the class is conducted in pantomime, without words. *My Dinner with Andre* (Shawn and Gregory, 1981) has sometimes served as a text for these sessions. In the discussion of such a class, students notice the remarkable effect a change in setting has on modes of self-presentation by class members.

Students are encouraged to take risks, to be creative, and to be unafraid of failure. In my meetings with the leaders I try to spot and cancel exercises that are silly or pointless; but even so, some silly and pointless things do happen—as when on one occasion the entire class found itself playing "Duck, Duck, Goose" to no apparent purpose. Even this turned out to be useful, for the class was then led to discuss the reasons for discomfort about wasting time and the problem of not being serious.

More commonly, truly epiphanic moments occur. I recorded the following example in my notes on a class organized about Shaffer's play *Equus:*

Here was the most powerful, memorable exercise of the day—conducted after snacks. Robin was selected to act as a religious figure-object. She was dressed in an academic robe, with a half-face mask of white and a scarf covering her lower face. The room was darkened and the lights were focused on the stage. She entered and sat on a tall stool on the stage. Andrew was the first supplicant—addressing her as the Tibetan prophet Bibi-tiki-lo, or some such. Improvised dialog: "At last I have found you, oh great Bibi-tiki-lo." "Who seeks Bibi-tiki-lo?" "A humble pilgrim, your greatness. My name is of no consequence." "What do you seek?" "Help with my tribulation." Etc., etc. All carried out with great dramatic impact and effect.

Then a second supplicant appeared, this time in the person of Debbie, who treated the figure as a therapist and acted very much as a patient in individual psychotherapy. "I've tried to keep in mind what you have told me, and it has helped. But I am still bothered by my feelings of anger toward my mother." Etc.

Then a third supplicant appeared, in the form of Lara, who inquired of the sleek and perfect goddess how she managed to refrain from eating herself fat. Where does she get such self control? And how can I attain it? "You must simply eat less and exercise more. Decide to control your own action and your own destiny." Etc.

The discussion after this exercise was rich and interesting. Because everyone in the room could see how easily reality could be manipulated with a little costume and a little light. Robin testified about how it felt to become the figure she was impersonating. This is worth recording, for she said that she became her mask. Others in the audience testified to the power of the mystique created by the robes and the lighting, even though they knew perfectly well what was happening. This epiphanic moment demonstrated to one and all the enormous power of staging in the creation of mood, sense, meaning, and emotion.

I could provide hundreds of examples of this sort. Each meeting of this course is an adventure, even for me, as a veteran of twenty years.

Some leader teams have invented exercises and plans that have become regular features of the course. One such plan is always placed at the first class meeting after spring break. I make no reading assignment over this vacation, but ask students to come to class in a costume of some sort, and to be prepared to act out the character of the costume for three minutes. When the class is assembled, after a brief warm-up, the room lights are dimmed and the stage is lighted. Class members are called up one by one to portray their characters, each remaining on stage for three minutes, entering and leaving the stage at a signal. After all have been on, snack break is declared, and students change into their normal attire. Then, after break, students are called back onstage, one by one, this time to portray themselves and to speak about themselves for three minutes.

The ensuing discussion is rich and powerful. Students testify about the relative difficulty of being themselves versus enacting a more distant role. Students remark on how much they have learned about their classmates, not only from their portrayals of themselves, but also from the costumes and personae they have chosen and enacted.

PSYCHODRAMA ILLUSTRATED

One class meeting is devoted to an exploration of the tradition of theory and practice organized under the rubric of psychodrama, invented and developed by Jacob Moreno.[2] A central feature of this class is an illustration of a psychodrama exercise. I serve as Director for this exercise, choosing one of the class leaders as an Auxiliary Ego. To play the Protagonist for the exercise, I ask for a student volunteer—one who has a conflict with another person and is willing to display it to the class.

The Protagonist and the Auxiliary Ego are seated on two chairs on the stage, with the rest of the class arranged as an audience. I then ask the Protagonist to provide some establishing features for the drama to be presented—the identity of the person who is the other in the conflict, the setting and time of day they are likely to meet, and any other relevant background features. The Protagonist and the Auxiliary Ego then begin to improvise a conversation, with the Director occasionally intruding to steer the conversation around and about the kernel of the conflict. After a few minutes of this the Protagonist and the Auxiliary Ego are asked to switch seats and roles, with the Protagonist now acting as the other person, and the Auxiliary Ego acting as much as possible like the Protagonist. They are asked to repeat the same scene, with this role reversal. (Moreno called this the *mirroring technique*.) After the Director ends this scene, the Protagonist is asked to stand behind the chair he or she occupied in the first scene, while the Auxiliary Ego returns to the original position. A member of the class is asked to sit in the Protagonist's original position and to say nothing. The Protagonist is asked to give a monologue based upon thoughts that occurred during the initial dialogue but were not expressed—employing a variant of what Moreno called the *double-ego technique*. At the next stage the Protagonist stands behind the Auxiliary Ego's chair, and projects what the other is imagined to be thinking but not saying. After these phases, the Protagonist and the Auxiliary Ego are asked to comment on their interpretations and feelings during the various phases of the exercise. Finally, the audience is asked to participate by offering observations and interpretations of the events portrayed.

Among the conflicts that have been portrayed and explored in this fashion are a dispute between a daughter and her mother over the daughter's proposed interracial marriage, a conflict between a student director and his lighting technician over her defection from the production without advance notice, a quarrel between a boyfriend and his girlfriend over her alleged infidelity, and a young man attempting to come out as gay to his father. These psychodramatic portrayals are intense, productive of high involvement, often emotionally trying. The exercise is done not for therapeutic purposes but as an illustration of a technique. Even so, the reactions of the Protagonists after these exercises are often ones of gratitude and relief. Years later, some Protagonists have reported to me the impressive power of this experience.

THE FINALE

Another class that has become standardized is the last one of the semester. Students are given the assignment ahead of time of writing evaluative comments about everyone else in the course. The instructions for this assignment are, in part:

> You are given a set of 22 cards, one for each person in our class. You are to write the name of each person on one side of the card. On the other side of the card you are to write a phrase, a word, or a name of something which is descriptive in some way, however indirect, of the

person whose card it is. You may say much or little. It is important that
what you say be well thought out—which on occasion may mean that
it is your first impulse. What you say should be a truth. It need not be
flattering, but it should not be hurtful.

The last class includes a number of other standard features, including a
potluck luncheon instead of snacks, a slide show of the course, and a
repetition of the silent greeting exercise conducted at the first class. The
final exercise of the class consists of a reading of the evaluations written
for each student by the other class members. At the end, all applaud all.
It is a bittersweet moment. It is the closing of the circle opened thirteen
weeks previously.

     While some lifelong friendships are formed in this course (and at
least two marriages have resulted—one couple now divorced), for most
of the students the end of the course means a dramatic transformation in
the close relationships established by this experience. As I argued in
Chapter 9, such relationships are largely conditional upon the dramatic
setting supporting them. When the course is over, so are most of the
relationships.

CONSEQUENCES

This course has had lasting and positive consequences for a substantial
portion of the students who have taken it. One criterion of success is
noticeable while the course is in progress: namely, students come to class
regularly and participate with enthusiasm. I have often conducted the
class for an entire semester with twenty-one students without a single
absence for a single session. Overall, the attendance rate is over 95
percent.

     A few years ago I sent a brief questionnaire to 238 alumni of the
course for whom some address was available. Responses were received
from 95 (40 percent) of the former students. The general tenor of the
responses was overwhelmingly positive (of course, respondents were self-
selected, and it may be that they had a positive bias). Alumni wrote of
the importance of the communication and trust established with their

classmates and the importance of participatory learning. The question-naire posed open-ended questions about memories, influences, and evaluation. The responses entered under these headings were copious and enlightening.

Memories

Many alumni remembered books and plays, though the specific material recalled varied widely. The most frequently remembered single experience was the "sharing of secrets" exercise. Many respondents had general memories of the experiential character of the class and of particular assignments they had as leaders.

About 10 percent of those responding reported no specific memories of the class at all, but just the general feeling of having enjoyed it—whatever it was. I think of these students as the somnambulists. This group is most strongly represented by an alumnus who wrote that he was quite sure he had never taken my course. As it happened, I had a copy of a written exercise he had prepared for the course—twelve years before. This I mailed to him along with a copy of the grade report form for the course. He then acknowledged that he must have taken it, but said he still had no memory of it whatsoever.

Here are some representative memories from those who were not sleepwalking during their college careers:

> I led a class on a reading from *Who's Afraid of Virginia Woolf?* Powerful scene, powerful memory—scary, challenging, very cathartic—kind of stepped outside of myself (surprised myself)—quite a satisfying experience. I remember that the culture of the class was safe, honest, collaborative . . . all the things a group needs to have.

> I remember my presentations—but more powerfully I remember the presentation of a student—he was good at everything he did. He was an "A" student, a good athlete, handsome, etc. He let his hair down and showed how lonely he was and how difficult it is to deal with the pressures of being "perfect" and "having it all." His talk humanized others and himself and has been a steadfast check against feelings of envy throughout my life.

I remember it was intimidating at times because it was so personal. Particular episodes: Everyone lying on the floor in the dark for anonymity, sharing things that were intensely personal, like little balloons floating up into the darkness. Also, creating a machine out of individual motions. Also *J.B.* and *Equus*—because religion and horses have been strong influences in my life. The final paper on masks, the best I ever wrote because I lived the material. Also a large black male telling us how hard it was to be instantly feared.

My memories of this class are stronger than any other class of my college career. This class never failed to engage students on an emotional level as well as an intellectual level. While other courses taught me to structure an argument and back up theory with facts, this class required me to do the same thing with personal issues, about which I was passionate.

Influences

The most commonly mentioned influence was an improvement in the skills required for leading and dealing with groups. Many respondents said the course had enabled them to see the difference between the surfaces of self-presentation and the underlying psychological reality. Quite a few said the course had helped them with their choice of a career. Some representative cases:

This class helped me to realize a number of things that influenced my career choice. I had thought I would go into clinical psychology. I realized that this was not an appropriate career choice. I have used the exercises from class in subsequent team-building activities and training sessions I have led in the past ten years.

This class had a significant effect on my later approach to group dynamics. In particular, it emphasized the limits of analysis in trying to guide group behavior. People sometimes just have to do what they have to do, and understanding their emotions on a visceral rather than an intellectual level can be crucial.

It gave me a lot of self-confidence, and most important, the courage to *risk*. Among my peers in that class I felt truly understood. And if not always understood, always taken seriously, always respected . . . I definitely improved my listening skills and came away with a more trained eye to see the drama in people's lives. I didn't want the experience to end. As an educator and mother, outward symbols of inner struggles have given me insight into the lives I reach out to touch. Recognizing these symbols and their power is a skill I worked on in the class.

Evaluation

Everyone who responded thought the course had been positively valuable. A few felt it had been dangerously personal and therefore uncomfortable. Criticisms were stated of certain exercises that did not seem serious enough or did not make sufficiently close connection to the readings. But the most common evaluative comment placed the course among the very best taken in the student's undergraduate career. Many praised the use of literature to teach psychology, with the insight that psychology can be taught through literature as well as by more conventional means.

> It was important for me to be learning psychology so experientially after lots of academic/memorizing classes. It was a great experience and an important approach to psychology that should be taught, but which *must* be taught by faculty with good communication skills and personal boundaries.

> This is a course that most embodies a "liberal arts" education to me. I used the course selfishly in my work as an actor. The reason I chose a liberal arts school is that it was important for me to have some idea of what I'm acting about. This course should be required material—for anyone in any field can benefit from an understanding of the roles we play in every aspect of our lives and how they affect others and ourselves.

> Excellent! The class made learning come alive—engaged my senses and challenged my intelligence. It developed skills that are extraordinarily useful—like tolerance, listening, articulation, sharing. The journalizing also required a skill of self-presentation, inspiring a sense of responsibility for one's self and one's role in a larger group. So much happens in

college. This class stands out as a time to process and engage some of what was being learned all along.

PROBLEMS AND LIMITATIONS

It is not, of course, all peaches. No one said that The Dramaturgical Approach to Psychology is good preparation for the Graduate Records Examination. Also, it has been something of a problem to connect the material of this course to the more conventional teaching of psychology that I and my colleagues perform in other venues. Fortunately, Wesleyan is a supportive environment for pedagogical experimentation, and I have never received the slightest reproach from colleagues for doing something so unorthodox. The only criticism from colleagues is that on occasion the class becomes quite noisy.

Another problem frequently encountered has to do with sensitivity to difficult issues and problems in the lives of individual students. It is one thing to read and enact dramas about suicide; it is quite another to know how to comfort students who have recently lost someone close to them to suicide. Rape, eating disorders, ambivalence about sexual activity and drug use, and violence can be studied at a distance. But when some of these issues come into focus as live problems for people in the room, the experience can be frightening and disorienting. Several students have demonstrated to the class that they can produce real tears on cue. On other occasions, the tears have been real in another sense—in the sense of being seriously connected to a deep experience of anguish. In no case, however, has support been lacking.

Occasionally students will enroll in the course who are what I think of as free riders—students looking for a course in which they can coast along and not be seriously at risk of failing. I don't recall anyone withdrawing from the course after the first two weeks of the semester, and I don't recall ever failing anyone. But a few students do not really work or contribute to the activities of the class. Usually the sanctioning of this passive attitude comes from other students—not from me—and it is usually effective at bringing about a modicum of wakefulness.

I have learned as well to respect the possibility of individual terrorism in a class of this sort. When a group of twenty-two adults engages in the sorts of exercises that characterize the course, a certain pious fiction becomes established that the whole enterprise is worthy of deference and respect, although from time to time some particular activity may be ludicrous. So on occasion a satiric critic within the class has given the raspberry, and one such note is usually sufficient to obliterate the fiction of pious purpose. But never has this been truly destructive. Certainly some students have felt intensely critical about some of the goings-on in the course, as well they should have. But the boat has always righted before crossing the finish line.

I do not think this sort of teaching can ever become the mode—for psychology or for any other discipline. For in fact I have relied on the knowledge students have acquired in other and more traditional classes to prepare them for the exposure to raw experience they encounter in The Dramaturgical Approach to Psychology. Even so, I believe that important lessons can be gained from this experience that can be generalized to other courses.

The other extreme of teaching for me is the introductory psychology course—where the class is usually over two hundred in number. It is difficult to create a direct experience with the material of psychology in a class so large. But approximations are possible. I do many demonstrations—at least one per class—whether I am talking about speed of neural transmission or the content of the id. For the former, forming a human chain and timing the impulse passed along by squeezing hands creates a direct experience of the phenomenon. For the latter, I have asked students to tell me on anonymous cards what they would fancy doing if they could be certain that they would be neither apprehended nor in any way punished for the activity. I then describe in the next class meeting a sampling from the writhing pit of serpents thus uncovered. Always and everywhere, no matter what one is teaching, one can dramatize—to make palpable and real what appears in textbooks only as an abstraction. The object of instruction is not to move material from the professor's head to those of the students, but to have the student come and get it. I do not believe in sleep learning. The first requisite of education is wakefulness. And dramatic transformation encourages wakefulness.

For Moreno, "the meaning of the universe" and God were the same thing. He said: "God is always within us and among us, as he is for children. Instead of coming down from the skies, he comes in by way of the stage door" (Fox 1987, 12). And, I might add, into the classroom.

FOR AND AGAINST PIETY

13

I do not see how it is possible, in the nature of things, for any true religion to continue long. For religion must necessarily produce industry and frugality, and this cannot but produce riches. But as riches increase, so will love of the world, in all its branches.

—John Wesley

Tear it down, bed slats and all,
Tear it down, hear the baby squall.
Tear it down, six feet tall . . .
Take me back to my folding bed.
If you don't I'm gonna tear it down.

—American song lyric

In *Animal House,* the character played by John Belushi, on meeting an old-fashioned fraternity man strumming a guitar and crooning "I gave my love a cherry without a stone," grabs the guitar and smashes it against the wall—all without words and with an expression of profound contempt. This dramatic act against piety represents a generation's rejection of propriety, pretension, and complacency—static forms of apparent well-being. The audience cheers, just as they would upon seeing a street urchin score a direct hit with a snowball against the top hat of a passing Swell. Similarly, the burning of draft cards or of bras or of American flags is an impious gesture. These acts of transformation are not intended merely as destruction of minor objects. Rather these acts acquire their dramatic significance because they represent a transformation away from unreflective and assured generalizations about goodness—they are acts against piety. And relief from piety—whether by destruction or deconstruction—can be a cause for cheer, at least for a while.

Another image evokes the positive force of piety as well as its origin as a word. Michelangelo's marble statue of the Virgin Mary with the crucified Jesus lying on her lap is called *La Pietà*—the Pity or the Mercy.[1] Mary's humanity is revealed by the grief she displays for her slain son, who is carved as a smaller figure than his mother, recalling to the viewer his status as Child of the Virgin as well as Lord. The show of mercy, of pity, of grief, the act of mourning over the death of another—these are gestures of piety. The *Pietà* represents the elemental form of authentic *human* caring—pathetic and forlorn, but human. (A form shared with other animals is the Madonna's embrace of the infant—natural and easy, like a ewe nuzzling a lamb.) Elemental human piety is a dramatic transformation—from the ordinary, through profound sadness, into the sublime. From this elementary form, a thousand varieties of human goodness are constructed.

The tradition of pietàs in Italy goes back to pre-Christian times, when representations of women holding palm branches or scepters were symbols of faithful attachment to gods, to country, and to one's relatives—particularly to one's parents. Religion has inspired more art over the ages than any other single source, and the objective of most religious art is to draw out and reinforce piety. The cross inspires reverence. It is not something you spit upon, although you might kiss it. Catholic cathedrals are alike in their representations of the wretched Jesus hanging from a cross—a reminder of misery amidst the splendor, but also a means of atonement and redemption. Visitors and worshipers alike are hushed. Sacred symbols and sacred spaces demand respect, even from unbelievers—at least for a while.

Piety is the most suspect of virtues, for human history and experience are full of evils masquerading as goodness. Dostoevsky's Grand Inquisitor is the model for the type—a withered old man, a wanton murderer, posturing as the protector of the faith and of humanity, discomfited only by genuine goodness, determined to put goodness to death. The Grand Inquisitor is a cynical enslaver of humanity—who is at the same time legitimately a priest. It is a chilling image—one earlier developed in the stories of the Marquis de Sade, where poor Justine thinks to find sanctuary within a monastery, only to be raped and abused there by the resident monks.

In our time, politicians, as well as fusty professors, preachers, and other slow-moving targets, provide prime material for satire, for the display of piety is often a thin mask for a life of self-indulgence and dissipation. Hypocritical evangelists, politicians, or priests who abuse altar boys seem always to be in the news. Nietzsche declared: "All the means which have been used heretofore with the object of making man moral, were through and through immoral" (1889/1968, 505). This is a devastating generalization, and even if it is false, as it doubtless is, it suggests that we have been conditioned by the evidence to look upon facades of goodness with suspicion.

"Tear it down," then, "bed slats and all!" Like the iconoclasts of the post-Enlightenment era, let us take our chisels to the holy statues—and not only of Christian saints: now Lenin and Stalin are removed from their pedestals. Even Washington, Jefferson, and Lincoln, we are told, were not as good as they were made out to be in an earlier age of innocent piety. Such paragons as Albert Schweitzer and Mother Teresa have had their detractors. Nothing is exempt from the critical force of those who see all displays of piety as masks over evil.

But the world will not be content with piles of broken idols. Dostoevsky observed: "So long as man remains free he strives for nothing so incessantly and so painfully as to find some one to worship" (1950, 301). In an antinomian and chaotic age, one longs for law and order, for structure, for institutional stability. Utopian societies are set up initially as a way of breaking free from the miserable hypocrisy and grinding confinement of the existing order. So the Protestant Reformation, so courageously begun by Martin Luther, soon became the Lutheran Establishment. So were born the Pietists, variant offshoots of the Lutherans in the seventeenth, eighteenth, and nineteenth centuries. And so were launched scores of Protestant denominations, each one initially a movement for revolutionary freedom, and virtually all consolidating into a piety that could be called false by the young and the restless.

In Mexico, Benito Juarez ushered in an era of reform in the mid-nineteenth century, eliminating the smothering control of the Catholic Church by instituting laws of reform, allowing secular marriages and secular burials, and seizing control of the Church's real estate. But Juarez, a Mason, soon became the Establishment, and his suppression of worship inspired the development of thousands of small household shrines throughout Mexico, at which common people could exercise their faith.[2] And revolutions were to sweep over Mexico again and again, in reaction to the established order; for no matter how liberating the revolution or what its label, it seems that oppression has been the inevitable sequel of liberation. This massive wheel is still in motion.

In the United States, the admirable Shaker sect was among the more successful religious utopian experiments. Mother Ann's Millennial Rules formed the foundation of a highly successful and genuinely pious community—victims, eventually, of their own success, for it was concerning the Shakers that John Wesley made the statement used as the first epigraph to this chapter, on how frugality will lead to prosperity and thus to the decline of religion.[3]

Michelangelo's first pietà was done on a commission from a sponsoring cardinal while he was yet a young man. It was a work of genius, but not yet a work that came from inner conviction. But upon his death at age eighty-nine, his last works, never finished, consisted of several pietàs, expressing an intrinsic and compelling urge of the old artist to give expression to the ineffable connection between hope for life and the spectacle of death. In the final and religious period of his life he tried to align his work and his inner convictions—to express an authentic piety. Genius was a constant in his life, but not piety.

Swings between piety and impiety can be understood from the combined perspectives of psychology and drama. The existing institutional order imposes constraints on the freedom of the individual, as Freud rightly observed in *Civilization and Its Discontents* (1930/1962). But about the other half of this psychological cycle Freud was less insightful, perhaps because he could not grant to the general run of humanity anything like genuine freedom or undisguised goodness. (Like the Grand Inquisitor, Freud had no illusions but could see the value of illusions for the masses. Freud's libido is both blind and crazy, and is only creative by accident.) The revisionist Freudian Erich Fromm provides a vision of the other side of the cycle in *Escape from Freedom* (1941/1968), wherein he argues compellingly for the constructivist urges of the deracinated, the disowned, the liberated. Out of the ashes of destruction, then, possibility is newly exposed, and watered with tears of grief and hope, new order is created.

Both individuals and collectivities move through the cycle of piety-impiety, and both the means and tokens of movement throughout this cycle are dramatic. Formal drama—that is, the drama of the theater—works in both directions. Satire and caricature work to tear piety down. Romance and historical epic work to establish piety. If there were no such thing as piety, then a major polarity for dramatic interest would be eliminated. Without the foil of the mask of goodness—perhaps authentic and perhaps false as hell—the opportunities for interesting transformations and revelations are much diminished. It would not do to unmask the pious Wizard of Oz and find him truly to be a wizard, but without this *possibility* there is no drama either. Hamlet's nobility is rooted ultimately in his loyal devotion to the memory of his dead father—true piety, we might say, as compared with the falseness of those who would cover their murders with a mask of easy innocence. What is Iago's aim, if not to undermine and destroy the goodness and the love he sees in Othello and Desdemona? Like Othello, Billy Budd is a good man, if seriously flawed. But he too must die a tragic death. To the likes of Iago, the pleasure of evil deeds is measured by the pain they bring to the good. Destruction has dramatic interest. And after destruction, of course, rebirth. New life also has dramatic interest.

THE FUNCTIONS OF CRITICISM

The opening act of *Cyrano de Bergerac* contains a play within a play, with a critical twist that is rarely seen in the drama of everyday life or even of everyday theater. Cyrano leaps upon the stage while a play is in progress to disrupt the performance of the actor, Montfluery, a pompous ass whom he regards as an insult to the performing arts. In a gesture of true panache, Cyrano flings his purse (containing *all* his wealth) onto the stage to compensate for the losses of the house, even as he evicts the bewildered Montfluery with his sword. This is the ultimate critical act—where such is one's rage at seeing a display of false piety that one must unmask it at once, no matter what the cost. Cyrano is not an impious man, for he is utterly devoted to his Gascon cadets, and his secret devotion to Roxanne has to be counted as among the most selfless instances of romantic love in the dramatic canon. Even so, he was a critic who had the courage of his convictions.

The norms of civility and propriety are evidence of a pervasive piety in the drama of everyday life. All moderately well socialized people come to have an automatic respect for the dramatic settings of performances.

Students do not, in general, disrupt professors in the middle of their lectures, no matter how tedious or odious the presentation may be.

I have been to hundreds of theatrical performances over the years, and only once in my memory have I observed an event even remotely similar to Cyrano's display of panache. Many years ago, an inaugural performance was held at Wesleyan of Robert Lowell's new translation of Racine's *Phèdre*. The performance opened and proceeded into the first act—whereupon a voice was heard bellowing from the left side of the audience, "This is awful!" The actors, somewhat stunned, regained their composure and resumed their dialogue. But within moments there was a new assault from the same quarter: "This is just awful! Why can't you actors speak your lines?" This time, the critic stood up to deliver his remarks and, upon completing them, strode resolutely out of the hall. Once again, actors and audience alike were stunned, but once again, albeit unsteadily, the actors resumed their enactment of the script. Years later, all is forgotten of Racine and Lowell. All that remains in memory is the impious and anonymous critic. It was a singular dramatic moment— a "tear it down" moment.

Babies do cry in church. But after a few wails, their mothers or fathers can be counted upon to do the proper thing and carry them out of the sanctuary. Assuredly many parishioners feel like crying or hissing in response to the sermons they are made to endure—but all save babies lack the courage of their convictions. Even babies soon learn to suppress their cries. Piety prevails. But the ubiquity of institutional piety means that the profession of critics always welcomes new applicants.

Criticism is more a part of theater than is commonly assumed. For criticism is an act of transformation—by praise genuine virtue is recognized, by blame false pieties are punctured. The term "criticism" itself suggests that in general the blame will outweigh the praise. G. B. Shaw said, "Criticism is not only medicinally salutary; it has positive popular attractions in its cruelty, its gladiatorship, and the gratification given to envy by its attacks on the great, and to enthusiasm by its praises" (1970, 13).

The critic learns to be content with pessimism, leavened by occasional bursts of appreciation. It has been said of Schopenhauer: "He wanted a world that he could bark at." Kenneth Burke asserts: "Once a man has perfected a technique of complaint, he is more at home with sorrow than he would be without it" (1964b, 88).

The critic has a job to do, an exceedingly important job. It is no accident that much emphasis is given in serious education in the liberal arts to what is known as critical thinking—the developed capacity to challenge tacit beliefs and suppositions, conventional ways of looking at the world. Without this element, education would consist of the simple transmission of knowledge, a matter of passing on traditionally accepted truths from one generation to the next. This process is boring and mindless. Unfortunately, the more brilliant the critic, the greater the angst he creates and endures. Unfortunately also, it is much easier to "tear it down" than it is to "build it up." Once you are accustomed to the massive impact of the wrecker's ball, it is hard to learn to manage and to tolerate the slowness of the loom or the stylus.

BREAKING FAITH, BREAKING FRAME, AND BREAKING WIND

Once I was a member of a search committee for a major administrative appointment. One of the candidates for the position was a member of the community, a man known for his intelligence, his gentleness, his integrity. As it happened, the chair of the selection committee was another local citizen, a man also known for intelligence, but in place of gentleness or integrity, he was driven by critical passion. At one crucial meeting the chair read a letter that was ostensibly written in support of the local candidate. In his reading, what was meant as praise was transformed by his tone into mockery. It was skillful, even brilliant, as a performance. For no one present could fail to be amused by the exposed *double entendre* of "I can't say enough in praise of ____," or the triteness of "I have known ____ for twenty years and have come to regard him as a paragon of institutional loyalty." It was all done by intonation and the lilt of voice. In the end, those on the committee who supported the local candidate did not have the presence of mind or wit to reply. The skillful deflation of piety could not be easily countered. But it seemed to me then, and seems to me now, to have been an act of bad faith, or of breaking faith. Even though skillfully delivered, it was the analogue of what is known in athletics as a cheap shot—a gratuitous attack on a vulnerable and perhaps naive target, meant to inflict punishment, even as it breaks faith with the rules of the game and the requirements of honor.[4]

Every social encounter is framed by a shared understanding of the rules of the game and the requirements of honor. People come to social occasions with their clothes on and are generally expected to keep them on. The violation of this norm is an instance of breaking frame—something that can cause shock, fear, or mirth. Once, while teaching a class on social psychology, I made a point of emphasizing the power of social conventions as constraints on individual behavior. I noted that no one ever walked through the classroom while a lecture was in progress, though the pathway through the classroom is a convenient shortcut, frequently utilized on other occasions. The following week, not only did a young man walk through the classroom while the lecture was in progress, but the interloper was naked, except for his ski mask. This breaching episode was reframed instantaneously as "streaking." This episode also is an example of what Jack Brehm (1966) calls *reactance*—the tendency of individuals to react against arbitrary constraints placed upon their actions. My invocation of the power of the frame was an invitation to break the frame—and so it happened.

In *Frame Analysis* (1974) Erving Goffman provides hundreds of instances of reframings of this sort. But the most important lesson to be learned from his analysis is that human beings seem incapable of regarding any social situation as not having some sort of frame, and that every frame is a manifestation of tacit piety.

A former client of mine is a woman who worked for a time as a seminude lap dancer in a nightclub. Even in this club—on the face of it, an extremely permissive and impious setting—quite an elaborate and punctilious set of rules of propriety is in force. Men may be touched but may not themselves initiate touch. Payment for dances is for a set amount and is to be provided immediately after a dance is finished. No kissing. Propositions for more advanced sexual contact are immediately and uniformly rejected. Of course, impious breaches occur in this setting as in all other social settings, and for this reason bouncers are in place to take action against offending clients or dancers, should the situation require that kind of reframing. My client told me that the specific rules regulating the conduct of dancers and patrons vary widely from club to club and from state to state. Participants who are well within the rules in one setting might find themselves severely sanctioned in another. This kind of variability in the moral framing of settings is somewhat more severe in its consequences than that imposed upon Baptists who don't quite know when to kneel and when to say "Amen" in an Episcopal ceremony.

In most social settings the implicit demands for proper comportment do not need bouncers or policemen for enforcement. Adults' compliance with the rules of propriety is automatic and unconscious. People generally speak in muted tones in libraries and in churches. You can shout encouragement to your favorite athlete at a baseball game or a boxing match, but at tennis matches and skating exhibitions you are expected to cheer only at certain well-marked times. Social enforcement of these rules is only modestly required.

It is a remarkable fact that one rarely if ever hears evidence of flatulence in a crowded auditorium. One does not, in contemporary suburbia, urinate on one's lawn during the daylight hours, or even at night if there is danger of being seen. No one has to tell people to refrain from this kind of behavior, for everyone recognizes public evidence of human eliminative functions to be unseemly. The wife of an octogenarian client reported to me with alarm his new and careless habit of relieving himself in their yard. She regarded this as a serious breach of propriety, a strong argument for moving him to a nursing home.

Modesty requires that ordinary human flatulence not be in evidence in any but the most familiar social settings. A young man of my acquaintance said that he knew that he and his wife-to-be were truly a couple when he could fart in her presence without embarrassment. This freedom does express familiarity and intimacy of a sort not present in all pairs of lovers. The mask of piety can be dropped in settings of complete familiarity, for in such settings one's goodness is not on trial. In nonfamiliar settings, a fart can at once destroy the agent's character and force a radical reframing of the proceedings, for such a display can be an ultimate critical gesture, although not one of panache.

To break faith is to depart from the moral requirements of the existing order with the purpose of exposing or undermining the standing of some individual within the order or of the order itself. In this sense, Gandhi broke faith with the occupying English power and Martin Luther King broke faith with the Jim Crow laws of the American South. But also Theodore Kaczynski broke faith with the laws of the United States as he engaged in his murderous one-man campaign against the corrupting force of modern technology. So did Timothy McVeigh and his accomplices in the bombing of the federal building in Oklahoma City. In all of these cases, and in cases of breaking frame and breaking wind as well, human piety is being challenged. In some cases, not in all, a new form of piety is being asserted, at least for a while. Human goodness is considerably more fragile and malleable than Michelangelo's marble. But even the marble is an invitation to destruction. Nothing of human creation, no matter how worthy, is immune to critical attack.

TOO MUCH PIETY

As the title of this chapter suggests, I have an ambivalent attitude about piety. My first association to the word is negative—as I imagine is true for most thinking people. Since an early exposure in my life to missionaries who taught that the only way of living a virtuous life was to commit oneself to preaching the Gospel among the heathen Chinese, I have had an aversion to True Believers of almost all forms—to Marxist colleagues who I am sure would mark me for doom come the Revolution, to politically correct students who would chide me for a lack of feminists in my syllabus, to psychoanalysts who consider all forms of disagreement with their doctrines to be resistance, to sociobiologists who would dismiss the force and form of human culture with a wave of the hand, to deconstructionists whose devotion to tearing things down is in some cases so nihilistic and mindless as to offend both common sense and common decency.

I am reassured in my suspicions about unreflective piety by some worthy company. The Babbitts of the world were forever exposed by Sinclair Lewis, the commissars by Arthur Koestler, the revolutionary pigs by George Orwell, the ill-willed stewards of goodness by Shakespeare.[5]

George Santayana presents a memorable sketch of the Unitarians he was made to visit in his youth:

If later I was taken to some Unitarian Church, it didn't matter. It seemed a little ridiculous, all those good people in their Sunday clothes so demure, so conscious of one another, not needing in the least to pray or to be prayed for, nor inclined to sing, but liking to flock together once a week, as people in Spain flock to the *paseo*, and glad to hear a sermon like the leading article in some superior newspaper, calculated to confirm the conviction already in them that their bourgeois virtues were quite sufficient and that perhaps in time poor backward races and nations might be led to acquire them. (1944, 165)

The thought occurs that a person can be ruined utterly by goodness, by too much piety. One has to be grateful for whatever it was in the youthful Santayana that kept him from being taken in by all those pious Unitarians in Boston. Perhaps it was his alien Spanish and Catholic soul that saved him. The lost are saved and the saved are lost, depending on how you look at it.

William James had a somewhat less placid and ironic reaction to a vision of perfect human goodness. He writes of spending a happy week at the Assembly Grounds on the borders of Chautauqua Lake in New York:

The moment one treads that sacred enclosure, one feels oneself in an atmosphere of success. Sobriety and industry, intelligence and goodness, orderliness and ideality, prosperity and cheerfulness pervade the air. It is a serious and studious picnic on a gigantic scale. Here you have a town of many thousands of inhabitants, beautifully laid out in the forest and drained and equipped with means of satisfying all the necessary lower and most of the superfluous higher wants of man. You have a first-class college in full blast. You have magnificent music—a chorus of 700 voices, with possibly the most perfect open-air auditorium of the world. You have every sort of athletic exercise from sailing, rowing, swimming, bicycling, to the ballfield and the more artificial doings of the gymnasium. You have kindergartens and model secondary schools. You have general religious services and special club-houses for the several sects. You have perpetually running soda-water fountains and daily popular lectures by distinguished men. You have the best of company, and yet no effort. You have no zymotic diseases, no poverty, no drunkenness, no crime, no police. You have culture, you have

kindness, you have cheapness, you have equality, you have the best
fruits of what mankind has fought and bled and striven for under the
name of civilization for centuries. You have, in short, a foretaste of
what human society might be, were it all in the light, with no suffering
and no dark corners.

And yet what was my own astonishment, on emerging into the dark
and wicked world again, to catch myself quite unexpectedly and involuntarily saying, "Ouf, what a relief! 'Now for something primordial
and savage, even though it were an Armenian massacre, to set the
balance straight again." (quoted in Barzun 1983, 177–178)

As I argued in Chapter 7, a continual paradise soon begins to cloy and is
at odds with the dramatic and psychological requirements of human life.
James remarked in another place: "The world is all the richer for having
a devil in it, so long as we keep our foot upon his neck" (1902/1984,
230).

The case against piety is solidly established. But it is an argument for
dramatic movement, for challenge and for transformation, rather than
for stasis in a world of diminished goodness. The hippies of the 1960s
were, alas, too much—too grubby, too stoned, too bereft of conversational talent, too unmusical, too *impious,* in a word, to constitute a
serious model for how to live in the world. The rubble and ruin that
result from tearing it all down present an invitation for the development
of a new and authentic piety. The image of Woodstock that remains for
me is of the mud and of the muddy people enclosed within it. Out of the
mud, grows the lotus—maybe.

KEEPING THE FAITH

There can be no definition of what constitutes authentic piety. For there
is no way of characterizing what constitutes goodness in a way that
transcends persons and historical contexts. But if a context can be suit-
ably defined, then I will argue that we can know an authentic piety—
genuine goodness—when we see it.

Philip Hallie spent most of the last twenty-five years of his life as a
philosopher in search of authentic goodness. His chronicle of the village
of Le Chambon, *Lest Innocent Blood Be Shed* (1979), describes the activi-

ties of a French village, led by their local pastor, André Trocme, in saving
hundreds of Jews from certain death at the hands of the Nazis during
World War II. In a posthumously published book, *Tales of Good and Evil*
(1997), Hallie augments this story by focusing on the life of a German
general, Julius Schmeling, who was complicit in the activities of the
Chambonnais in saving Jews, and who thus provides a case of someone
enlisted in an evil cause who is nonetheless capable of genuine goodness.
He also tells of Joshua James, a precursor of the U.S. Coast Guard, who
devoted his life to saving men at sea, and of Katchen Coley, who helped
to establish an institutional structure in a Connecticut community to
help former prison inmates find their way back to legitimate lives. Hallie
does not present these as cases of perfectly good people—for in fact all
three have manifest flaws. But he does succeed in training our vision on
good works being done by good people—people who take the difficult
pathway of extending themselves unselfishly toward the objective of
helping their fellow human beings, and who manifest in this way a
genuine piety, piety in its root sense of pity or mercy.

Hallie's tales are about ordinary people engaged in their everyday
rounds of activities who seem pulled by some special sense of mission to
be of service to others who need them. I believe that many such tales
could be told. I know of ministers who have a true sense of trying to help
the people of their congregations cope with difficult moments of transition in their lives—births, weddings, baptisms, funerals, divorces, loss of
jobs, sickness, despair. I know physicians who willingly sacrifice their
own well-being and ease for the welfare of their patients. I know of
psychotherapists who genuinely care about their clients—who secretly
pray for them, who extend their love to them, while respecting utterly
the boundary that prohibits the exploitation of the return of that love. I
know of nurses who care for the elderly, the infirm, the dying, with real
mercy, real tenderness. I know of teachers and professors who touch the
minds and hearts of their students with the passion for learning—with
no thought of return either of gratitude or of credit, but for the simple
joy of teaching. These are people, and their numbers are legion, who
keep the faith.

Authentic piety is manifest in other ways as well. I know a man
whose wife of over fifty years died in their home after a long illness,

leaving him alone. They had not been separated for more than ten days in their entire life together. On a sunny afternoon, he and I went for a walk along a familiar pathway by the ocean. We sat on a bench where he and his wife had often sat together, sharing a lunch and sharing their thoughts and plans and hopes. As we sat and talked, his voice choked a bit as he spoke of her; he cried, quite involuntarily, but without shame. His wife has left him, but his love and devotion for her remain. He keeps the faith.

One spring day I witnessed an unusual event on my campus. Walking by the student center early in the morning, I noticed two students standing at a podium erected in front of a plaza. It was raining softly. One of them was holding an umbrella over the other. The second student was reading names, one after another, into a microphone, to a nonexistent audience. Later, on my way to class, I walked by the same spot. Same scene. Later, after class, the reading of names continued— with different students. As I left campus in the afternoon, I saw a continuation of the same solemn ritual as the rain continued. It was part of a commemoration of the International Holocaust Day of Remembrance. These Jewish students were simply keeping the faith; I, for one, was touched and moved by their display of piety.

I do not know if there are any individuals who are thoroughly and genuinely pious. I only know that there are instances—dramatic instances—of authentic piety. For all I know, many of the people whose good works and pious moments I have here mentioned might at other times break faith with their cause, just as Peter broke faith with Jesus on the night of his betrayal. But I know that some acts of piety are authentic, even in the theater, the place where pretense is supposed to rule.

The late Paul Horgan, my erstwhile Wesleyan colleague, a devout Catholic, a superb artist and author, and a man as complicated as any other, wrote this seven-line credo:

> Believe in God.
> Worship art.
> Love as it is given to you to love.
> Foster life.

Cherish children.
Work to the limit.
Submit with courage.
Amen

P. H.
22 February 1980[6]

This same Paul Horgan was a devoted fan of the Marx brothers, whose stock in trade was making riotous fun of the Lord and Lady Plushbottoms on the world's stage. For me, Horgan's piety is above reproach, but he knew the value of tearing it down as well.

Raspberries, then, for the vain, the unctuous, the complacent true believers. Hosannas for those who keep their faith and display nobility of spirit, even if only for a while.

THE GIVING OF GIFTS

14

Now concerning spiritual gifts, brethren,
I would not have you ignorant.

—Paul the Apostle

> In all human societies at all times it is and
> has been considered right . . . that people
> should benefit those who benefit them.
>
> —Roger Brown

A great actor, Laurence Olivier, has written of the sublime joys of exercising his craft. He makes a gesture and holds it—knowing precisely how long he can maintain a posture for maximum effect. He makes his audience laugh, makes them cry, knows that he is the immediate cause of their thoughts, feelings, and reactions. From the time he was a child, he had both the urge to say "Look at me!" and the talent to elicit the sure applause and approval of his audience. In his old age, he paused to write a memoir—a reflection on theatrical glory:

> Breathing in the thick, warm air, feeling the expectancy of the house as it awaits your next moment. Timing a pause for perfection. Feeling the lungs bellow in and bellow out as the voice hits the heights of its power. Never giving too much; always making them want more . . . Frightening them, exciting them, holding them in the palm of your hand, Lilliputians and Gulliver. Cuddling them, cajoling them, caressing them . . . I can no longer work in the theater, but the thrill will never leave me. (1986, 370)

These are inspiring words. They speak of magic—of being an agent for the transformations of reality accomplished by theater. Olivier had an awesome capacity to experience and express such pinnacles of human delight—those transitory moments in front of the footlights when the actor knows he has achieved the miraculous feat of creating for a mass of people a shared mood, an apotheosis of ordinary experience.

"Ah, yes," we say, as we leave his theater or close his book, "the man had vast talent." But a second thought follows quickly: Where does that leave people whose theatrical gifts are puny by comparison? To be in the presence of such a luminous star is momentarily enthralling—but a sense of abject inferiority can follow closely. Giftedness is not universal; the consequences of the giving of gifts are mighty both for the gifted and for those less well endowed.

NATURAL GIFTS AND MATERIAL GIFTS

"The giving of gifts" is ambiguous in a way that serves the purpose of this discussion. Olivier's gift, like that of Shakespeare or Mozart or Mother Teresa, has an unseen donor. One might equally well say such gifts are God-given or biologically given: the two amount to the same thing—accounting for a miracle by reference to a mystery. Let us call these natural gifts, as distinguished from material gifts, where the donor is a person with an intention.

How are we to understand the giving of natural gifts—the arbitrary, seemingly capricious distribution of talents, aptitudes, strengths, genius, charisma? Psychologists are supposed to be experts at the task of delineating and describing individual differences among human beings. A vast trove of research and theory has been produced to describe and explain differences in intelligence, in motivational needs, in vocational interests, in personality traits, and in creativity. But all of this is largely useless in helping us understand the significance of the giving of gifts. Psychology is richly descriptive of the many dimensions of human variability. Psychology is conspicuously silent in accounting for the immense power of gifts as determinants of an individual's sense of well-being and of the admiration or hatred of the surrounding social host.

Natural or material, gifts exalt and gifts humiliate; gifts bring pride, and also envy, hatred, greed, jealousy. People are literally the creative products of the gifts they receive. But people can also be destroyed by their gifts, or by the perverse effects of the gift-giving process gone awry. The giving of gifts is of major importance in the drama of everyday life.

To refer back to the distinctions between self and identity that I drew in Chapter 1, a person's self is *given to be*—a hand dealt by nature. But the self—a natural gift—is only realized through interplay with the social host. Identity is established as a person progresses down the stream of life, and now a different form of gift comes into play. Let us imagine little offerings by the social host to the person—material gifts to the baby. As the person matures, gift-giving with the social host becomes reciprocal, and by means of these exchanges the person's identity takes shape. Each exchange of gifts acts as a link between the person and a portion of the social host.

Human families are manifestly tied and held together by social exchange—including the giving of gifts. To speak of *one* human family is to express an empty piety, for this supposes a generalization of human charity far beyond its demonstrable limits. Indifference, as I argued in Chapter 3, is the normal social attitude; indifference does not produce presents. Because of our indifference, we do not pay our taxes with a willing heart.[1] Our generosity is selective, as is our love for our fellows.

This second sense of gift—material gifts—is mundane, but is equal to natural gifts in psychological importance. Cain and Abel both presented offerings to their Creator—products of their respective labors as farmer and herdsman. Cain's gift was rejected while Abel's was accepted. This caused Cain to hate Abel—to rise up and kill him. Why, we ask, was one gift accepted and the other rejected? Is it whimsy, caprice, an unnamable Karma that accompanies one gesture of offering but not the other? In the end, the origin of this difference is beyond knowing, just as it is for natural gifts. But the consequences are deep and permanent. Because of his rejection and humiliation, Cain murdered his brother. Because of his murder, he was cast out of Eden and became a marked man. Much depends upon the success or failure of the ritual of offering and accepting gifts. To offer a gift is to express caring for the other. The offer is also a question: "Will you accept my caring and love me in return?" The rejection of a material gift can be a profound insult—a cold isolation of the giver from the desired other. If a *father* rejects the proffered gift of one *son* and accepts that of his *brother,* then truly the first son is damned. The rejection of a gift is a rejection of the giver—and by implication the giver translates this rejection into a sense of inadequacy of self. The adequacy of self, in turn, is always the secret central issue in a person's inner life.

This is why an actor, such as Olivier, always seeks more applause. His giftedness is affirmed by the audience's response to his performance-offering to them. The inner self is affirmed by successful exchange of the actor's talent for the audience's applause. Natural gifts and material gifts are in this way connected.

GIFT CYCLES

A gift is first formed outside of the recipient's knowledge or control. Biologically given capacities are laid down in silence at the moment of conception and are slowly realized as development occurs. A present for a loved one is contrived in secret and then revealed in a grand gesture. Whether we are speaking of biologically given gifts or of the material presents given on birthdays and on special occasions, it is essential to note that gifts typically come disguised as secrets. Every secret, even if it is just the unknown prize at the bottom of a box of Cracker Jack, provides the potential for dramatic revelation.

The secret, in the normal round of events, is unwrapped—though many a secret gift of the natural sort remains unrealized, undeveloped, unknown. Surely thousands with the gifts of a Mozart have never seen a piano, and thousands with the talents of a Willie Mays have never swung a baseball bat. "Know thyself," says the Greek sage. Yet the terms of knowing cannot exceed what the environment and the opportunities of the social host afford, for talents can be realized only in their exercise. We must see ourselves reflected in mirrors, or by studying the shadows we cast on the walls of our caves. All mirrors are partial and incomplete, and sometimes appropriate mirrors are lacking altogether. Natural gifts become manifest unevenly—the talents of the self are revealed in jagged patterns. Material presents are less likely to be ignored, and their fragile wrappings yield easily to eager fingers. The revelation of gifts—natural or material—comprises dramatic moments, with strong consequences for the actors involved.

ON BEING CHOSEN

As any aspiring actor can attest, it is a thrill to audition for a part and then to be chosen for the role—the greater the competition, the more exalting the success. Every September, Americans are treated to a standard tableau at the conclusion of the Miss America Pageant. After a week of competitive displays of talent, beauty, and conversational aplomb, a crisis is arranged for the delectation of the viewing public. Three finalists are chosen for the final countdown, and after the elimination of the two runners-up, the winner, Miss America, dissolves in tears—an ostensibly involuntary response that occurs on cue, without fail. The winners at the Academy Award ceremony are more variable in their reactions, but rarely is the honor refused. Olympic medalists ascend a platform to receive their awards while flags wave and anthems play. Nobel laureates deliver solemn speeches. Politicians take oaths of office and throw inaugural balls. For the winners, material gifts affirm inner giftedness, and there is general rejoicing. Losers often join in the applause, in this way masking their disappointment at their failure to have their gifts affirmed, the social value of their identities enhanced. There are always more auditions, or perhaps they may search for another calling, or test for sacred luck more rapidly and safely at the casinos.

Winners follow the paths of winners, losers the paths of losers. This is generally true, even though the winning of a prize or an honor may be quite divorced from the possession of real merit. In the dim past of every royal family, someone won a lottery. It is the work of propaganda and selective memory to transform mere accident into something like the Divine Right of Kings. Once again, the arbitrary becomes essential.

It has been said that behind every great fortune lies a crime. The benefits of great fortunes are passed down from generation to generation and enjoyed as natural gifts. Crime or manifest stupidity can often be found as the consequence of great fortunes as well—as when the Romanovs are duped by Rasputin and benignly trust in Divine Providence to save them, even as they are being murdered by the Bolsheviks, or when a Du Pont murders a wrestler he has sponsored, or when Barbara Hutton squanders her inherited fortune on a series of gigolos and dies impoverished and pathetic. Too much plenty, as I argued in Chapter 7, can transform success into a miserable failure. These cases are interesting because they form exceptions to the general rule that winners follow the paths of winners, losers the paths of losers.

I have reviewed the credentials of thousands of candidates for appointments, awards, and promotions—for faculty positions, for tenure, for student elections to Phi Beta Kappa, for foundation awards and fellowships, for publication contracts, for college presidencies, for elections to secret societies. Out of these experiences, one generalization holds true: awards of merit are powerfully influenced by evidence of previous awards of merit. Thus candidates for faculty positions tend to win appointments if they have degrees from prestigious universities, have won competitive fellowships, have letters from distinguished scholars, and have publications in recognized journals. With the right string of credentials, a candidate comes to campus surrounded by a kind of aura, and with just a bit of cleverness can win the prize. I know from having participated in many selection meetings for Phi Beta Kappa that at the margins some students are included and excluded from election to this society in a way that is arbitrary and capricious. Yet claiming Phi Beta Kappa on one's résumé might, in marginal cases, win one admission to a famous graduate school, and a degree from a famous graduate school might, at the margins, influence a decision to accept a manuscript for publication. This might influence the decision, at the margins, of a selection committee for a faculty appointment—and so on, perhaps to the awarding of a Nobel Prize.

The workings of these cycles of blessing are not passive and blind, for the person who enjoys an initial success internalizes the message of that success and is emboldened to enlarge upon it. I offer an example from my own history:

I once received this comment on an essay from a respected high school English teacher: "You have a gift, very rare and very precious—the gift of expressing yourself in writing." I remember trying to restrain my ecstasy on the revelation of this gift, but surely I was influenced by it. The next year, in a college freshman English course, I confidently handed in my first essay to the distinguished scholar Samuel French Morse. The comment from Professor Morse was equally memorable: "Someone in high school probably told you that you could write." The grade was C–. In conference, Professor Morse gave me a superb gift. He told me that the craft of writing is never mastered—that one must always maintain the attitude of the student, for the challenge of writing well is limitless. Thus admonished, I learned a useful lesson of humility in connection with the gift of writing. I was not born with any talent at all for writing, but merely with some capacity to learn to write. My editors, my peers, and my students continue to teach me. But writing is at least a skill I might enlarge, and Professor Morse was later to approve some of the product of this enlargement. No amount of tuition, work, encouragement, or award of prizes would enable me learn to draw or paint in an acceptably artistic fashion—it is not in me.

There is a certain ambiguity of blessing for peoples and nations as well as for individuals. The Jews are the chosen people. But one result of being chosen is to be reviled and blamed, by those not chosen, for a wide range of human misfortune, and as a consequence to be subject to remorseless pogroms and ultimately the Holocaust. The United States of America is the richest and most powerful nation in the world. But we are hated as imperialists and blamed for a list of disasters—including global warming and economic difficulties—by large segments of the developing world. The white race in the United States is clearly dominant in terms of economic and political power, as are men. An inevitable result is a smoldering resentment among minority groups and women directed at white men. For collectivities as for individuals, resentments about gifts are pervasive. Now and again such resentments will consolidate into overwhelming currents of protest, resulting in a readjustment in the orderings of power and influence. International wars are one main consequence of this consolidation of collective bad feeling. But affirmative action programs and civil rights legislation are also means of redressing collective grievances about asymmetries in the givens of power.

MUTUALITY

Gifts are not always so pernicious. A horizontal and equitable cycling of gifts can be peaceful and balanced—bringing satisfaction to all. The main principle operating in the regulation of gifts is the norm of reciprocity—the principle that over time, what one partner contributes to the other ought to be roughly the same as the contribution in the other direction. If one friend consistently outfumbles the other in picking up restaurant checks, it is likely that these friends will cease dining out together. The evidence for the operation of the norm of reciprocity is overwhelming. Roger Brown (1986) cites sources from industrial relations, from experimental social psychology (one is more likely to help a stranger in distress if one has just found a dime in a phone booth), and from studies of marriage compatibility—all supporting the fundamental principles of social exchange theory. One good turn deserves another, and another almost always is given.

Giving more than you get causes anger—a feeling of exploitation. A particularly deadly form of this problem is often encountered in marital counseling—where the man feels that he supplies all the money for the household and does not receive enough service and favor in return, and where the woman is equally convinced that she has sacrificed everything for the marriage, works like a dog to keep up the house and care for the children, and receives neither salary nor gratitude from her self-indulgent husband. Such couples are better advised to seek lawyers rather than a psychologist, especially if this double breaking of the principle of reciprocity has a long history.

Getting more than you give produces guilt, perhaps followed by contempt or hostility. It is demoralizing to be paid a high sum for trivial or nonexistent services—to have a job where nothing is expected of you. The famous studies on "the psychology of insufficient rewards," wherein students who were highly paid for a task liked it less than students who were modestly paid for the same task, is a case in point.[2]

Exceptions get all the news and notice. But, by and large, the norm of reciprocity operates in most social systems, maintaining a decent degree of cohesion for the system as a whole, and positive morale for the individuals within it.

The effective functioning of a team or an ensemble of individuals can be a transcendent experience. On an athletic team, the norm of reciprocity means that all members must invest themselves heartily for the welfare of the team as a whole. The same is true of musical ensembles seeking artistic greatness, or teams of research workers striving on a common project. The crews of ships or partners in law enforcement agencies or members of mountain-climbing expeditions can and do report the extraordinary quality of mutually shared success. Olivier attests to the magnificent feeling associated with participating with a cast that has worked hard together to deliver a dramatic masterpiece:

> To achieve true theater, you can't have one man up front and the acolytes with their backs to the audience simply feeding the great star with lines. What you must have is every character believing in himself and, therefore, contributing to the piece as a whole, placing and pushing the play in the right direction. The third spear carrier on the left should believe that the play is all about the third spear carrier on the left. (Olivier 1986, 44)

In two stanzas of a poem entitled "Vacillation," Yeats describes a unique pleasure in reciprocity—a pleasure that the poem's narrator can, oddly enough, experience by himself, when alone:

> My fiftieth year had come and gone,
> I sat, a solitary man,
> In a crowded London shop,
> An open book and empty cup
> On the marble table-top.
>
> While on the shop and street I gazed
> My body of a sudden blazed;
> And twenty minutes more or less
> It seemed, so great my happiness,
> That I was blessed and could bless.[3]

Blessings are always transactions, as are exchanges of love. Yeats's narrator experiences happiness in a cycle of blessing, just as lovers experience their greatest happiness in the presence of each other.

Brazilians have the custom of wearing an ancient symbol, the *figa*, as an amulet—a way of warding off evil and of bringing good fortune. (The *figa* is a small carving of a human right hand, with the thumb inserted between the middle and ring fingers.) But the rule is that one may not just go out and buy a *figa* and then wear it. It must be given to the wearer as a present. One may invoke the blessing of God or another spirit, but one may not bless oneself. As it is with blessings, so with love: love is a cycle of mutuality or it is nothing at all.

GRACE AND PERFECT FRIENDSHIP

In *Ethics* Aristotle considers the kinds of friendship. He suggests that some friendships are based on utility and some on pleasure. Some people are our friends because they are useful to us, others because their company brings us pleasure. The exchanges within such friendships are encompassed by the norm of reciprocity. But Aristotle notes a third kind of friendship—a rare type, he says, but the best. This he calls "perfect friendship": a desire to bring good to the other because one loves that person, and not for any expectation of return. In a perfect friendship, one no longer keeps accounts of the exchanges back and forth, no longer cares who owes a favor, who gave the larger gift. Advantages of this sort are forgotten: "In friendships based on goodness there are no complaints, for the measure of the benefit seems to be the intention of the giver" (*Ethics,* Book 8; Burnham 1900, 284). Perfect friends have achieved that state wherein it is truly more blessed to give than to receive; consequently, in such friendships no complaints are heard about not receiving enough.

Genuine acts of altruism are performed in this world—by kidney donors to unrelated recipients, by widows who silently drop their mite in the plate, by the likes of Mother Teresa, who defy all easy applications of the norm of reciprocity: "Our life of poverty is as necessary as the work itself. Only in heaven will we see how much we owe to the poor for helping us to love God better because of them" (Mother Teresa 1975, 35).

Mother Teresa's friendship with humanity was perfect. Let no one say that she was secretly self-serving and inauthentic, lest these words be stripped of their meaning. If grace is the bestowing of unmerited favor, then giving to unrelated or unknown parties without thought of return is a graceful act. Mother Teresa's life is testimony to this possibility. This poor Albanian missionary had the gift of giving. She did not reject worldly plenty, but set about to redistribute it as best she could, without being absorbed or spoiled by her contact with riches. She was a net giver to humanity. It is possible.

UNEQUAL GIFTS

Mother Teresa is worthy of the distinction of the Nobel Peace Prize, because her kind of unselfish character is rare. The common case is that of people who look always to their own advantage, no matter what the cost to others or to the collective good. The common case is that of people who count their pleasure by the pain of others. A colleague reports that when he read a scathing review of another's book, "My heart leapt like a faun!" It is said that the only occasion for truly wishing success to another in the culture of Hollywood is when that other is about to die. To see another favored, as Cain witnessed the favor of Abel, is to risk an immediate and pernicious cankering of the soul, to be relieved only through a murderous act.

From this perspective, we can see why the publication of a work like *The Bell Curve* (Herrnstein and Murray 1994) is so troubling. This compendious work purports to be about the giving of gifts, and its authors' intention is to prove the hypothesis that some persons are more intellectually gifted than others, and that specific groups can be identified as enjoying more or less of the unmerited favor of intellectual ability. The problem with this idea is not that it is wrong. If one accepts both the silent and the stated premises of the authors, they make a reasonable demonstration of their case. The problems with the idea are two: first, it gives emphasis to one potentially valuable dimension of human ability at the expense of all others. Second, its impact is divisive—it gives aid and comfort to those in our society who are most inclined to be piggishly selfish, the polar opposites of Mother Teresa. The argument is not so much wrong as it is wrongheaded and rude. It is rather like developing a genealogy to demonstrate to all the world that one's family is superior to all other families. This prating and posturing about one's giftedness begins to look stupid, thus creating the curious paradox of intelligent authors acting in a most unintelligent way. Who can admire the Sun King, even if he *is* the Sun King?

Talents are many and specific. Olivier was perhaps the most gifted actor of the twentieth century, but would not have claimed to have the highest I.Q., even among actors. J. S. Bach was a brilliant musician, as were many of his relatives, but I know of none who won a physics prize. I have learned to write a bit, but cannot learn to draw. Woodrow Wilson would have been classified as dyslexic, if the category had been around in the nineteenth century, and did not learn to read until he was eleven— yet he was brilliant. Adlai Stevenson was an indifferent student, and yet went on to display outstanding political gifts. Intelligence tests are good predictors of scholastic achievement, but are not strongly related to general indices of success in life, even if this is crassly measured by earned income.

It turns out that 90 percent of the players in the National Basketball League are black, 67 percent of professional football players are black, 17 percent of major league baseball players are black, and virtually all winners of Olympic medals in races of less than 1,500 meters are black, while only white athletes have won Olympic swimming medals at all distances.[4] These numbers, of course, would have been entirely different a generation ago, when the opportunities afforded to racial groups in our society were quite different than they are now. But no matter what the structure of opportunities, it will be the case that some families of human beings will excel at certain kinds of things and not at others.

Why is it so tempting to be disputatious about gifts? The historian and philosopher Ortega y Gasset argues in *The Revolt of the Masses* that until the nineteenth century human beings, high and low, were so oppressed by the difficulties of their circumstances, economic and physical, that complaining about one's given condition in life was both futile and rare. But with the growth of technologically induced ease, a growing middle class could raise the question of why its gifts were not even greater: "What before would have been considered one of fortune's gifts, inspiring humble gratitude toward destiny, was converted into a right, not be grateful for, but to be insisted upon" (1932/1957, 55).

We forget to be grateful for what appears to be given as a natural right—the air we breathe, the food we eat, the medical care that is provided (now taken for granted by the affluent). And we look about and inspect the gifts that others are given—still greater than ours—not only air and food and medical care, but mansions and fortunes, or great good looks, or stunning oratorical skills, or the ability to dance like the wind, to sing like a nightingale, or to prove abstruse mathematical theorems. All of us must recognize, sooner or later, that our gifts are severely limited, and this can create for us, as it did for Cain, a disposition to rail against the forces of nature. Our sense of injustice, intimately connected to our *amour propre,* our self-admiration, leads easily to a sense of outrage. With maturity comes the recognition of the finitude of our given condition, and this recognition is enough to drive our passions. And so people argue over gifts, like so many spoiled children turned into vicious little beasts squabbling over their surfeit of Christmas presents, not thinking to share their surplus with the poor kids around the corner. This is the foundation of identity politics.

In his essay "Representative Men" Emerson attempts to come to grips with the problem of the unequal distribution of gifts. His solution, in keeping with his democratic belief in the equality of all, is to assert that each person has a unique potential, a unique gift, that is in some sense divine: "Each great person represents, for Emerson, the full flowering of some one aspect of our common nature. Great persons are not superior to us; they are exemplary, symbolic, or representative of us" (Richardson 1995, 414). Thus Emerson could accept and could urge acceptance of what appeared to be gross inequality in the distribution of human talents, for these flowerings of nature, seen in others, are intimately connected with our own inner natures, and afford us pleasure in their realization.

The Apostle Paul proposes a similar solution to the problem of acceptance in his discussion of gifts of the spirit (I Corinthians 12). He draws an analogy between a body of believers and the human body, suggesting that one part of the human body, the hand or the foot, need not despise another, the head or the heart, for its superior position or function. Rather, one body is composed of many parts, and the parts act in concert, producing a functional whole. Each part of our social body, in this idealization, can accept itself and each other part for its given nature and function, rejoicing in the cooperative achievements of the ensemble thus created.

This is a beautiful idea. If only Cain and Abel had considered themselves to be part of the same body, then Cain could have rejoiced at Abel's favor. They were obviously not perfect friends, even if they were brothers. One might wish for a human brotherhood, banishing all envy and pettiness, but this seems a vain piety in our ever more competitive times of plenty, when even the most conventional and expected forms of common feeling can disappear.

A story by a student in my course The Dramaturgical Approach to Psychology illustrates this more somber possibility, and shows as well how a gift can be an instrument of pain. It is the story of a father and a son—the son, like most of us, desperately seeking his father's approval and blessing. The father, a busy financial tycoon living in Manhattan, rarely had time to attend the son's athletic events at his exclusive private school, much less to be present for Parents' Day and similar occasions. The son, successful in school but with an inner emptiness because he could not display his success to his father, asked the father to swear that he would attend the son's graduation ceremony, where the son was to receive a special award. The father, out of guilt and deferred obligation, solemnly promised to be present. When graduation day came, the boy returned to his opulent apartment to make preparations for the big event. Instead of his father, he found a note and a sealed bulging envelope on the silver platter in the foyer. The note read: "Dear Stanley—I am very sorry to tell you that I had to fly out of town on short notice. A huge financial deal is in its final stages in Chicago, and I simply had to go to meet my obligations to my partners. I hope your graduation goes well. The envelope contains your graduation present—a token of my love for you. Dad." In the envelope were the keys to a Porsche, and when Stanley looked out the window he saw, down at the curb, a new, sparkling red Porsche convertible. Stanley wept—hard, bitter tears of resentment, not of gratitude. It was a gift that revealed a poverty of spirit.

Our level of participation in the drama of everyday life is determined by the gifts we are given. Blessings and curses are mysterious and perhaps arbitrary in their origins. One may be exalted by gifts or one may be destroyed by them. Talents are distributed as potentials for development—some to be realized, others never to be discovered. The giftedness of others can be the object of simple admiration, or it can produce both envy and a sense of injustice. Economists can shrug and say, "Life isn't fair." Psychologists must ponder the consequences of the giving of gifts more deeply, for gifts matter to the inner self more than wages.

THE QUESTION OF AUTHENTICITY

Mere imaginings are often taken as real. Thus, the members of the Heaven's Gate community who committed collective suicide, in apparent anticipation of being picked up by a spacecraft, were merely enacting the logical consequences of their believed-in imaginings. It is as if they entered into a dramatic frame—and having entered, could not escape its force. Within that frame, their imaginings seemed authentic; outside that frame, they are ludicrous.

Replicated objects and events increasingly dominate the universe of perception. In a world of indirect experience, it is difficult to be sure what is authentic and what is merely imagined and made up. An understanding of authenticity depends on an understanding of dramatic framings.

REPLICAS

The modern age is characterized by the recognition of the value of the replicable event and object. Mass production, standardization of parts, photography, sound recording, facsimile transmission, electronic communication, instant access to massive databases, and even the cloning of living tissue are all products of the twentieth century.

Most of us live in a world that is, in this sense, largely unoriginal. We spend our days in commerce with copies of things—photographs, recordings, reproduced art, cinema, television, and mass-produced objects, including computer screens and books. The postmodern era is characterized by a hypertrophied concern with easy and precise replication along with instant access to all of the recordings of all the events, words, and persons of all the past. We also have the capacity to record and replicate ourselves and our products, words, and activities for the benefit of the citizens of the future—and, of course, for the personal satisfaction to be derived from our own immortality. Cheap and efficient reproduction of things means ease of acquisition. Our imaginations and our acquisitive appetites seem to have no limits, even if our closets, bookshelves, and hard drives do. The pervasiveness of loneliness, stress reactions, and depression in our time must be related to these observations. We live more and more in a world overfilled with replicas. Nature recedes—as do enduring relationships with living others. Boredom grows amidst the clutter as our drama weakens.

Replication involves losses and raises questions—including some questions that are of the highest psychological significance. Some information is lost in copying anything from an original, and multiplying the generations of reproduction inevitably means the loss of information and detail. Restoration projects are conducted with great technical skill and precision, and perhaps the restoration will seem an improvement on the original, as in the process of "colorizing" films originally printed in black and white. But time inevitably brings information decay. Even our language is not exempt from this effect—witness the difficulty our ears have in understanding Shakespeare, just as he must have strained to understand Chaucer.

PROBLEMS OF VERIDICALITY

The more significant psychological problems with replication are of a different nature. The availability of precise copying techniques raises the possibility and likelihood of falsification—of the counterfeit, the ersatz, the shoddy, the *manqué*, the phony, the imitation. The question of authenticity is the inevitable sequel. Can we be sure that the bills in our wallet are truly legal tender? Can we be sure that the news reports we read and see in the media are true representations of reality, and not concocted and tendentious stories? What about scientific findings—can we believe what they tell us about life forms in a Martian meteorite? How about biography, history, and our own personal stories? Now we are told that Thomas Jefferson was a rogue, emancipation a charade, and that avowed memories of personal history—such as those of sexual abuse—are of questionable validity.

In one form or another, these are all problems of veridicality—of matching the qualities of some reproduction with some original object or criterion of truth.[1] Another problem of veridicality is the problem of dramatic context. Contexts cannot be replicated; it is impossible to reproduce the climate of circumstance and conventions of perception and understanding for any event. Who knows how Gilbert Stuart's portrait of George Washington was seen and understood by its contemporaries? The reproductions are excellent and the original is still in good shape. But the historical climate of the period, its modes of seeing and knowing and evaluating—these essential ingredients of understanding are lost to us forever, for they cannot be captured in mere words and pictures. They have to be experienced. Our experience is, ineluctably, that of today, not of the eighteenth century.

No film or slide show or enthusiastic orator can take us back—not even a year, not to mention two centuries. To be sure, the illusion of such historical transport is possible to attain, as when we are gripped by the power of an excellent historical narrator to convey a sense of remote times and places. But Mr. Kenneth Burns, the TV producer, does not have the experience of the Civil War or of nineteenth-century baseball in his bones. He does have a considerable amount of experience with dusty archival material and lively old storytellers. From this, he applies his talent to make an era seem to come alive. We lack the criteria to determine whether his portrayals are true. My claim is that the recreation of climate and context is certainly false. To repeat, dramatic contexts *cannot* be replicated. We shall never know Hamlet as he was known in the seventeenth century. Hamlet, as a fictional creation, is with us still. But the winds and smells and climate of the time of his invention are irrevocably lost.

Perpetual and pervasive doubt seems the only legitimate stance to take. Indeed, apologists for a postmodern mentality would urge us to forget about it, suggesting that the whole question of authenticity is misplaced, for it smacks of essentialism. We all know by now that nothing is essentially anything. Nothing is real, apart from our partial and idiosyncratic construction of the Real. Plato is dead, thanks be, along with thousands of other quondam white male claimants to authority.

However sustainable this position is from a logical point of view—and I admit it has merit—it is psychologically inadequate. Postmodernism is a warmed-up version of nihilism, verging on solipsism, and such views have been around for centuries. The reason they haven't generally been taken up has nothing to do with their logical inadequacy; rather the reason is that they are psychologically insufficient, or as I would prefer to say, that postmodernism makes its believers dramatically impoverished. Moreover, the view that the entire world of our existence is socially constructed is pragmatically unsound. As Melville said, "The sea is, after all, the sea—and drowning men do drown." It is of little use or comfort to cancer victims to tell them that they are suffering from a fatal social construction.

James told us: "Man needs a rule for his will, and will invent one if one be not given to him" (1890, vol. 2, 315). It will not do to suspend belief on everything that we cannot personally and completely check out. We take our aspirin from the bottle so marked and devoutly hope that we are not deceived. We marry and have children on the basis of vows not scientifically tested, and hope we will not be deceived, though here we often are. We pay large sums of money to educational institutions to educate our young, on the basis of glossy catalogs, nostalgic memories, and a nervous hope that somehow our offspring may thus be prepared better to arrange themselves in an uncertain and chaotic future. We invest our money in what are presented as legitimate companies, on the basis of the quality of the stories that can be told about those enterprises and their brokers. Doubt is legitimate. But serious and pervasive doubt is also paralyzing, for it takes one out of play. We are urged to "Just do it." And, of course, we do—or at least we try—for we want to be in the drama of life.

The question of authenticity must be addressed from the point of view of drama. The dramaturgical perspective provides us with the keys to understanding why the problems of replication and the larger question of authenticity are so psychologically persistent.

A WORLD OF REPLICAS

Commentators thought that the invention of motion pictures a century ago would produce a major change in the meaning of death, for now moving replicas of living forms could be maintained indefinitely. Technological advances now make possible the faithful reproduction of form and sound, as well as virtual realities, in which one might experience additional sensory dimensions in commerce with a replica of some remote or dead object. Recent advances in the cloning of living cells have produced more questions about the finitude of life. The possibility of cloning indefinitely large numbers of precise genetic replicas of human beings changes the ground rules of the ancient drama of life. Cloning and related feats of genetic engineering open up the possibility of developing human cultures that might be as efficient as a termite colony. We can finally envisage the elimination of sex, and with it an enormous source of worry and preoccupation. Freud can be shown to be quite wrong about sex as a drive: its elimination will not remove the source of energy for all human activities, but rather will remove a noisome impediment to true psychological efficiency.

Human cloning raises other questions of authenticity. Human clones are inevitable. The scientific knowledge to clone humans is at hand, and while ethical strictures and pieties abound as to why this should not be attempted, no one can restrain curious science. Someone will perform the feat of producing a human being from the genetic material of one parent within a few years—although this may not become a matter of public knowledge for some time. The prospect is dramatically exciting. The question will arise as to whether a person so produced is an authentic human being—for alternatively such a creature might be regarded as a source of spare parts for human beings (especially its parent) or as a robot. By the habits of millennia, we have developed the custom of judging the legitimacy of human material by its parentage.

Can the charter of humanity be automatically extended to artificially produced clones, or are they to be regarded as a particularly degraded form of bastard? What role are they to play in the human drama?

Techniques of replication can be seen as attempts to defeat time, to create permanence, and thus to extend and expand away from the present moment and place and the confinement of finitude. But replication introduces the possibility of imitation. Replicated objects and experiences are not identical to their originals but differ in some way—perhaps in detail, perhaps in essence. Some imitations present themselves as such—as copies of original objects—as prints and photographs and statues do not pretend to be the objects they represent.[2] Other imitations are fobbed off as the real thing—gold bricks meant to be taken for real gold, wooden nutmegs for real nutmegs, fake Rembrandts for real Rembrandts, and yes, reported episodes of sexual abuse as representing genuine sexual abuse.

The worlds of Disney and other theme parks provide instructive cases illustrating the importance of successful replication in our times. A Disney park is an artificial construction and is distinctive only in the consummate care devoted to imitative accuracy. They are places for pleasure, diversion, amusement—fun for the whole family. They are, quite obviously, successful—the most popular tourist destinations in the entire nation, perhaps in the world. They are clean and efficient and affordable. In touring Disney World, one can have the experience of seeing real historical figures as well as real ghosts. One can experience real adventures, all the while knowing that nothing there is really real. Visionaries in the Disney corporation are doubtlessly thinking about combining their technology with a kind of psychic manipulation, perhaps by means of a variant of hypnosis, in order to create the illusion of an altered identity. In this way, it should be possible to participate convincingly in replications of Lincoln's assassination, or the Battle of Hastings, or the Crucifixion.

The most important products of the imagination of the late twentieth century, after theme parks copying Disneyland, are the Mall and the Internet—both conspicuous examples of the wild success of replication.

Malls are ruled by the principle of good function, and they allow easy access to a world of mass-produced objects, marketed in an attractive and effective way by chains of stores—many with branches around the globe. This makes malls quite similar throughout the developed world, differing only in size and in the dominant language. The same credit cards are taken everywhere.

Sherry Turkle's book *Life on the Screen* (1995) provides an excellent description of the possibilities and consequences of living in a world of replicas. Turkle describes the use of MUDs (Multiple User Domains) on the Internet as a focus of human interaction. For their avid participants, RL (Real Life) is not nearly as interesting or involving as life within a MUD. Virtual sex is but one of the many forms of imaginative involvement with others—others of an indeterminate RL gender, for there are cases of men pretending to be women pretending to be men, straights pretending to be gay, and other interesting constructions. Such a life has its moments of wistful consummation, for as Turkle points out, virtual sex games are played "sometimes with both hands on the keyboard, sometimes with one." Relationships in a MUD must be more satisfying than the unreciprocated fantasies of off-line people. On-line, one can share fantasies with utter strangers, develop relationships that must never be acted upon in the messy flesh. It releases one from the confines of physicality. One can be perfect, or at least more interesting, if one never need be seen in the flesh.

Human life did not start off being a movie, but it is fast becoming one. My Wesleyan colleague Joseph Reed, in *American Scenarios* (1989), provides an intense yet breezy journey through major genres of American film (the Costume Picture, the Inventor Movie, the Horror Movie, the High School Picture, the Epic, the Empire, the Western, and so on). He develops the theme that we take our attitudes, gestures, ways of thinking, dressing, conversing, loving, hating, and fighting from the movies. Yes, of course: "In a way . . . it is all a movie: we continually live one movie or another, or a scene, or a genre fragment as we move through anything from mundane encounter to major transition, from a chance meeting to those moments when we enter a room to discover that all the parts have been handed out before we arrived and we must take the one that's left" (3).

A number of scholars and critics of contemporary American culture base their analyses in large part on their viewing of films from the archives. An example is another Wesleyan colleague, Richard Slotkin, whose books and essays on the American West and on our tradition of violence have become modern classics (Slotkin 1973, 1985, 1992). I remember thinking, and perhaps even saying, "Richie, you've seen too many movies. You can't base an analysis of American attitudes about violence on your viewing of John Wayne. Real life is not a movie!" But I was wrong: he can and has based a convincing analysis of these and other issues on his viewing of John Wayne on film, along with countless other imitations of the past.

Even so, my reservations remain: in the world of my youth, not urban but rural, movies were not reality but an escape from reality. Reality was a crib full of corn, collecting eggs from the hens, the wonderful smell and feel of recently harvested wheat in a granary. Reality was the cold grease and streaking water on the block of an old engine that wouldn't stay repaired. Reality was a runny nose and a chipped tooth. A broken scooter was reality, as were our cow and our goat. I explored reality with my chemistry set, and though I could never make anything truly impressive happen with it, I did get a glimpse of the alchemical vision of the relation between magic and science. My father's hands were the most real things in the world to me—a working man's hands that could do anything, hung on the arms of a preacher. I was surer of his hands than I was of his head, which seemed to me full of unseen and unacknowledged things.

So I had a hard time learning to take movies seriously as sources of instruction and of modeling—for as a preacher's kid I wasn't allowed to see many. My context in living was different from that of my contemporary colleagues Reed and Slotkin. It took me a while to recognize the truth in their position. James reminded us: "Each world whilst it is attended to is real after its own fashion; only the reality lapses with the attention" (1890, vol. 2, 293). Attention shifts as we enter the movie house and once again as we leave it. Reality is convincing as long as attention lasts, and as we continue attending to the movies, their reality becomes pervasive. For some of us, the movie continues to seem more real than ordinary Main Street as we come out of the theater blinking in the sunlight after a Saturday matinee.

Even so, there is a distinction to be made between the primary reality of cows and piles of grain and the derivative reality of Western movies, for the latter reality is based on replicas. The question of authenticity becomes paramount. A cow is, after all, a cow. Whitehead (1929) said: "The second-handedness of the learned world is the secret of its mediocrity. It is tame because it has never been scared by facts" (79). I think Whitehead had a point—and I doubt that there are many postmodernists or deconstructionists on farms or in factories. But farmers and factory workers have their own forms of mediocrity, and they are surely and commonly scared by the facts of primary experience. As it happens, any world view can defeat any other world view, if your world view happens to be at the immovable center of your existence. Tests for authenticity are perhaps easier on the farm than they are in the library, but difficult cases are to be found in both worlds.

TESTS FOR AUTHENTICITY

James proposed that if a stick inserted in a glass of water looks bent and broken, then it is possible to draw the stick out of the water to inspect its linear quality, or to insert one's hand into the water to feel it, and gain thereby the advantage of another sensory dimension in determining the real nature of things. These are examples of pragmatic tests for authenticity.[3] An illusion is only an illusion if some pragmatic test exists to show by some comparative criterion that one version of perceived reality is more convincing than another. Thus we can see that our impression that the moon is larger on the horizon than it is at its zenith is an illusion if we devise a technique to measure the actual equal angles subtended by the moon at its zenith and on the horizon.

The difficulty is that for many interesting questions and problems there are no pragmatic tests to show whether an appearance or an assertion is illusory or not. The experimental psychologist always makes sure a comparative criterion is at hand for determining whether something is learned, perceived, or remembered correctly. The clinical psychologist can never be sure about the authenticity of what is reported, for the comparative criteria are usually not available. As a consequence, the clinician must make judgments about authenticity based upon the rather more shaky grounds of plausibility, consistency, coherence, and perhaps fit with what is generally thought to be true. Loftus (1975) has shown that eyewitness testimony is often wrong, and by extension suggests that many cases of purported eyewitness identification may also be wrong. Lie-detection studies have revealed the inaccuracy of techniques for the identification of truthful and false assertions (Lykken 1998). One can't always just feel along the stick to determine what is true. Sometimes pragmatic tests don't exist, or if they exist, they are indirect and problematic.

The discovery of the Dead Sea Scrolls in the mid-twentieth century provided a new way of refining the general understanding of the authenticity of the Bible. A team of biblical scholars called the Jesus Seminar has been earnestly meeting in order to determine which of the many words attributed to Jesus Christ in the Gospels might be regarded as authentic (see Funk, Hoover and The Jesus Seminar 1993). To this day, major controversies abound over such issues as control of the Dead Sea Scrolls, the legitimacy of the Jesus Seminar's authority to designate certain sayings of Christ as authentic, and such related questions as who really wrote the biblical texts, when they were written, who copied them out, and how they ought to be read. Not only deconstructionists but also ordinary skeptics assure us that all such questions are indeterminate, footless, and ultimately a waste of time. But such a verdict is naïve in that it ignores dramatic significance: for these are among the manifold human efforts to find out God. Any news from this front—no matter how speculative or ultimately flawed—is fraught with deepest importance for those of us (and that is most of us) who are caught up in the drama of the question of origin. It matters not that there are no answers: the quest is the thing.

Suppose your drama is a different one—suppose you are a psychoanalyst. Again, the question of authenticity is paramount. What did Freud really say, and have the Strachey translations betrayed him? More important—what did he really think? Did Freud truly believe in the universality of the Oedipus complex, the generality of the seduction theory, the importance of the nose as a determinant of physical and psychological health? Was his early advocacy of cocaine as a panacea for human ills based on his own experimentation with this drug, and if so, could the early formulations of psychoanalytic theory have been facilitated by drug-induced ecstasy—so that *The Interpretation of Dreams,* like Robert Louis Stevenson's *Dr. Jekyll and Mr. Hyde,* might be a product of an imagination inflamed by cocaine? What really was the problem between Freud and Jung? And speaking of Jung, what about this Toni Wolf business? Was she really his conduit to the Anima, and was he really in the habit of having sexual intercourse with his female clients and then transforming them into collaborators? And speaking of sexual infidelity and back to Freud, did the master have carnal knowledge of his own niece, and why did he seem so repressed about homosexuality?

Again, deconstructionists and ordinary skeptics might warn us away from such titillating but footless questions, arguing (*pace* Freud) that such matters are indeterminate. But some cracking good stories are to be found in this domain for those who are heirs to the psychoanalytic legacy and who, in their own way, are bent on finding out God. Serious scholarly work on these questions is guaranteed to continue and to be avidly read. The flap about Freud's seduction theory between Jeffrey Masson (1984) and Janet Malcolm (1980), involving intrigue, banishment from favor, secret papers, suppressed letters, Anna Freud's desire to protect her father, and sundry elements of loyalty and heresy—all of this elaborate drama was about the question of authenticity, was ultimately without a particle of practical importance for those of us (and that is most of us) outside its dramatic range, and was and is indeterminate. Even so, it is a fascinating story, full of dramatic appeal.

The problem of authenticity is of high importance if beliefs about the world and about ourselves are derived from some remote source, as most of our beliefs are. We do not speak face to face with God or Jesus or even have commerce with Freud. Rather, virtually all of our contact with the Ur-sources in our lives is mediated by replicas—copies of materials. How do psychologists, in general, derive knowledge? Like other scientists, we read books and journals, and therein we learn of experiments, surveys, clinical studies, and learned theories from respected authorities. We do not, in general, replicate first hand the studies we teach or regard as authoritative for our own understanding of the psychological world. The replication of knowledge is a tricky business and highly subject to distortion.

One of the first articles I ever published was a study of the effect of demand characteristics in a psychological experiment that purported to be about sensory deprivation (Orne and Scheibe 1964). This study was done under the direction of Martin Orne at Harvard Medical School in the summer of 1961, while I was a graduate student at Berkeley. The study became known in certain quarters even before its publication, for it was one of the first to demonstrate the potentially confounding effects of subtle implicit instructions in common social psychological experimentation. When I returned to Berkeley in the fall of 1961, I had a conversation with a fellow student who had heard about the study from a friend at Harvard, but who did not know that I had performed the experiment. His account of the experiment to me—an account I allowed him to give without giving away my own involvement—was a classic example of leveling and sharpening. The gist of his account was true, but the effects he reported to me were far more dramatic than what we had actually found, and the experimental manipulations he described only vaguely resembled what we had actually done.

I should also note that while other studies have demonstrated the effects of demand characteristics on the outcomes of psychological experiments, the best and closest attempt to replicate our original study failed to produce findings similar to ours (Barabasz, Barabasz, and O'Neil 1991). The effect we described was not terribly robust, at least under the conditions of the replication experiment. But that has not stopped generations of psychologists from citing our study rather uncritically as demonstrating a general and authentic truth. It is quite difficult for me to imagine that our results would not replicate precisely, but this is an example of identity politics, or of the invulnerability of my personal world view to an alien competitor.

The same can be said, of course, about a host of other psychological studies and reported truths. I remember trying to replicate Gibson's visual cliff phenomenon with kittens and with babies. Both crawled out on the glass, apparently over open space. I tried to demonstrate the consistency of Piaget's observations about conservation of mass with my own children. The results were far messier than the theory. Rosenthal's studies of experimenter bias proved to be, in some hands, rather hard to replicate (see Barber 1969). I noticed another kind of replication problem recently in an article on how Skinner's views on cognitive processes were reported in common introductory texts (Jensen and Burgess 1997). Virtually all of the fifteen introductory texts missed what the authors of the article regarded as a fundamentally correct version of Skinner's account of cognition. The authors complained that the views of the twentieth century's most prominent experimental psychologist were not being represented in an authentic manner. In summary, some experiments that are thought to be of central importance to psychology do not replicate very well, and some conceptual approaches of major theoreticians are not necessarily represented or reproduced with accuracy.

EPHEMERAL EVENTS

I know a professor of music who does not use recordings in his teaching and who does not even listen to recorded music. I know another professor who no longer writes for publication, though he is a brilliant thinker and lecturer and has much to say. Yet another professor refuses to have his picture taken—not because he fears that his spirit will be captured thereby, but rather because he thinks that any recorded visual image of him is false the moment after it is taken, and he does not want to be falsely represented. These are tender and strange souls, one might say—and yet they have in common a strong respect for the value of the ephemeral, verging on a reverence for it, coupled with an aversion to replicas.

The ephemeral is defined as being "of the day"—impermanent, transient. The anthropologist Edmund Carpenter (1978) describes Alaskan Eskimo mask makers who, having created a mask out of some inner impulse, use it once and then burn it. Similarly, Japanese and Tibetan Buddhists create paintings and images that are not to be seen, and Navaho sand paintings are to be destroyed almost as soon as they are finished. Carpenter suggests that these examples are unified by a concern for the spirit of the act of artistic creation, and that this is entirely different from veneration of the material product of artistic creation. Eskimos would not create their own museums.

The freshness of real theater is its enduring appeal. No matter how

successful and virtual the photographed and recorded replicas of theatrical performances become, there will always be audiences who prefer to
take their theater "live" and actors who prefer to perform in that way.

The theatrical director Mark Lamos has said: "The performing arts
actually benefit from their ephemeral nature. They live on most perfectly
in memory. Their legacy is primarily verbal and requires transmittance
from 'one who was there,' actually allowing a narrative condition to
continue" (1996b, 1). Dramatic authenticity, on this view, is of the
moment, is real, powerful, but evanescent. A presentation occurs in the
unique context of a particular moment, with a particular cast in particular conditions to a particular audience. Memory, of course, is what gives
the ephemeral event some lasting value—for what occurred can be described and talked about with others—including others who were not
present for the original event. So it is with trips to foreign and exotic
places, or sicknesses endured and overcome, or accidents, or conventions
and meetings, or ceremonies—weddings and graduations and funerals
and other dramatic rituals.

James Averill (1988) and Theodore Sarbin (1986b) have argued that
emotions ought to be described as situated actions. Fear, happiness, and
anger are not abstract states that can be described independently of the
circumstances wherein they are experienced. Here is an example: I am
seated in a church, witnessing a ceremony for ten adolescents who have
just concluded a two-year initiation-into-adulthood program (see
Roberts 1982). A hymn is sung; these are some of its words: "I was there
to hear your borning cry, I'll be there when you grow old." Year after
year, parents break down in tears while singing this song. They know it is
coming. Their own children are no longer involved in the initiation
program. But they cry despite themselves—they cannot help it. At the
ceremony, I cried. But as I repeat this story I do not cry—nor do I feel a
twinge of a tendency to cry. You had to be there. Emotions are authentic
but ephemeral. We move on. Events recede, even as the living memory of
them is carried forward into the present, and occasionally events are
revivified, *mutatis mutandis,* by sympathetic conversation. Emotions are
dramatically embedded, but not less real or authentic for this qualification.

The posture of respect for the ephemeral does present some problems, particularly in a world where contexts and conditions change so rapidly as to obliterate memory, where the actual exercise of memory in verbal discourse disappears because of the ubiquity of useful replicas of events and facts, where a learned person may find no interested venue for the display of learning, but where stand-up comics find plenty of customers ready to enjoy the disconnected and ephemeral experience of laughing at the expense of others. Living memory is absolutely crucial to the existence of a sense of historical continuity, and this, I am not the first to argue, is central to civilization. When memory breaks down —and the plethora of replicas can paradoxically encourage its breakdown—we've got problems.

Arthur Miller (1996) has reflected on his writing of *The Crucible,* a play meant as a treatment of the evils of McCarthyism, using the Salem witch trials as an allegorical vehicle. He says it is hard to convey the sense of fear that pervaded the 1950s: "I remember those years—they formed *The Crucible*'s skeleton—but I have lost the dead weight of the fear I had then. Fear doesn't travel well; just as it can warp judgment, its absence can diminish memory's truth. What terrified one generation is likely to bring only a puzzled smile to the next" (158). Miller then describes an audience's reaction to an old film of Hitler at the Nuremburg rallies. They giggled at Hitler's absurd posturing and his overacting.

Not something to giggle at, surely. But taken away from the spirit of the times, reframed on a screen in a darkened room many years later, with Hitler dead and the Nazi movement discredited, and watched with savvy friends, it all seems faintly amusing. One wonders how he did it—this comical little man with the Charlie Chaplin mustache and the slicked black hair—how did he inspire a great nation to perform massive atrocities and to inspire fear in the entire world? Apparently, you had to be there. The chilling thought occurs that the recording of history is a literal impossibility—that even with the most sophisticated and wide-angle recording devices it is not possible to capture and preserve the ephemeral historical circumstances surrounding events. Since the meaning and consequences of actions cannot be understood outside of their dramatic context, and since that context cannot be captured, we can only achieve an approximate understanding of what the contemporary reaction was to important events. Not that our present reaction to historical events is necessarily weakened by the passage of time. I conjecture that those who witnessed the execution of Jesus or of Joan of Arc or who saw Lincoln give the Gettysburg Address may have been less filled with awe and wonder than those of us who came after them and see things through the mythology created around the larger historical context. Many stories become wonderful only upon their retelling. Historical authenticity, it turns out, differs from the ephemeral authenticity of the moment, and there are merits and demerits to each.

In a wonderful book called *Within the Context of No Context* (1997), George Trow develops the argument that America has become a culture without context, and that television is the major vehicle for bringing about this state of affairs. Television has overwhelmed such formerly important events as political conventions—converting them into nonevents, where the commentary by experts becomes the main feature as the convention itself becomes utterly devoid of interest or importance. Television has shortened our attention span and obliterated our sense of historical continuity. It has tickled and titillated us into a state of vulnerable and supine stupidity. If one grows up watching twenty hours of television a week, the current norm for American children, then surely replicas become the prime reality, and it becomes faintly absurd to try to disentangle what is meant by authenticity, for on television there are no pragmatic reality checks. MTV represents a simple extension of the medium. The cuts are rapid and as incongruous as a dream. No attempt is made to maintain a consistent story line or to make sense. It is a visual representation of total fantasy, and since it is made with great skill, with arresting images and carefully coordinated sound, it can be captivating—probably much more developed and interesting that any internal fantasy the viewer might produce.[4]

Robert Bly (1996) provides a complementary vision:

> When a young man in our culture arrives at the end of adolescence, the river of secularity typically carries him over the waterfall and he's out in the big world. The speakers at his high school graduation will say, "The future belongs to you." But the speaker does not mention to whom the

student belongs. He belongs to nothing; he belongs to the river; he belongs to the trash at the bottom of the waterfall. He belongs to light beer, and sitcoms about bars, and forgetting. In ten years his muscles will be looser then they were at graduation, and high school will be very nearly his last experience of form . . . He will find around him a group centered on the acquisitive instinct, by which I mean that impulse toward taking and consuming. (79)

The obliteration of memory and reason can be so great as to bring about the acceptance at face value of the fake altruism of talk show hosts, as they invite strange people onto their stages for the stated purpose of displaying for the first time the hidden reality of sexual deviates, criminals, and assorted weirdos—but with the authentic purpose of drawing large audiences, who seem able to yawn and be titillated simultaneously.

A sociological analysis of the content of several of the most popular talk shows concluded as follows:

> Television shows offer us an anomic world of blurred boundaries and at best normative ambiguity. Cultural distinctions between public and private, credible and incredible witnesses, truth and falseness, good and evil, sickness and irresponsibility, normal and abnormal, therapy and exploitation, intimate and stranger, fragmentation and community are manipulated and erased for our distraction and entertainment. Nothing makes conventional sense in this deconstructed society. (Abt and Seeholtz 1992, 174)

The ephemeral is potentially both wonderful and horrible. Those who can bring their memory, their reason, and their emotional capacity to an event are prepared to be transported by the singularity of the moment, perhaps to achieve an indescribable ecstasy. These peak experiences can then become the bases for waves of narrative extension, and may become even more wonderful through the retelling. Those who come to the same event with dulled memory, lazy reason, and emotional indifference are merely subjects for manipulation; not sentient human beings, but dead to the authentic significance of the moment. Termites live in the moment, without sentiment, without a sense of history, without moral sensitivities.

STATIC AND DYNAMIC AUTHENTICITY

As I argued in Chapter 4, restlessness is a product of the urge to avoid boredom, and restlessness produces, among other things, theater. The essence of drama is transformation—the transformation of the quotidian world into something that commands interest and stimulates conversation, the rippling out of novelty away from its time and place or origin. The Russian master of theater Nicolas Evreinoff (1927) described the instinct to produce theater as a protest against mechanical repetition. But Evreinoff observed also that professional theater can turn toward this evil rather than against it, and that the repetitive acting and sure-fire speech patterns and gestures of the professional actor can lack all spontaneity and can become stale and a torture to behold.

By extension, the drama of an entire culture can become excruciatingly boring, when manners become so standardized as to permit no variation, roles so standardized as to admit no cadenzas, beliefs so conventional as to allow no dissent. Enter Ibsen, enter Brecht, enter Artaud, enter Beckett, enter Albee, enter Mamet, enter Tennessee Williams, enter Pinter, enter commedia dell'arte—enter all those playwrights and dramatic traditions that would challenge the established order. Drama becomes the instrument of salvation from sameness, and when the drama itself becomes stale, it becomes necessary to produce something like a political revolution, even if the revolution amounts to no more than turning over the sore body politic in its bed.

This introduces a twist into my developing argument about replicas and authenticity. Replicas depart from authenticity and produce boredom. Boredom is a negative motivational pole and produces restlessness, and this can produce theater. Theater is authentic only if it is novel, spontaneous, and fresh, and becomes inauthentic as it comes to match exactly some preexisting model. Thus, the criterion for authenticity is transformed away from the matching-to-criterion standard that was articulated earlier. Instead, authenticity in the drama of everyday life has to do with our capacity to improvise with creativity and originality on the materials and themes we have been given to play on, with the companions who adventitiously form our company.

Both criteria for authenticity have utility. I think of static authenticity as that of matching an example to some standard, as when a rock is examined to determine if it is a diamond. These are pragmatic tests. The authenticity of historical events is finally indeterminate, because of their context dependence, because of the reactivity of human beings to the context of the moment, and because contexts are ephemeral. Dynamic authenticity is the more difficult case but the more delightful. Great and original performances can take place around us at any moment, if we are alert to them and are ourselves, on occasion, willing to depart from common and safe pathways.

DRAMATIC CYCLES

Consider an unsatisfactory dramatic cycle. I have a client who is a seventy-eight-year-old man. He is married, retired, and financially comfortable. He is commonly bored, and sometimes irritated at his wife, who tends to be controlling and overbearing. He has two means of escape. One is to read books. He consumes thick novels, one after the other. Occasionally, to break the monotony, he will buy a half-pint of vodka and drink it down in his garage or cellar, for his wife will not permit him to drink and he has to sneak his libations. This cycle is unsatisfactory in several respects. His alcohol use is harmful and potentially fatal. Already my client has had several bad falls because of alcohol, one of which resulted in a severe head trauma. Second, his reading habit is not part of a complete cycle of meaning. He reads novels as if he were pouring water into the desert sand. The material goes nowhere. He doesn't talk about what he reads—not to his wife, not to his therapist, not to his few friends—it just pours in and disappears. He is bored with his life, and the only things he can think of doing to break the boredom are either self-destructive or else boring in themselves. As his therapist, I strive to create an authentic completion of cycles for him. I listen to his stories and respond to them with as much vitality and interest as I can muster. Together he and I sustain dramatic cycles, and this seems to help him to maintain at least some meaning in his life.

What does a complete and satisfactory cycle look like? A colleague once described to me the ideal connections among teaching, research, and publication—as phases or parts of a cycle or series of cycles. One is first and always a student. As a student one learns, and in order to demonstrate and make fast the learning, one recites what one has learned. But more, one is stimulated by what one learns to inquire beyond what is initially given as the product of the past. This is research or scholarship, and, like theater, it is a product of restlessness and a lack of satisfaction with mere repetition. This scholarship, if blessed by success, leads to classrooms as well as to books and journals—for both provide means for performing and then being corrected for what one thinks one has learned from one's research. Always there are new questions. Always there are new fields to explore. Always there are new audiences, before whom one may lay out the provisional results of one's inquiry. And those audiences, by their reactions of indifference, hostility, or cordial appreciation, are informative about the authenticity of one's work. This is a satisfactory cycle. It is a dramatic cycle, something worth seeking every day. This book is product of such a search.

REPRISE

Everyday life is a drama. In virtue of the choices made by human players, time successively molds definition out of mere possibility—the arbitrary becomes essential. Our performances always take their significance out of the frames and boxes that provide their context, and it is sometimes hard to know that these frames and boxes are not coextensive with the whole world, but are necessarily affordances of the theater of the moment. Drama implies not only an actor but at least two actors, or an actor and an audience, or a hypothetical other. The play necessarily involves cycles between and among these parties. Drama is not stasis but transformation—a change in form or quality resulting from the playing out of cycles of exchange.

A dance provides a clear example of all of this. A dance is a stylized set of gestures, a realized essence chosen with some degree of arbitrariness from myriad possibilities. The dance takes place in a particular place in a particular context, conditioning its meaning. Dances involve partners or audiences, or an all-seeing other, and involve cycles of reciprocation among the participants. Finally, the dance is itself a transformation—the ensemble creation of a new human pattern of expression and experience for the partners, who now are not just people, but dancers.

The drama of everyday life is taken seriously—or not, depending on the disposition of actors to be loyal to their professed commitments and true to their promises, and, of course, depending on the way settings change. Genuine human caring is created out of the natural background of profound indifference by the connective properties of dramatic narrative. The motivational significance of drama is revealed by its capacity to relieve human beings from the boredom of sameness and repetition, even as boredom is never completely lost as a phase in the dramatic cycle.

We are material creatures, animal bodies—and as such we must be clothed and made up in order to be suitable for participation in the drama of everyday life. We are conditioned by millennia of scarcity to seek to acquire goods and properties that will enrich and extend our dramatic ambit. But increases in human productivity and material efficiency have made it possible for substantial numbers of players to acquire more stuff than they need, with curious and paradoxical effects. In the stock market, fear and greed operate in a way that is quite independent of actual need for wealth, producing a set of dramatic cycles of despair and of euphoria—with fear taking bigger steps than greed as the dance proceeds, but with greed never failing to return. Our material and animal natures are also manifest in eating and in sex—but the real significance of these activities is in the dramatic extravagance built upon biological necessity.

Like many other primates, human beings are social and thrive within relationships. Dramatic encounters may last for minutes or for a lifetime, but all relationships are provisional on the scripts for the dance, recognized and legitimate or secret and illicit. The world of gambling is a social arena that is liminal—between the legitimacy of seeking gain and the sinful forcing of God's hand. The mental hospital is a radically different social arena, wherein the enveloping force of schizophrenia as a constructed dramatic category for disordered functioning created an institutional tyranny that is only now yielding its force. The classroom is another example of a social arena that conditions and controls the relationships among its inhabitants, often in a way that discourages the ostensible purpose of teaching and learning and produces only boredom. But the classroom, properly animated, is potentially a most lively venue for conducting dramatic exercises of intellectual and personal discovery for students and teachers alike.

The self has concerns other than bread and company—namely concerns about its own meaning and value. Human beings are given life and the capacity to reflect about it. But reflection quickly produces a recognition that the gifts of life are by no means equal but vastly disparate, raising serious questions about cosmic justice and injustice. By the exchanging of gifts human beings negotiate their credits and debits; and by exercising these dramatic cycles they establish their solidarities—with their fellows as well as with the cosmos. Human goodness is a fragile accomplishment, and considerable pleasure can be had in dramatic reduction of the apparent goodness masking false piety—tearing it down. But keeping the faith with the extension of caring beyond the confines of the self, even though that caring may be in the quite arbitrary form of religious commitment, represents genuine piety, a possibility that distinguishes our species from ants and rats. Finally, personal authenticity is hard to achieve in a world that is overfilled with imitation, replicas, and vast storehouses of scripts that have already been lived. Even so, an authentic drama of the moment is possible; even psychotherapy may bring about living freshness for people who have grown dull and listless amid the clutter and confusion of our modern arenas.

Words are prosaic devices, ill suited for the function they are called upon to serve—the raiding of the inarticulate, the production of sense out of inchoate thought, the creation of an order that is at once solid and provisional. And so this extensive set of words does not completely solve the problem that has tormented my imagination for a long time—the problem of how to convince the world that psychology would profit immensely from applying the perspective of drama to its central concerns. But I have said what I really think and I have said it in a way that suits me. Perhaps these words will at least advance the cause of uniting psychology and drama in a useful and illuminating way. I am grateful for the engagement with the dance of ideas and for the encouragement of many partners. I hope that the traces left here will encourage others to try a few new steps of their own.

1 A Quotidian Psychology

1. See, e.g., Neisser's (1982) studies of living memories.
2. See Sarbin (1986c); Gerrig (1993).
3. See Fox (1987) for a worthy collection of Moreno's writings, and for commentaries by Carl Whitaker and Jonathan Fox about his life and work.
4. For autobiographical accounts of these events, see Sarbin (1994a); Scheibe (1994).
5. Later Burke (1969) would develop his "Five Key Terms for Dramatism"—Act, Scene, Agent, Agency, and Purpose—in a way that is fully consistent with the contextualist position but radically different from traditional psychological assumptions.
6. Lewis (1939) was a major influence on Sarbin's thinking about these matters, as was Turbayne (1970).
7. A sign of what I mean by "post-polemical" is provided in a book by John Ellis (1997) decrying and criticizing the corruption of the humanities by the deconstructionist movement and the politics of race, gender, and class. As Kermode (1997) notes, Ellis's criticisms, however well taken and supported, are easily ignored by their intended targets. No one seems disposed to get terribly excited about these well-worn issues. Instead, academicians simply proceed with their business.
8. Sarbin (1984) makes a distinction between dramaturgical and dramatistic enactments. By the former he means such things as consciously playing a role that is not to be taken seriously as one's real identity—as when children play at make-believe. By the latter he refers to enactments that are dramatic transformations taken seriously—such as getting married or performing as a teacher. Both kinds of enactments qualify as dramatic, in that they both involve transformations. On the question of seriousness see Chapter 2.
9. "Coming Up on the News, the Top Story Is Murder: Network Coverage of 'Blood and Guts' Soars," *Hartford Courant,* Aug. 13, 1997, 1.
10. See Scheibe (1995) for a discussion of this position.
11. See Jung (1965): "The discovery I made in the course of associating with my rustic schoolmates. I found that they alienated me from myself. When I was with them I became different from the way I was at home" (19).
12. See Novak (1996) for an eloquent description of how the idea of calling applies to the contemporary world of business.
13. See Noll (1994) for evidence of the self-interested editing of the autobiography.

14. "Man became first an actor, a player; and then came religion; 'Commedia Divina' was preceded by 'Commedia.' It is for this reason that religious myths are essentially dramatic and theatrical—this applies to the history of all people at the dawn of their existence" (Evreinoff 1927, 30).

15. This from Thoreau's journal: "I love and could embrace the shrub oak with its scanty garment of leaves rising above the snow, lowly whispering to me, akin to winter thoughts, and sunsets, and to all virtue . . . innocent and sweet as a maiden is the shrub oak . . . I felt a positive yearning toward one bush this afternoon. There was a match found for me at last. I fell in love with a shrub oak" (in Hallie 1997, 112).

16. See Whorf (1956). Another cycle was started by an early visit he made to Mexico and his fascination then with the evidence of ancient Mayan culture.

17. From Asch's obituary in the *New York Times,* Feb. 29, 1996.

2 Seriousness

1. This is a change in footing, in Goffman's (1981) terms.

3 Indifference

1. Something about mere quantity produces indifference. Stalin is said to have observed, "One death is a tragedy; a million deaths is a statistic" (in Remnick 1995, 61).

2. *Hartford Courant,* March 28, 1997, A9.

4 Boredom

1. Several pioneers in motivation theory are noteworthy for breaking away from the homeostatic model. Maslow (1954) posited "growth motives" as well as the more acceptable "deficiency motives," asserting that motives for self-actualization have nothing to do with answering biological needs and everything to do with what a person can be and must be—poet, musician, artist, dramatist, scientist. Harlow (1950) broke away from the true faith of drive reduction by showing that monkeys like to play, fiddle with puzzles, and form attachments in a way that has nothing to do with drive reduction. Berlyne (1960) showed that curiosity is a motive not just in human beings but, as should have been obvious, in rats and cats as well.

2. I am indebted to Theodore Sarbin for conversations and suggestions about these matters.

3. Love stories tend to end rather than begin with marriage. Few literary or dramatic treatments of successful marriages can be found—they seem not to

make good stories. The association between marriage and boredom is noted in Honoré Daumier's 1869 lithograph "Six Mois de Mariage," wherein a married couple are shown yawning as they sit together in their living room (Klapp 1986, 26).

4. Farm work is hard work, leaving little space for boredom. Fewer than 2 percent of the U.S. population lived on farms in 1991; early in the twentieth century about 35 percent of Americans lived on farms. *New York Times,* Oct. 10, 1993, sec. 1, 23.

5. In "Servant to Servants," line 56 (Frost 1912, 83).

6. Csikszentmihalyi gives much deserved credit to the Dutch historian Jacob Huizinga (1949), who provided a brilliant argument for the primacy of the principle of play in the construction of human life and civilization.

7. "Congress insured that a war-conditioned generation would embrace the interstate program by naming it, 'the National System of Interstate and Defense Highways'" (Goddard 1994, 194).

8. Ortega y Gasset, who appreciated the charm of hunting, said: "The essence of man is purely and simply danger. Man always travels among precipices, and whether he will nor not, his truest obligation is to keep his balance" (1957, 32).

5 Cosmetics and Costumes

1. This is not to say that appearances are unimportant to other animals—only that the problem of *managing* appearances by means of cosmetics and costumes emerges with the human aesthetic of beauty. See Thornhill and Gangestad 1996; Singh 1995.

2. Orwell was not speaking of his own rather remarkable face, for he died at age forty-six.

3. The title of Peiss's book *Hope in a Jar* (1998) is derived from Charles Revson's characterization of what he marketed with Revlon products.

4. E. H. Angle is credited with inventing this specialty in 1899.

5. An odd similarity emerges in the ratios of various statistics that reflect the cosmetic preoccupations in our society. The ratio of cosmetic-surgery operations in 1990 favored women over men by about 9 to 1 (see Hull and West 1991). A similar ratio applies to the occurrence of eating disorders, such as anorexia and bulimia (see Smolak, Levine, and Striegel-Moore 1996).

6. *Statistical Abstracts of the United States, 1996,* table 618.

7. I am indebted to Mara Kailin, Wesleyan '94, who in a senior tutorial performed the research reported here.

8. See Gladwell (1996) on the extraordinary detailed knowledge that market researchers have developed about the behavior of men and women as shoppers.

6 Fear and Greed

1. On September 3, 1929, the Dow Jones Industrial Average (DJIA) reached its pre-crash high of 381.17. It did not exceed that level until November 23, 1954, when it closed at 382.74. Recovery from the October 19, 1987, free-fall (from a previous-day DJIA high of 2,246) took until January 24, 1989 (when the DJIA closed at 2,256).

2. This principle was first articulated by Daniel Bernoulli in the eighteenth century (see Bernstein 1996). Kahneman and Tversky (1984) have published the major empirical validations of risk aversion. Plous (1993) provides a thorough discussion of this phenomenon, together with the related issues of "framing" and "psychological accounting."

3. About 52.1 percent of daily changes in the DJIA are at least finitely positive (corresponding figures are 53.21 percent for the S&P 500 and 57.1 percent for the NASDAQ). This inexorable tendency of the market to move upward is the best argument for a "buy and hold" strategy of investment in instruments that follow the indexes.

4. I say "near" the index averages rather than "equal to" because there is some finite cost involved even in a fully indexed portfolio. Part of the total return for any portfolio is made up of cash return—dividends and interest. Reinvesting this income necessarily involves some transaction costs. Mutual funds that are said to be indexed always have a modest management fee. Also, the actual composition of stocks making up an index will change over time (new companies enter, old ones leave), and this also entails some transaction costs. However, the transaction costs of an index fund are perhaps an order of magnitude smaller than those of actively managed portfolios.

5. This is also related to the "illusion of control" phenomenon described by Langer (1975). Langer found that office workers participating in a lottery preferred to retain lottery tickets if those tickets had numbers or symbols that they had chosen. Lottery tickets that were arbitrarily given were surrendered more easily. Similarly, portfolio managers are psychologically invested in their selections because the selections are, after all, theirs—creating an illusion of control.

6. Two additional points need to be made, both of them psychological. First, money managers concede that an indexing strategy may make sense in a rising market. But they claim that active management is superior in a flat or falling market. My contention is that the reason they feel this way is another example of the asymmetry of gains and losses. While the market is rising, good enough is good enough—and if an index is performing at a 20 percent rate, greed doesn't push for more. However, in a flat or falling market the aversion to loss is so great as to create the (false) expectation that active management will be superior. Second, if passive management were to become the norm and all market analysts were to be fired, an enormous opportunity would be created for active

management—for the lack of research that is sequel to passive management would make any live piece of good information extremely valuable. So the trend to passive management would be self-correcting. (I am indebted to conversations with David Scheibe for these observations.)

7. The character Gordon Gekko, played by Michael Douglas in the film *Wall Street,* echoed Boesky's remark. This is a case of art imitating life.

8. The distribution is split at the median, not at the mean or at 0 percent. Therefore, many days when the market finished with a very small positive gain (less than .024 percent on the DJIA) are counted as DOWNs, not UPs.

9. Using the normal approximation to the binomial for large Ns. The tests are all two-tailed, with correction for multiple comparisons.

10. We further confirmed the reliability of these dependencies by correlating the array of 32 probabilities for strings of five previous days derived from the first-half analysis with the corresponding probabilities for the second-half analysis. The resulting correlations were .50 for the DJIA, .44 for the NYSE, .76 for the NASDAQ. All of these correlations are significant ($p < .01$). Not only does the market have a memory, that memory has worked in roughly the same way over the course of the twentieth century.

7 Too Much Plenty

1. See Goodall (1971) and the film "Among the Wild Chimpanzees" (Jampel 1984) for a description of this work.

2. We are, as a population, growing fatter. Current estimates are that 31 percent of men and 35 percent of women in the United States are overweight. Overweight prevalence grew by about 8 percent from 1978 to 1990 (Kuczmarski et al. 1994).

3. Shenk (1997) points out that most Americans now handle information, not goods, and that the quantity of available information is creating a condition he calls "information obesity." Tenner (1996) argues that advancing technical knowledge in health, the environment, the office, and sports has not eradicated problems in those domains but only increased them. These authors do not argue for a retreat to the cave of ignorance, but rather that we need to manage our knowledge wisely in order to avoid perversely negative effects of progress.

4. Henry and Short (1954) argued that suicide increases as social conditions improve and homicide increases as social conditions worsen. Lester (1985) has shown that this relationship is not quite so simple. Even so, depression is a besetting problem of affluence, and no one has argued that those in society most afflicted with scarcity are moved thereby to kill themselves.

5. Brickman, Coates, and Janoff-Bulman (1978) found that lottery winners are neither more nor less happy than matched controls. *Time* ran a feature article on November 4, 1991, to the effect that most lottery winners continued to live

ordinary lives. Only 23 percent quit their jobs. Numerous magazine profiles provide examples of the destructive consequences of winning the lottery. There seems to be a taste for stories about wealth spoiling the lives of common folk.

6. In a classic experiment on this phenomenon, Ross, Amabile, and Steinmetz (1977) found that a person is considered smart when allowed to ask questions within his or her domain of knowledge. The opposite occurs when a person is subjected to questions from another's domain of knowledge. Thus it is that professors are probably unduly credited with being intelligent, for they have the conventional right to ask all the questions.

8 Eating and Sex

1. In Stendahl's novel *The Red and the Black,* young Julien, after lusting for months after his patron's wife, possesses her in a night of wild abandon. But this is his sad reaction to his conquest: "'Heavens! Is to be happy, to be loved, not more than that?' Such was Julien's first thought on his return to his own room. He was in that state of astonishment and uneasy misgivings into which a heart falls when it has obtained what it has long desired. It has grown used to desiring, finds nothing left to desire, and has not yet acquired any memories" (1926/1995, 107).

2. Sex and eating are functions that we share with other animals. Perhaps in the actual performance of these functions we are as unconscious as they are. Consider this quotation from the novel *Billy Bathgate:* "You can't remember sex. You can remember the fact of it, and recall the setting, and even the details, but the sex of the sex cannot be remembered, the substantive truth of it, it is by nature self-erasing, you can remember its anatomy and be left with a judgment as to the degree of your liking of it, but whatever it is as a splurge of being, as a loss, as a charge of the conviction of love stopping your heart like your execution, there is no memory of it in the brain, only the deduction that it happened and that time passed, leaving you with a silhouette that you want to fill in again" (Doctorow 1989, 226).

3. "One cannot think well, love well, sleep well, if one has not dined well" (Woolf 1929/1981, 18).

4. Harré (1981) comments on the loose relationship between marriage and sex in many cultures: "Marriage appears only as the ritual ratification, and so transformation, into a relation within the social order, of the last and most durable of what may have been a series of several sexual relationships entered into without ceremony" (264). Harré sees marriage as an optional ceremonial elaboration of sexual contact—one of several modes of making dramatic sense of sexual encounters.

5. Larry Don McQuay, a habitual child molester incarcerated in a Texas prison, made a plea to be castrated: "I [might] be walking the streets of your city, your

community, your neighborhoods. And without a doubt there will be children around. You tell me what is likely to happen if I am not castrated before I am released" (Austin *Star Telegram,* April 13, 1998).

6. From an interview in the *Observer* (London), Feb. 19, 1989.

7. Nurse Wolf, a case described by Theroux (1998), does not allow men to take sexual liberties with her, but she takes a positive delight in beating, scolding, and humiliating her servile and rich clients.

8. "I do not know if there are more numerous erotic encounters, but I am sure that there are no new ways of copulating. The body and its passions are not historical categories. It is more difficult to invent a new position than to discover a new planet. In the realm of eroticism and passion, as in the arts, the idea of progress is particularly ludicrous" (Paz 1972, 80).

9   While We Were Dancing

1. Brown (1996) is one of the few psychologists to have the temerity to speak in favor of prostitution. When his lover of many years died, Brown found consolation in the availability of young men from an escort service.

2. Sarbin (1986a) makes a distinction between "contract and covenant." A contract is an agreement between parties involving their achieved roles—as a salesman forms a contract with a customer. A covenant is an agreement between or among parties involving their ascribed roles—as a matter of honor among men and women, as citizens of a nation, as believers in a religion.

3. Bersheid and Walster (1978) found that the likelihood of an engagement being broken off was directly related to the distance separating the homes of the engaged couple.

4. The Latin means "Friends together to the altar."

5. Melville goes on: "Upon the whole, it might rather be thought, that he, who, in view of inconsistencies, says of human nature the same that, in view of its contracts, it said of the divine nature, that it is past finding out, thereby evinces a better appreciation of it than he who, by always representing it in a clear light, leaves it to be inferred that he clearly knows all about it" (1887/1984, 70).

6. As the song says, "In a restless world like this is, / Love is ended before it's begun. / And too many moonlight kisses / Seem to melt in the warmth of the sun." "When I Fall in Love" by Edward Heyman and Victor Young; Chappell and Co/Intersong USA (ASCAP).

7. *Saturday Review,* Jan. 22, 1972, 28.

10   Gambling

1. Before the Mashantucket Pequot tribe was granted special permission by the State of Connecticut to develop its bingo parlor and later a full-scale casino,

only two half-sisters occupied the 216 acres of reservation land. After the bonanza, the ranks of the tribe swelled considerably.

2. No mechanical or mathematical reason exists for the three-to-four-second delay between the pushing of a button and the revelation of the payoff. But there are two reasons—one historical and the other psychological—for the delay. The old mechanical machines, first invented around 1910, used rotating wheels—activated by a spring-release mechanism from the handle, so that the player could not affect the speed of spin. A mechanical contraption stopped the wheels one by one, left to right, after a random period of time. Thus the delay was an essential part of the slot machine's operation. These machines were in common use until the early 1980s, and this created an expectation in the public about how slot machines work. So when electronic machines were invented—much preferable because of their increased reliability and lower maintenance—they were created as analogues to the old machines. The psychological reason for the delay has to do with suspense and the resolution of suspense. The brief period of spinning wheels is one of suspense—analogous to the brief period at the track when the horses are running, in roulette to the movement of ball and wheel, in craps to the dice in motion, in poker to the dealing of the cards. In these brief moments of tension between the buildup of hope and fear and the resolution in satisfaction or pain, the Fates can be active. These little cycles of buildup, tension and suspense, then release are the essence of the product sold by all gambling games. This cycle and variations on it are common to all drama.

3. Walker (1992), after an exhaustive review, concludes: "The results of studies which attempt to describe the personality traits of people who are attracted to gambling are disappointing" (100). Results are inconsistent from study to study, with no strong personality profile emerging for the typical gambler. Similarly, studies of pathological gamblers do not produce strong generalizations about personality, other than the causally equivocal proposition that such people have real problems.

4. In 1996 the average attendance at NASCAR-sanctioned races was over 170,000—by far the largest average for any spectator sport in the United States. *Business Week,* Feb. 24, 1997.

5. The flavor of this conflict is conveyed in Brenner and Brenner's (1990) summary of the history of lotteries: "Until the beginning of the seventeenth century the use of lots was generally regarded as a direct appeal to divine providence. The clergy condemned their use in resolving trivial matters . . . All games depending upon hazard or chance were to be strictly shunned, not just because they were said to encourage habits of idleness and improvidence, but because they were disrespectful to God" (7). While public lotteries were commonly used in the eighteenth century as a way of raising funds, their use became increasingly controversial, and by the end of the nineteenth century they had been banned in most European nations, including England, and in the United States

and Canada. New Hampshire was the first state to reintroduce lotteries, in 1963. At present, thirty-seven states have legalized lotteries.

6. A cursory exploration of Internet offerings under the twin key words "gambling" and "sex" produced hundreds of hits. A representative example is something called J. L. Enterprises. Its web page contains the following words of hype: "Do You Love Sex? We Can Get You Excited! Do You Want To Have the Finest Sex Videos? We Have All Of Them! Can You Handle Powerful Gambling Systems? We Wrote Them! Does Sex and Gambling Turn You On? We Will Make It Happen For You! Gambling has been around almost as along as sex. When you combine both Sex and Gambling, you have the most powerful Aphrodisiac known to man. Now take both of these elements to the gambling town of your choice, and fulfill your every desire while making large sums of money at the same time. Does it get any better?"

7. While Brenner and Brenner (1990) insist on describing this fraction as "tiny," in my opinion that adjective is misleading and even tendentious. For they concede that perhaps one percent of the gambling population are gambling addicts. If, by conservative estimates, 50 million people in the United States gamble each year, then their one percent would yield 500,000 pathological gamblers—not a tiny number.

8. Even those who are big winners at gambling often discover that having the money is not what it is really about. A feature article reports on Jack, the winner of a $1 million state lottery: "He still buys tickets, just for the old kick. A typical $1 or $2 impulse player, he'll spring when the jackpots rise up into the stratosphere, then hold onto the tickets, without checking the numbers for a while. 'That way, you can keep the fantasy going as long as you like.'" Louis Gould, "Ticket to Trouble," *New York Times Magazine,* April 23, 1995.

11   The Disappearance of Schizophrenia

1. See Scheibe and Shaver (1967); Scheibe, Kulik, and Hersch (1969); Scheibe, Dowds, and Kulik (1969); Scheibe, Kulik, and Martin (1969); Scheibe, Kulik, Hersch, and LaMacchia (1969).

12   Drama in the Classroom

1. The mechanics of this exercise is of some interest both formally and practically. The problem is this: Given N individuals, what is the most efficient means of assuring that contact is made with each of the $N(N - 1)/2$ possible pairs? The solution is this, and I believe it is uniquely correct:

If the number is odd, place students in two lines, facing each other, in such a way that everyone is facing a partner, but with the odd person (the Dummy) at one end of the two lines, facing down the alley thus formed. The commands are two: "Greet"—at which point students make eye contact and touch right palms with the persons directly across from them (save the Dummy, who has no one to greet); and "Shift"—at which point students move exactly one position to their left—with the person on the end of the left line shifting over to the first position in the right line, the person at the end of the right line near the Dummy assuming position as the new Dummy, and the Dummy taking first position in the left line. N − 1 pairs of commands are given, at about 3-second intervals. If the number of students is even, then the Director joins and gives commands from his shifting position. If the number of students is odd, then the Director is stationary and gives the commands from outside the formation, and greets each student as he or she assumes the position of Dummy. Aside from the verbal commands, this exercise is conducted in complete silence. This exercise has some mathematical as well as psychological fascination. It is in some sense a problem in topology, and my colleague Wistar Comfort has provided a proof that this is the most efficient mode of universal and mutual greeting.

2. See Fox (1987) for a collection of Moreno's principal theoretical and practical writings.

13 For and Against Piety

1. Dated 1499, it is on display in St. Peter's Basilica in Rome.

2. In the old colonial city of Zacatecas, the Museum of Zacatecas contains an extensive collection of sacred folk art—all of it a product of the zealous desire of citizens of that city to create shrines in their own homes, since they were forbidden to worship in churches.

3. Kanter (1972) notes that successful communal experiments in the United States were either celibate, as in the case of the Shakers, or had a kind of enforced free love, as in the case of John Humphrey Noyes's Oneida community. Both tactics succeeded in removing the sanctity of the married couple and hence eliminated a form of potential conflict within the community of believers.

4. The biblical injunction against bearing false witness is directed against breaking faith—acting dishonorably in order to harm another. Thus the first Christian martyr, St. Stephen, was stoned to death for blasphemy by a mob swayed by the testimony of false witnesses (Acts 6–7).

5. In *Twelfth Night*, Sir Toby says to Malvolio: "Out o' tune, sir! Ye lie. Are any more than a steward? Does thou think / because thou art virtuous, there shall be no more cakes and ale?" (Act 2, Scene 3, lines 114–115).

6. Paul Horgan, "Credo," *American Scholar* 65 (Summer 1996): 415. Reprinted by permission of the Estate of Paul Horgan.

14 The Giving of Gifts

1. Except, of course, for war taxes—as William James noted in "The Moral Equivalent of War" (1910/1984). A passion for self-defense quite effectively abolishes indifference.

2. See Festinger and Carlsmith (1959) and Bem (1972) for interpretations of this phenomenon by self-perception theory.

3. W. B. Yeats, "Vacillation," from *The Collected Works of W. B. Yeats,* vol. 1: *The Poems,* revised, ed. Richard J. Finneran (New York: Scribner, 1997).

4. See "Whatever Happened to the White Athlete?" *Sports Illustrated,* Dec. 8, 1997.

15 The Question of Authenticity

1. Experimental psychologists studying the problem of false memory turn this into a rather easy matter through the simple expedient of controlling the truth. Thus in Deese's (1959) original study, falsely remembered items are identified simply by comparison of remembered lists with originally learned lists—the false intrusions are obvious. In the world outside the laboratory the criterion problem is not so easily solved, and in fact is so intractable that the controversies about false memory syndrome and its connections to sexual abuse and dissociative disorders will never be resolved by a simple appeal to fact.

2. Morgan le Fay fashioned a sword and scabbard in the exact likeness of Excalibur. The real sword was given to Accolar and the false to Arthur. As a consequence, Arthur was almost killed. The appearance was identical, but the functional characteristics were quite different—for only the authentic object carried magical qualities. Quite obviously, Sir Thomas Malory, the teller of the Arthurian legend, was a Platonist and not a Pragmatist.

3. See Barzun (1983), the chapter entitled "The Test of Truth," for an excellent discussion of the applications and misapplications of the principles of pragmatism as tests for truth.

4. Sut Jhally (1995) has analyzed the portrayal of women on MTV in a video called *Dreamworlds.* Jhally makes the point that MTV is dominated by male producers, and that the collective image of women is that they are sex-starved, aggressively after the male stars, and without independent interests or abilities. It is truly a self-serving male fantasy, but it also may be seen as an attempt to create a reality where none existed before—the synthesis of authenticity.

REFERENCES

Abt, V., and Seesholtz, M. 1992. The shameless world of Phil, Sally and Oprah: Television talk shows and the deconstruction of society. *Journal of Popular Culture 28,* 160–182.

Adams, H. 1918. *The education of Henry Adams: An autobiography.* Boston: Houghton Mifflin.

Ainsworth, M. D. S. 1989. Attachments beyond infancy. *American Psychologist 44,* 709–716.

Allgeier, E. R., and Allgeier, A. R. 1984. *Sexual interactions.* Lexington, Mass.: D. C. Heath.

Averill, J. R. 1988. Disorders of emotion. *Journal of Social and Clinical Psychology 6,* 247–268.

Balint, M. 1959. *Thrills and regressions.* London: Hogarth Press.

Barabasz, M., Barabasz, A., and O'Neil, M. 1991. Effects of experimental context, demand characteristics, and situational cues: New data. *Perceptual and Motor Skills 73,* 83–92.

Barber, T. X., Calverley, D. S., Forgione, A., McPeake, J. D., Chaves, J. F., and Bowen, B. 1969. Five attempts to replicate the experimenter bias effect. *Journal of Consulting and Clinical Psychology 33,* 1–6.

Bartholomew, K. 1990. Avoidance of intimacy: An attachment perspective. *Journal of Social and Personal Relationships 7,* 147–178.

Bartsch, S. 1994. *Actors in the audience: Theatricality and doublespeak from Nero to Hadrian.* Cambridge, Mass.: Harvard University Press.

Barzun, J. 1983. *A stroll with William James.* New York: Harper and Row.

Bayley, S. 1992. *Taste: The secret meaning of things.* New York: Pantheon.

Bem, D. J. 1972. Self-perception theory. In L. Berkowitz, ed., *Advances in experimental social psychology,* vol. 6, 1–62. New York: Academic Press.

Berlyne, D. E. 1960. *Conflict, arousal, and curiosity.* New York: McGraw-Hill.

Bernstein, P. L. 1996. *Against the gods: The remarkable story of risk.* New York: John Wiley.

Berscheid, E. 1985. Interpersonal attraction. In G. Lindzey and E. Aronson, eds., *Handbook of social psychology,* vol. 2, 413–484. New York: Random House.

Bersheid, E., and Walster, E. H. 1978. *Interpersonal attraction.* Reading, Mass.: Addison-Wesley.

Bloom, A. 1988. *The closing of the American mind.* New York: Touchstone/Simon and Schuster.

Bly, R. 1990. *Iron John: A book about men.* Reading, Mass.: Addison-Wesley.

———. 1996. *The sibling society.* Reading, Mass.: Addison-Wesley.

Bordo, S. 1990. "Material girl": The effacements of postmodern culture. *Michigan Quarterly Review 29,* 653–677.

Borges, J. L. 1964. *Dreamtigers.* Trans. M. Boyer and H. Morland. Austin: University of Texas Press.

Bowlby, J. 1988. *A secure base: Parent-child attachment and healthy human development.* New York: Basic Books.

Boyle, M. 1990. *Schizophrenia: A scientific delusion?* New York: Routledge.

Boynton, R. S. 1996. God and Harvard. *New Yorker,* Nov. 11, 64–73.

Brehm, J. W. 1966. *A theory of psychological reactance.* New York: Academic Press.

Brenner, R., with Brenner, G. 1990. *Gambling and speculation: A theory, a history, and a future of some human decisions.* Cambridge: Cambridge University Press.

Brickman, P., Coates, D., and Janoff-Bulman, R. 1978. Lottery winners and accident victims: Is happiness relative? *Journal of Personality and Social Psychology 36,* 917–927.

Brisset, D., and Edgley, C., eds. 1990. *Life as theater: A dramaturgical sourcebook.* New York: Aldine de Gruyter.

Brodsky, J. 1995. *On grief and reason.* New York: Farrar, Straus, and Giroux.

Bromat, E. J., Dew, M. A., and Eaton, W. 1995. Epidemiology of psychosis with special reference to schizophrenia. In M. T. Tsuang, M. Tohen, and G. E. P. Zahner, eds., *Textbook in psychiatric epidemiology,* 283–300. New York: Wiley-Liss.

Brown, R. 1986. *Social psychology,* 2d ed. New York: Free Press.

———. 1996. *Against my better judgment: An intimate memoir of an eminent gay psychologist.* New York: Harrington Park Press.

Burke, K. 1964a. *Perspectives by incongruity.* Bloomington: Indiana University Press.

———. 1964b. *Terms for order.* Bloomington: Indiana University Press.

———. 1969. *A grammar of motives.* Berkeley: University of California Press.

Burnham, J., ed. 1900. *The ethics of Aristotle.* New York: Ayer.

Burnham, J. C. 1993. *Bad habits: Drinking, smoking, taking drugs, gambling, sexual behavior, and swearing in American history.* New York: New York University Press.

Burns, A. S., and Burns, K. 1987. *The Shakers: Hands to work, hearts to God.* New York: Aperture Foundation.

Carpenter, E. 1978. Silent music and invisible art. *Natural History 87,* 90–99.

Carstensen, L. L. 1993. Motivation for social contact across the life span: A theory of socioemotional selectivity. In J. E. Jacobs, et al., eds., *Nebraska symposium on motivation,* vol. 40, *Developmental perspectives on motivation: Current theory and research in motivation,* 209–254. Lincoln: University of Nebraska Press.

———. 1995. Evidence for a life-span theory of socioemotional selectivity. *Current Directions in Psychology 4,* 151–156.

Cash, T. F. 1995. *What do you see when you look in the mirror?* New York: Bantam.

Cash, T. F., and Pruzinsky, T., eds. 1990. *Body images: Development, deviance, and change.* New York: Guilford Press.

Chesterton, G. K. 1912. *A miscellany of men.* New York: Dodd Mead.

Coelho, P. 1993. *The alchemist.* San Francisco: Harper.

Cohen, J. 1960. *Chance, skill, and luck: The psychology of guessing and gambling.* Baltimore: Penguin.

———. 1973. *Psychological probability; or, The art of doubt.* Cambridge, Mass.: Schenkman.

Coleridge, S. T. 1817/1997. *Biographia literaria.* London: Everyman/J. M. Dent.

Comfort, A. 1972. *The joy of sex: A gourmet guide to the art of lovemaking.* New York: Crown.

Crittenden, P. M. 1985. Social networks, quality of child-rearing, and child development. *Child Development 56,* 1299–1313.

Csikszentmihalyi, M. 1988. *Beyond boredom and anxiety.* San Francisco: Jossey-Bass.

Cunningham, M. R. 1986. Measuring the physical in physical attractiveness: Quasi-experiments on the sociobiology of female facial beauty. *Journal of Personality and Social Psychology 50,* 925–935.

Cunningham, M. R., Barbee, A. P., and Pike, C. L. 1990. What do women want? Facialmetric assessment of multiple motives in the perception of male facial physical attractiveness. *Journal of Personality and Social Psychology 59,* 61–72.

Deese, J. 1959. On the prediction of occurrence of particular verbal intrusions in immediate recall. *Journal of Experimental Psychology 58,* 17–22.

Der, G., Gupta, S., and Murray, R. 1990. Is schizophrenia disappearing? *Lancet 335,* 513–516.

Diamond, J. M. 1997. *Why is sex fun? The evolution of human sexuality.* New York: Basic Books.

Dillard, A. 1974. *Pilgrim at Tinker Creek.* New York: Harper's Magazine Press.

———. 1982. *Teaching a stone to talk: Expeditions and encounters.* New York: Harper and Row.

———. 1989. *The writing life.* New York: Harper and Row.

Doctorow, E. L. 1989. *Billy Bathgate: A novel.* New York: Random House.

———. 1997. *Ragtime.* New York: Modern Library.

Dostoevsky, F. 1950. *The brothers Karamazov.* Trans. C. Garnett. New York: Modern Library.

———. 1960. Notes from underground. In *Three short novels.* Garden City, N.Y.: Anchor.

———. 1972. *The gambler, with Polina Suslova's diary.* Chicago: University of Chicago Press.

Drosnin, M. 1985. *Citizen Hughes.* New York: Holt, Rinehart, and Winston.

Dull, D., and West, C. 1991. Accounting for cosmetic surgery: The accomplishment of gender. *Social Problems 38,* 54–69.

Eagles, J. M. 1991. Is schizophrenia disappearing? *British Journal of Psychiatry 158,* 834–835.

Eliot, G. 1985. *The lifted veil.* New York: Penguin.

Ellis, J. 1997. *Literature lost: Social agendas and the corruption of the humanities.* New Haven: Yale University Press.

Emerson, R. W. 1904. *Society and social aims.* Boston: Houghton Mifflin.

Evreinoff, N. 1927. *The theatre in life.* London: George G. Harrup.

Farmer, R., and Sundberg, N. D. 1986. Boredom proneness: The development and correlates of a new scale. *Journal of Personality Assessment 50,* 4–17.

Festinger, L., and Carlsmith, J. M. 1959. Cognitive consequences of forced compliance. *Journal of Abnormal and Social Psychology 58,* 203–210.

Fox, J., ed. 1987. *The essential Moreno.* New York: Springer.

Freedman, R. 1986. *Beauty bound.* Lexington, Mass.: Lexington Books.

Freud, S. 1901/1965. *The psychopathology of everyday life.* Trans. A. Tyson, ed. J. Strachey. New York: Norton.

———. 1930/1962. *Civilization and its discontents.* Trans. and ed. J. Strachey. New York: Norton.

Friday, N. 1996. *The power of beauty.* New York: HarperCollins.

Fromm, E. 1941/1968. *Escape from freedom.* New York: Avon.

Frost, R. 1962. *The complete poems of Robert Frost.* New York: Holt, Rinehart and Winston.

Fuentes, C. 1964. *The death of Artemio Cruz.* New York: Farrar, Straus, and Giroux.

Funk, R. W., Hoover, R. W., and the Jesus Seminar. 1993. *The five gospels: The search for the authentic words of Jesus.* New York: Macmillan.

Galbraith, J. K. 1984. *The affluent society.* Boston: Houghton Mifflin.

Geddes, J. R., Black, R. J., Whalley, L. J., and Eagles, J. M. 1993. Persistence of the decline in the diagnosis of schizophrenia among first admissions to Scottish hospitals from 1968–1988. *British Journal of Psychiatry 163,* 620–626.

Gergen, K. J. 1973. Social psychology as history. *Journal of Personality and Social Psychology 26,* 309–320.

Gergen, K. J., and Gergen, M. M. 1983 Narratives of the self. In T. R. Sarbin and K. E. Scheibe, eds., *Studies in social identity,* 254–273. New York: Praeger.

Gerrig, R. 1993. *Experiencing narrative worlds: On the psychological activities of reading.* New Haven: Yale University Press.

Gladwell, M. 1996. The science of shopping. *New Yorker,* Nov. 4, 66–75.

Goddard, S. F. 1994. *Getting there: The epic struggle between road and rail in the American century.* New York: Basic Books.

Goffman, E. 1959 *The presentation of self in everyday life.* Garden City, N.Y.: Doubleday Anchor.

———. 1961. *Asylums: Essays on the social situation of mental health patients and other inmates.* Garden City, NY: Anchor.

———. 1963. *Stigma: Notes on the management of spoiled identity.* Englewood Cliffs, N.J.: Prentice-Hall.

———. 1967. *Interaction ritual: Essays on face-to-face behavior.* Garden City, N.Y.: Anchor.

———. 1971. *Relations in public.* New York: Basic Books.

———. 1974. *Frame analysis: An essay on the organization of experience.* New York: Harper and Row.

———. 1981. *Forms of talk.* Philadelphia: University of Pennsylvania Press.

Goldberg, R. 1995. *Citizen Turner: The wild rise of an American tycoon.* New York: Harcourt Brace.

Goldhamer, H., and Marshall, A. 1953. *Psychosis and civilization: Two studies in the frequency of mental disease.* Glencoe, Ill.: Free Press.

Golub, S. 1984. *Evreinov: The theater of paradox and transformation.* Ann Arbor: UMI Research Press.

Goodall, J. 1971. *In the shadow of man.* Boston: Houghton Mifflin.

Gray, J. 1992. *Men are from Mars, women are from Venus.* New York: HarperCollins.

Grob, G. N. 1991. Origins of DSM-I: A study in appearance and reality. *American Journal of Psychiatry 148 (4),* 421–431.

Hacker, A. 1997. *Money: Who has how much and why.* New York: Scribner.

Hacking, I. 1995. *Rewriting the soul: Multiple personality and the sciences of memory.* Princeton: Princeton University Press.

Hallie, P. 1979. *Lest innocent blood be shed: The story of the village of Le Chambon, and how goodness happened there.* New York: Harper and Row.

———. 1997. *Tales of good and evil, help and harm.* New York: HarperCollins.

Harlow, H. F. 1950. Learning and satiation of response in intrinsically motivated complex puzzle performance by monkeys. *Journal of Comparative and Physiological Psychology 43,* 289–294.

Harré, R. 1981. The dramaturgy of sexual relations. In M. Cook, ed., *The bases of sexual attraction,* 251–274. New York: Academic Press.

Hays, D., and Hays, D. 1995. *My old man and the sea: A father and son sail around Cape Horn.* Chapel Hill, N.C.: Algonquin Books.

Henry, A., and Short, J. 1954. *Suicide and homicide: Some economic, sociological, and psychological aspects of aggression.* Glencoe, Ill.: Free Press.

Herrnstein, R. J., and Murray, C. 1994. *The bell curve: Intelligence and class structure in American life.* New York: Free Press.

Herzfeld, M. 1992. *The social production of indifference: Exploring the symbolic roots of Western bureaucracy.* New York: Berg.

Hirschey, G. 1994. Gambling nation. *New York Times Magazine,* July 17, 34–61.

Hoek, H. W. 1995. The distribution of eating disorders. In K. D. Brownell and C. G. Fairburn, eds., *Eating disorders and obesity: A comprehensive handbook,* 207–211. New York: Guilford Press.

Hughes, R. 1996. The case for elitist do-gooders. *New Yorker,* May 27, 32–34.

Huizinga, J. 1949. *Homo ludens: A study of the play-element in culture.* London: Routledge and K. Paul.

Hull, D., and West, C. 1991. Accounting for cosmetic surgery: The accomplishment of gender. *Social Problems 38,* 54–69.

James, W. 1890. *Principles of psychology.* 2 vols. New York: Holt.

———. 1900. *Talks to teachers on psychology: And to students on some of life's ideals.* New York: Holt.

———. 1902/1984. Varieties of religious experience. In B. W. Wilshire, ed., *William James: The essential writings,* 222–261. Albany: State University of New York Press.

———. 1910/1984. The moral equivalent of war. In B. W. Wilshire, ed., *William James: The essential writings,* 349–361. Albany: State University of New York Press.

Jampel, B. 1987. *Among the wild chimpanzees.* Video. Pittsburgh: WQED and National Geographic Society.

Jensen, R., and Burgess, H. 1997. Mythmaking: How introductory psychology texts present B. F. Skinner's analysis of cognition. *Psychological Record 47,* 221–232.

Jhally, S. 1995. *Dreamworlds II: Desire/sex/power in music videos.* Video. Northampton, Mass.: Media Education Foundation.

Jung, C. G. 1965. *Memories, dreams, reflections.* Trans. R. Winston and C. Winston, recorded and ed. A. Jaffe. New York: Vintage/Random House.

Kagan, J. 1994. *Galen's prophecy: Temperament in human nature.* New York: Basic Books.

Kahneman, D., and Snell, J. 1992. Predicting a changing taste: Do people know what they will like? *Journal of Behavioral Decision Making 5,* 187–200.

Kahneman, D., and Tversky, A. 1984. Choices, values and frames. *American Psychologist 39,* 341–350.

Kanter, R. M. 1972. *Commitment and community: Communes and utopias in sociological perspective.* Cambridge, Mass.: Harvard University Press.

Kermode, F. 1997. The academy vs. the humanities. *Atlantic 280,* 93–95.

Kerr, J. 1993. *A most dangerous game.* New York: Knopf.

Klapp, O. E. 1978. *Opening and closing: Strategies of information adaptation in society.* Cambridge: Cambridge University Press.

———. 1986. *Overload and boredom: Essays on the quality of life in the information society.* Westport, Conn.: Greenwood.

Kuchta, D. 1996. The making of self-made man: Class, clothing, and English masculinity, 1688–1832. In V. de Grazia, ed., *The sex of things: Gender and consumption in historical perspective,* 54–78. Berkeley: University of California Press.

Kuczmarski, R. J., Flegal, K. M., Campbell, S. M., and Johnson, C. L. 1994. Increasing prevalence of overweight among U.S. adults: The national health and nutrition examination survey, 1960–1991. *JAMA 272,* 205–211.

Laing, R. D. 1961. *The self and others: Further studies in sanity and madness.* Chicago: Quadrangle.

Lamos, M. 1996a. Reflections. In program notes for "Loot," Hartford Stage Company, Feb. 10–March 16.

———. 1996b. Reflections. In program notes for "The servant of two masters," Hartford Stage Company, Sept. 28–Nov. 2.

Langer, E. J. 1975. The illusion of control. *Journal of Personality and Social Psychology 32,* 311–328.

Lenzner, R. 1985. *The great Getty: The life and loves of J. Paul Getty, richest man in the world.* New York: Crown.

Lepper, M. R., Greene, D., and Nisbett, R. E. 1973. Undermining children's intrinsic interest with extrinsic rewards: A test of the overjustification hypothesis. *Journal of Personality and Social Psychology 28,* 129–137.

Lester, D. 1985. The quality of life in modern America and suicide and homicide rates. *Journal of Social Psychology 125,* 779–780.

Levy, L. W. 1993. *Blasphemy: Verbal offense against the sacred, from Moses to Salman Rushdie.* New York: Knopf.

Lewis, C. S. 1939. Bluspels and flalansferes: A semantic nightmare. In *Rehabilitation and other essays,* 133–158. London: Oxford University Press.

Lewis, R. W. B. 1991. *The Jameses: A family narrative.* New York: Farrar, Straus, and Giroux.

Lightfoot, C. 1997 *The culture of adolescent risk-taking.* New York: Guilford Press.

Loftus, E. F. 1975. Leading questions and the eyewitness report. *Cognitive Psychology 7,* 560–572.

Lubenow, G. C. 1997. IGS Observer. *Public Affairs Report 38,* May, 17.

Lykken, D. T. 1998. *A tremor in the blood: Uses and abuses of the lie detector.* New York: Plenum.

Malcolm, J. 1980. The impossible profession—I. *New Yorker,* Nov. 24, 55–133.

Malkiel, B. G. 1973. *A random walk down Wall Street.* New York: Norton.

Mann, T. 1955. *Confessions of Felix Krull, confidence man: The early years.* New York: Random House.

Maslow, A. H. 1954. *Motivation and personality.* New York: Harper.

Masson, J. M. 1984. Freud and the seduction theory. *Atlantic,* Feb. 3, 33–53.

Melville, H. 1887/1984. *The confidence man.* Vol. 10 of *The writings of Herman Melville.* Evanston and Chicago: Northwestern University Press and Newberry Library.

Miller, A. 1996. Why I wrote *The crucible. New Yorker,* Oct. 21 and 28, 158–160.

Miller, R. 1985. *The house of Getty.* New York: Holt.

Monette, P. 1992. *Becoming a man: Half a life story.* New York: Harcourt Brace Jovanovich.

Monk-Jorgensen, P., and Mortensen, P. B. 1992. Incidence and other aspects of the epidemiology of schizophrenia in Denmark, 1971–87. *British Journal of Psychiatry* 161, 489–495.

Needleman, J. 1991. *Money and the meaning of life.* New York: Doubleday.

Neisser, U. 1982. *Memory observed: Remembering in natural contexts.* San Francisco: Freeman.

Nietzsche, F. 1889/1968. Twilight of the idols. In W. Kaufmann, ed., *The portable Nietzsche*, 463–564. New York: Viking.

Noll, R. 1994. *The Jung cult: Origins of a charismatic movement.* Princeton: Princeton University Press.

Novak, M. 1996. *Business as a calling: Work and the examined life.* New York: Free Press.

O'Brien, T. 1994. *In the Lake of the Woods.* Boston: Houghton Mifflin/Seymour Lawrence.

Olivier, L. 1986. *On acting.* New York: Simon and Schuster.

Orne, M. T., and Scheibe, K. E. 1964. The contribution of nondeprivation factors in the production of sensory deprivations effects: The psychology of the "panic button." *Journal of Abnormal and Social Psychology* 68, 3–12.

Ortega y Gasset, J. 1914/1961. *Meditations on Quixote.* Trans. E. Rugg and D. Martin. New York: Norton.

———. 1932/1957. *The revolt of the masses.* New York: Norton.

———. 1957. *Man and people.* New York: Norton.

———. 1973. *An interpretation of universal history.* Trans. M. Adams. New York: Norton.

Orwell, G. 1946/1968. Why I write. In S. Orwell and I. Angus, eds., *The collected essays, journalism and letters of George Orwell*, vol. 4, *An age like this*, 1–7. New York: Harcourt, Brace and World.

Paz, O. 1972. Eroticism and gastrosophy. *Daedalus 101 (4)*, 67–86.

Peiss, K. 1990. Making faces: The cosmetics industry and the cultural construction of gender, 1890–1930. *Genders 7*, 143–167.

———. 1998. *Hope in a jar: The making of America's beauty culture.* New York: Metropolitan Books.

Pepper, S. C. 1942. *World hypotheses: A study in evidence.* Berkeley: University of California Press.

Pfister, J., and Schnog, N., eds. 1997. *Inventing the psychological: Toward a cultural history of emotional life in America.* New Haven: Yale University Press.

Phillips, A. 1993. *On kissing, tickling, and being bored: Psychoanalytic essays on the unexamined life.* Cambridge, Mass.: Harvard University Press.

Plous, S. 1993. *The psychology of judgement and decision making.* Philadelphia: Temple University Press.

Reed, J. W. 1989. *American scenarios: The uses of film genre.* Middletown, Conn.: Wesleyan University Press.

Remnick, D. 1995. Letter from Chechnya: In Stalin's wake. *New Yorker,* July 24, 46–62.

Richardson, R. D. 1995. *Emerson: The mind on fire, a biography.* Berkeley: University of California Press.

Roberts, W. O. 1982. *Initiation to adulthood: An ancient rite of passage in contemporary form.* New York: Pilgrim Press.

Rombauer, I. von Starkoff. 1931/1997. *The joy of cooking,* 6th ed. St. Louis: A. C. Clayton.

Ross, L. D., Amabile, T. M., and Steinmetz, J. L. 1977. Social roles, social control, and biases in social perception processes. *Journal of Personality and Social Psychology 35,* 485–494.

Sacks, O. W. 1989. *Seeing voices: A journey into the land of the deaf.* Berkeley: University of California Press.

Safer, D. J., and Krager, J. M. 1994. The increased rate of stimulant treatment for hyperactive/inattentive students in secondary schools. *Pediatrics 94 (4),* 462–464.

Santayana, G. 1944. *Persons and places.* New York: Charles Scribner.

Sarbin, T. R. 1950. Contributions to role-taking theory: I. Hypnotic behavior. *Psychological Review 57,* 255–270.

———. 1964. Anxiety: Reification of a metaphor. *Archives of General Psychiatry 10,* 630–638.

———. 1967a. On the futility of the proposition that some people should be labeled mentally ill. *Journal of Consulting Psychology 31,* 447–453.

———. 1967b. The concept of hallucination. *Journal of Personality 35,* 359–380.

———. 1968. Ontology recapitulates philology: The mythic nature of anxiety. *American Psychologist 23,* 411–418.

———. 1977. Contextualism: A world view for modern psychology. In A. W. Landfield, ed., *Nebraska symposium on motivation:* vol. 24, *Personal construct psychology,* 1–42. Lincoln: University of Nebraska Press.

———. 1982. The Quixotic Principle: A belletristic approach to the psychological study of imaginings and believings. In V. L. Allen and K. E. Scheibe, eds., *The social context of conduct: Psychological writings of Theodore Sarbin,* 169–186. New York: Praeger.

———. 1984. Role transition as a social drama. In V. L. Allen and E. van de Vilbert, eds., *Role transitions: Explorations and explanations,* 21–38. New York: Plenum.

———. 1986a. Two models of care: Contract and covenant. In E. E. Rutherford, ed., *Ethics and practice of care in public and private settings: Proceedings of the American Association for the Advancement of Science.*

———. 1986b. Emotion and act: Roles and rhetoric. In R. Harré, ed., *The social construction of emotions,* 83–97. Oxford: Basil Blackwell.

————. 1986c. *Narrative psychology: The storied nature of human conduct.* New York: Praeger.

————. 1994a. Steps to the narratory principle: An autobiographical essay. In D. J. Lee, ed., *Life and story: Autobiographies for a narrative psychology,* 7–38. Westport, Conn.: Praeger.

————. 1997. The poetics of identity. *Theory and Psychology 7,* 67–82.

Sarbin, T. R., and Juhasz, J. B. 1982. The concept of mental illness: A historical perspective. In I. Al-Issa, ed., *Culture and psychopathology,* 71–109. Baltimore: University Park Press.

Sarbin, T. R., and Kitsuse, J. I., eds. 1994. *Constructing the social.* London: Sage.

Sarbin, T. R., and Mancuso, J. C. 1980. *Schizophrenia: Medical diagnosis or moral verdict.* New York: Pergamon.

Sarbin, T. R., and Scheibe, K. E. 1980. The transvaluation of social identity. In C. J. Bellone, ed., *Organization theory in the new public administration,* 219–245. New York: Allyn and Bacon.

Saroyan, W. 1939. *The time of your life.* New York: Harcourt, Brace.

Scheibe, K. E. 1979. *Mirrors, masks, lies and secrets: The limits of human predictability.* New York: Praeger.

————. 1986. Self-narratives and adventure. In T. R. Sarbin, ed., *Narrative psychology: The storied nature of human conduct,* 129–151. New York: Praeger.

————. 1994. Yet another preacher's kid finds psychology. In D. J. Lee, ed., *Life and story: Autobiographies for a narrative psychology,* 39–60. Westport, Conn.: Praeger.

————. 1995. *Self studies: The psychology of self and identity.* Westport, Conn.: Praeger.

Scheibe, K. E., Dowds, M., and Kulik, J. 1969. Effects of mental hospital volunteer work on career choice. *Psychological Reports 25,* 35–40.

Scheibe, K. E., Kulik, J. A., and Hersch, P. 1969. Personal characteristics of college volunteers in mental hospitals. *Journal of Consulting and Clinical Psychology 33,* 30–34.

Scheibe, K. E., Kulik, J., Hersch, P., and LaMacchia, S. 1969. College students on chronic wards. *Monographs of Community Mental Health Journal 5.*

Scheibe, K. E., Kulik, J., and Martin, R. 1969. Effects of mental hospital volunteer work on students' conceptions of mental illness. *Journal of Clinical Psychology 25,* 326–329.

Scheibe, K. E., and Shaver, P. R. 1967. Transformation of social identity: A study of chronic mental patients and college volunteers in a summer camp setting. *Journal of Psychology 66,* 19–37.

Schwager, J. E. 1992. *The new market wizards.* New York: Harper.

Shattuck, R. 1996. *Forbidden knowledge: From Prometheus to pornography.* New York: St. Martin's.

Shaver, P. R., and Clark, C. L. 1996. Forms of adult romantic attachment and their cognitive and emotional underpinnings. In G. G. Noam and K. W. Fischer, eds., *Development and vulnerability in close relationships,* 29–58. Mahwah, N.J.: Erlbaum.

Shaver, P. R., and Hazen, C. 1993. Adult romantic attachment: Theory and evidence. In D. Perlman and W. H. Jones, eds., *Advances in personal relationships,* vol. 4, 29–70. London: Jessica Kingsley.

Shaw, G. B. 1970. Preface: Mainly about myself. In *The Bodley Head Bernard Shaw: Collected plays with their prefaces,* ed. D. H. Laurence, vol. 1, 11–34. London: Bodley Head.

Shawn, W., and Gregory, A. 1981. *My dinner with Andre: A screenplay.* New York: Grove Press.

Shenk, D. 1997. *Data smog: Surviving the information glut.* San Francisco: Harper Edge.

Shor, R. E., and Orne, E. C. 1962. *Harvard group scale of hypnotic susceptibility.* Palo Alto: Consulting Psychologists Press.

Singh, D. 1995. Female health, attractiveness, and desirability for relationships: Role of breast asymmetry and waist-to-hip ratio. *Ethology and Sociobiology 16,* 465–482.

Skinner, B. F., and Morse, W. H. 1958. Fixed-interval reinforcement of running in a wheel. *Journal of the Experimental Analysis of Behavior 1,* 371–379.

Slotkin, R. 1973. *Regeneration through violence: The mythology of the American frontier, 1600–1860.* Middletown, Conn.: Wesleyan University Press.

———. 1985. *The fatal environment: The myth of the frontier in the age of industrialization, 1800–1890.* New York: Atheneum.

———. 1992. *Gunfighter nation: The myth of the frontier in twentieth-century America.* New York: Atheneum.

Smolak, L., Levine, M. P., and Striegel-Moore, R. 1996. The developmental psychopathology of eating disorders: Implications for research, prevention, and treatment. Mahwah, N.J.: Erlbaum.

Spence, D. P. 1982. *Narrative truth and historical truth: Meaning and interpretation in psychoanalysis.* New York: Norton.

Stendhal, M. H. B. 1926/1995. *The red and the black.* Trans. C. K. S. Moncrieff. New York: Modern Library.

Sternlieb, G., and Hughes, J. W. 1983. *The Atlantic City gamble.* Cambridge, Mass.: Harvard University Press.

Sundberg, N. D., and Bisno, H. 1983. Boredom at life transitions—adolescence and old age. Paper presented at the meeting of the Western Psychological Association, San Francisco, April.

Sundberg, N. D., Latkin, C. A., Farmer, R. F., and Saoud, J. 1991. Boredom in young adults: Gender and cultural comparisons. *Journal of Cross-Cultural Psychology 22,* 209–223.

Szasz, T. S. 1961. *The myth of mental illness: Foundations of a theory of personal conduct*. New York: Hoeber-Harper.

Taylor, A. 1996. How I flunked retirement: An interview with Lee Iacocca. *Fortune*, June 24, 36–43.

Tannen, D. 1990. *You just don't understand: Women and men in conversation*. New York: Morrow.

Tenner, E. 1996. *Why things bite back: Technology and the revenge of unintended consequences*. New York: Knopf.

Teresa, M. 1975. *A gift from God*. New York: Harper and Row.

Theroux, P. 1998. Nurse Wolf. *New Yorker*, June 15, 50–60.

Thornhill, R., and Gangestad, S. W. 1996. The evolution of human sexuality. *Trends in Ecology and Evolution 11*, 98–102.

Trow, G. W. S. 1997. *Within the context of no context*. New York: Atlantic Monthly Press.

Trump, D. 1987. *Trump: The art of the deal*. New York: Random House.

———. 1997. *Trump: The art of the comeback*. New York: Times Books.

Turbayne, C. M. 1970. *The myth of metaphor*. Columbia: University of South Carolina Press.

Turkle, S. 1995. *Life on the screen: Identity in the age of the Internet*. New York: Simon and Schuster.

Tversky, A. 1995. The psychology of decision making. In A. S. Wood, ed., *Behavioral finance and decision theory in investment management*. Charlottesville, Va.: Association for Investment Management and Research.

Tversky, A., and Kahneman, D. 1986. Rational choice and the framing of decisions. *Journal of Business 59*, S251–S278.

Updike, J. 1989. *Self-consciousness: Memoirs*. New York: Knopf.

———. 1994. The critic in winter. *New Yorker*, Nov. 29, 159–164.

———. 1996. *In the beauty of the lilies*. New York: Knopf.

Veblen, T. 1934. *The theory of the leisure class: An economic study of institutions*. New York: Modern Library.

Vygotsky, L. 1962. *Thought and language*. New York: Wiley.

Walker, M. 1992. *The psychology of gambling*. New York: Pergamon.

Weinberg, S. 1989. *Armand Hammer: The untold story*. Boston: Little, Brown.

Whitehead, A. N. 1929. *The aims of education and other essays*. New York: Macmillan.

Whitehead, B. D. 1997. *The divorce culture*. New York: Knopf.

Whorf, B. L. 1956. *Language, thought, and reality: Selected writings of Benjamin Lee Whorf*. Ed. J. B. Carroll. Cambridge, Mass.: MIT Press.

Wilson, E. 1993. *The sixties: The last journal, 1960–1972*. Ed. Lewis M. Dabney, New York: Farrar, Straus, and Giroux.

Wilson, E. O. 1975. *Sociobiology: The new synthesis*. Cambridge, Mass.: Harvard University Press.

Wolf, N. 1991. *The beauty myth: How images of beauty are used against women.* New York: Morrow.

Wolfe, T. 1983. *The right stuff.* New York: Farrar, Straus, and Giroux.

Woolf, V. 1929/1981. *A room of one's own.* San Diego: Harcourt Brace.

Wordsworth, W. 1805/1947. *Prelude.* Ed. E. De Selincourt. New York: Oxford University Press.

Wright, R. 1994. *The moral animal: The new science of evolutionary psychology.* New York: Pantheon.

CREDITS

The song quoted in the Preface is "Corrente" by Chico Buarque de Hollanda. Used by permission of Chico Buarque and Grupo Editorial Musical Arlequim.

A portion of Chapter 1 was presented as an invited address for Division 24 of the American Psychological Association Convention, Chicago, 1997.

The section of Chapter 2 with the heading "Seriousness and Venturing Forth" is based on Scheibe, "Self-narratives and Adventure," in T. R. Sarbin, ed., *Narrative Psychology: The Storied Nature of Human Conduct* (New York: Praeger, 1986). A preliminary version of this chapter was published as "Dramapsych: Getting Serious about Context" in S. C. Hayes, L. J. Hayes, H. W. Reese, and T. R. Sarbin, eds., *Varieties of Scientific Contextualism* (Reno: Context Press, 1993), adapted here with permission.

Chapter 3 is adapted from Scheibe, "On a Certain Emotional Blindness in Human Beings," *Journal of Narrative and Life History 5*, no. 3 (1995).

A preliminary version of Chapter 11 was presented in a symposium entitled "'Normal' and 'Abnormal' in Psychological Discourse, I: Sociocultural Influences on Practice" at the American Psychological Association Convention, Toronto, 1996.

Chapter 15 was originally published as Scheibe, "Replicas, Imitations and the Question of Authenticity" in T. R. Sarbin and J. de Rivera, eds., *Believed-In Imaginings* (Washington: American Psychological Association, 1998).

Figure 6.1 is excerpted, with permission, from *Behavioral Finance and Decision Theory in Investment Management,* copyright 1986, Association for Investment Management and Research, Charlottesville, Virginia. All rights reserved.

Chapter 9, note 6, quotes "When I Fall in Love" by Edward Heyman and Victor Young, © Victor Young Publications, Inc. © Renewed, assigned to Chappell & Co. and Intersong-USA, Inc. All rights administered by Chappell & Co. All rights reserved. Used by permission. Warner Bros. Publications U.S. Inc., Miami, FL 33014.

The song quoted in Chapter 13 is "Tear It Down," words and music by Clyde McCoy and Raymond Leveen, copyright © 1945, 1973, by MCA Music Publishing, A Division of Universal Studios, Inc. All rights outside the USA and Canada controlled and administered by MCA Music Publishing, a division of Universal Studios. International copyright secured, copyright renewed, all rights reserved.

The quotation in Chapter 14 from "Vacillation" by W. B. Yeats is reprinted with permission of Scribner, a division of Simon and Schuster, Inc., from *The Collected Works of W. B. Yeats,* vol. 1: *The Poems,* revised, edited by Richard J. Finneran. Copyright 1933 by Macmillan Publishing Company. Copyright renewed © 1961 by Bertha Georgie Yeats.

ACKNOWLEDGMENTS

I have had the rare good fortune of maintaining for almost forty years a relationship of friendship and collaboration with my mentor from graduate student days. Ted Sarbin first taught me the value of drama as an approach to understanding psychology. He has read and commented on every chapter in this book. I have continued to benefit from his wise counsel and from the example of his life.

My wife, Wendy, has also read and commented on all the chapters. She has been supportive of this project, even though I have gone through fits and moods in the act of composition. Her calm and steady confidence has helped me along the way.

John Harney encouraged me at a critical point and helped me to place the manuscript with Harvard University Press. There, I have had the pleasure of working with Elizabeth Knoll, my editor. She has been my interlocutor as well, and has saved me from a host of literary and conceptual sins. Also, I am deeply grateful to Mark Freeman, a reviewer recruited by Elizabeth, who supplied a key suggestion regarding the ordering and organization of the chapters.

Over the years I have taught well over three hundred students in a course called The Dramaturgical Approach to Psychology (see Chapter 12). This maturing pedagogical experiment has provided me with a major warrant for writing this book. I have benefited much from my students. While the outline was mine, they supplied much of the content. In a sense, the book is a recitation for them.

Another warrant derives from my clinical practice. I have logged thousands of hours on the counseling side of the couch. This has given me the irreplaceable privilege of access to the lives and minds of people with serious troubles. I have come to appreciate Freud's claim for the instructive value of the clinical crucible.

Professional colleagues, friends, and students have given me the richness of their conversation about the unconventional set of topics covered here. Along the way they have rectified mistakes, set me off in worthy new directions, or just given me a reference I needed. I list their names here, not in order of priority or importance, nor alphabetically, nor even capriciously, but in an order that seems to me sonorous and musically interesting. Names are wonderful in their sound and significance and, even if unknown, are worth reading aloud: Theodore Sarbin, Wendy Scheibe, John Harney, and Elizabeth Knoll I have mentioned before, but must repeat. And the rest: Antonio da Costa Ciampa, Adrienne Woike, Kinshasa Bennett, Natalie Brender, Daniel Scheibe, Jill Morawski, Gene Borgida, Bill Francisco, Bob Richardson, Phil Simshauser, Al Turco, Joyce Lowrie, Nick Kafes, Bill Roberts, Tom Allen, Rolf Kroger, Dick Miller, Charles Lemert, George Creeger, Ted Sarbin Jr., Ruth Striegel-

Moore, Amy Abbazia, Camille Smith, Stephen Bank, Mary Boyle, Kathleen Ring, Joseph Reed, Linda Wood, Doris Hallie, Ernest Lowrie, Mara Kailin, Jason Kaden, Norman Sundberg, Stephen Petrill, Annie Dillard, Dara Greenwood, Carlo Brumat, David Scheibe, David Zita, Reuven Brenner, Mehadin Arafeh, Anita Malufe, Michael Angelides, Shawn Green, John Hobbs, Scott Plous, and members of the Jacob Group.

Finally, I want to acknowledge the atmosphere of freedom, encouragement, and support for exploring new ways of teaching and learning at Wesleyan University over the more than thirty-five years of my career. I have never found a place I would rather be.